S0-BIK-082

DE ARCHITECTURA

ARCHITECTURE OF THE INDUSTRIAL AGE

1789-1914

FRANÇOIS LOYER

Lecturer in the History of Architecture,
University of Haute-Bretagne, Rennes

Translated from the French by R.F.M. Dexter

Library of Congress Catalog Card Number: 83-42959

Printed in Switzerland

Contents

Introduction

The French Revolution, following hard upon the American Revolution that prefigured it, remodelled the social and political order of all Europe. The sweeping changes it brought about opened the way to the rise of a new type of civilization. With the nineteenth century began the industrial age. It grew as the century advanced, overthrowing the cultural and social organization of the West and spreading over the whole world. [1] The first phase of this transformation ended in 1914 with the Great War, as it was then called, which symbolically marks the end of pre-industrial civilization.

Such a transformation was naturally a matter of concern to thinking minds and even to public opinion, for every day brought changes in the environment and in social relations: the nineteenth century, in Europe, was the age of the rural exodus and recurring revolutions. These changes naturally affected people in different ways. Some saw them as tokens of progress (and the cult of progress grew steadily throughout the century); others lamented them as a change for the worse, blighting the countryside, threatening the heritage of the past, distorting moral and ideological values.

Art, because it is the conscience of the group, has much to tell us, by the very ambiguity of its message, about the uncertainty with which the industrial phenomenon was viewed. Praise of modernity is strangely coupled with nostalgia for the past. For the nineteenth century [2] was the first to look back yearningly to the past, faced as it was by the threatened loss of its patrimony. In the visual arts and the crafts it was possible to ward off destruction by collecting valued works. Not so where architecture and the townscape were concerned: these had to meet the needs of daily usage or had to be financially profitable. Architecture, more than any other art, was liable to become antiquated; and, again more than any other art, it was apt to embody the aspirations, the "modernity," of the new generations, increasingly conscious in the nineteenth century of belonging to the industrial age.

So it is that the nineteenth century was history-conscious more than any other had been. Far from turning its back on the past, it contended with it, confronted it. Whether nostalgia for the past or rejection of it, both meant a certain dependence on history which indeed was implicit in the very process of change, whereas cultures founded on more settled economic and sociological conditions have been able to live without any difficulty in the contemporaneity of their art.

The sixteenth century was the founder of eclecticism.[3] It was the first to borrow its system of forms from the past–from Roman antiquity, an idealized past which the artists of the classical period held up before them. So the eclecticism of the nineteenth century was nothing new. But its view of history was affected now by a double transformation. In the first place, archaeology dealt now with a real antiquity, not an imagined one; in excavating a site like Pompeii, it demystified history, seeing it as a parallel and precedent to today, not as an example or model; undiscriminating enthusiasm was superseded by critical analysis. Secondly, the scope of historical research was enlarged far beyond Mediterranean antiquity, to include a

whole series of earlier cultures; the ancient world of Greece and Rome was no longer the one supreme reference; it was challenged and had to compete with others.
Paradoxical as it may seem, it was this enlarged view of a worldwide past that helped to create the spirit of modernity, as one aspect of the past was used to offset another. That history should have been taken as a model for the future may seem strange today, for such a justification is no longer necessary now. But it was a different matter in the nineteenth century, when the struggle to overcome the conventions of classical idealism was far from being won. By its implicit rationalism, the Gothic revival was a most effective weapon against the ideological oppression of academic thought.
Paradoxically again, the Gothic revival was no less effective in the service of the contrary cause, which saw in the abstractions of classical idealism a menace against tradition. As an antidote to the debased forms of the present, neo-Gothic could also serve to mythify the past, to guarantee its legitimacy, to establish its power at a time when far-reaching changes might have obliterated its very memory. In short, for both sides history came to act as the vestment of ideology: it was there to justify whatever forms and style were chosen for contemporary architecture. But if the nineteenth century was so history-conscious, it is because it had in the last resort to free itself from the past in order to lay the economic, technical and social foundations of the new civilization on the rise. And in breaking free of that past it was well aware of the alienation it would have to endure. Is it any wonder then that it occasionally revolted? Industrial civilization was not all gains and benefits! It was with repeated outbreaks of violence that the nineteenth century lived through this conflict between the values of the old and the new civilization.

Project for a modern Metropolis,
1914.
Watercolour drawing by Mario Chiattone.

◀ Interior of a Metropolitan Church,
view at dusk.
Late 18th century.
Drawing by Etienne-Louis Boullée.

I

ACADEMICISM

To single out the notion of planning as the guiding idea of neoclassical art in its architectural and urban production may seem far-fetched, when it is pervaded by so many other preoccupations as well–the idealism of antiquity, the philosophical aesthetic, the archaeological discovery of the Greek world, the cult of Palladio or the sense of the picturesque. Yet the ensemble of these ideas, which belong to the repertory of forms, achieves synthesis only within a global vision of the world dominated by the sentiment of Reason.

The heir of the Century of Enlightenment, Neoclassicism indeed expressed itself as a daring attempt to dominate the world by logical thought. The clarifying effort which marked the modern sciences at their birth, through a vast system of classification, found its equivalent in the principle of architectural and urban *ordonnance*, applied to every creation, however minor.

A keen sense of the fitness of things, of suiting the means and forms employed to the purpose of a building, runs through the entire artistic production. It places each work on a precise level of intention, of relative importance, within a global hierarchical vision of the whole of that production, and does so outside any notion of rivalry or transgression.

Planning the landscape 1789-1830

In neoclassical art we find no work that is out of place; no work, that is, whose artistic resources are not in direct proportion to its position in the whole of the group. The portrayal of social status is effectively less prevalent than before. Even if challenged by a certain aristocratic production, it is the economic order as a whole which organizes the city, defines the role of public buildings, restructures the rural landscape, traces the main lines of communication; moreover, it gives to all of them a magnificent ordered arrangement and makes them works of art as much as of utility.

Thus it was to a comprehensive vision of the world that neoclassical art, through apparently competing and at any rate distinct forms, constantly referred: the vision of a planetary order shaped by human thought.

Thought then willingly submitted to that order, in harmonious relationship with the mind's diverse activities (which meant that art, far from competing with industry, formed with it an indissoluble unity, the Beautiful being the normal expression of the mind, and the ugly a failure or dead end). It was not by chance that the Supreme Being was the Great Architect of that universe which the Freemasons dreamt of building by uniting their minds in perfect harmony. Unlike Platonic speculation, philosophical idealism built its vision of the world on the effort at harmony self-imposed by human thought against the perversion of error and disorder. This deliberate intention gave to every production an exemplary character, a moral bearing such that the slightest action contributed to the general edification.

Finally, the idealism of the Enlightenment, like all of classical European art, put together this vision of the world on an inaccessible model: that of an antique, Hellenic or Roman Eden. The essential quality of this model would always be that it subsisted only in fragments, leaving the field free for aesthetic invention, which proved the fact by its continual theoretical reconstructions. The strange manner in which Neoclassicism rediscovered Pompeii, without taking any account of its architectural reality, or interpreted the ruins of Athens from engravings,[1] stands as a witness. Moreover, Quatremère de Quincy, the great theoretician of Neoclassicism on the wane, had the courage when challenged by the archaeological reality of Paestum to firmly condemn its *error*, reality being necessarily inferior to the Idea.[2] Far more than the ruins of Athens or Rome, it was, after all, the thought of Palladio which constituted the most nearly perfect model of the neoclassical aesthetic as a system of visual organization of space: the mirror of its economic planning.

Transformation of the city

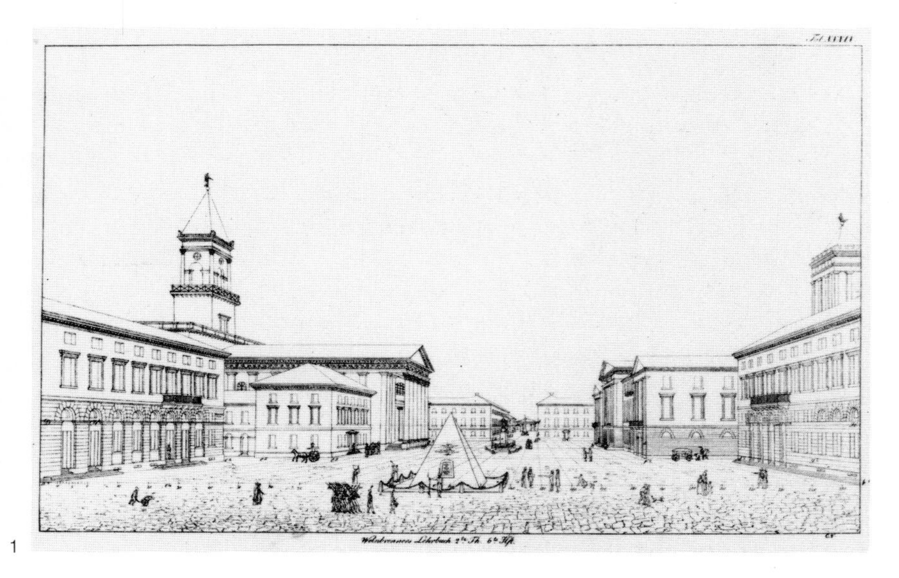

1

1. Karlsruhe: Marktplatz and Via Triumphalis, 1804-1824.
Architect: Friedrich Weinbrenner.
Weinbrenner, *Architektonisches Lehrbuch II*, 1824.

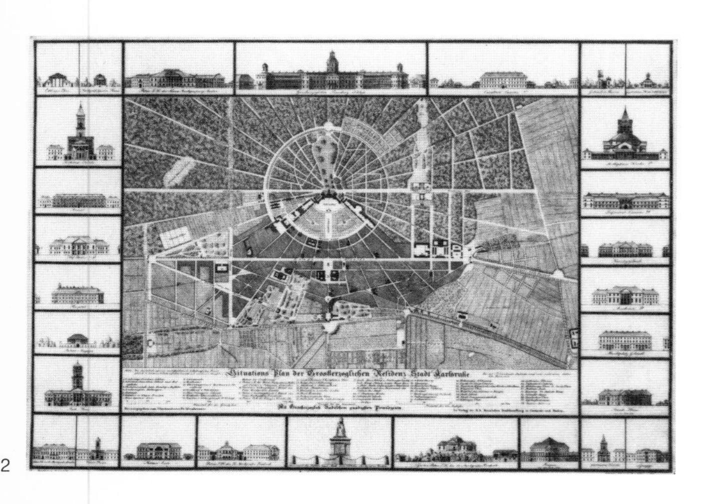

2

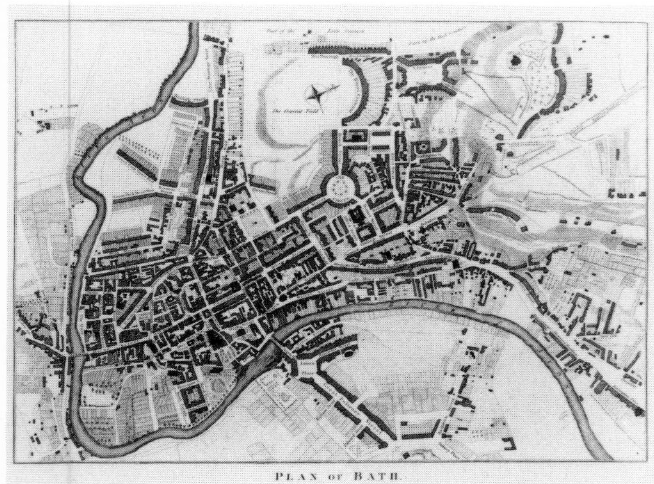

3

2. Karlsruhe: Circular plan of 1724, after Friedrich Weinbrenner, 1822.
3. Bath: Plan of Charles H. Masters, 1801.

Restructuring the city has been a constant preoccupation since the sixteenth century, as testified by the Rome of Sixtus V, unanimously considered as the model of Baroque urbanism.[3] Its system of axes and pivots made it possible to organize the principal open spaces of the city while leaving them with pleasing proportions and facilitating the recognition of different sites by the monuments that accentuated them. The seventeenth and eighteenth centuries bent their efforts to remove from this system the multiplicity of centres of interest, whose competition harmed the general interest. The Versailles model and its successors (such as the circular plan of Karlsruhe in 1724) managed to concentrate urban structure entirely around its political and monumental centre.

The neoclassical aesthetic went the opposite way from this absolute, autocratic unifying of space by proposing to establish multiplicity as a model (and not as the accidental result of economic forces). The plan of Bath, in England, shows it very well. The exploitation of the topographical accidents of the site makes it possible to articulate the city in a sequence of autonomous segments, whose own centres of interest do not necessarily coincide with the major thoroughfares. Broad organizing lines and spatial landmarks maintain a dialogue without confusion. They give each part of the city a form of autonomy by the additions of skilfully interlinked structures. No element ever obtrudes. Even the famous Circus by John Wood the Elder (1754) obeys the general law by rejecting the axiality and centrality of its Baroque models (the Place des Victoires in Paris) in favour of a neutral centre–a simple lawn–and radiating roads as from a roundabout with three exits. As for the nearby Royal Crescent by John Wood the Younger (1767), it gets its centre of interest from the landscape (like a vast semicircular theatre turned towards the panorama of the valley).

The rejection of political significance, with which all classical art had been previously fraught, is evident in this urban practice, which paved the way for the great conceptions of the nineteenth century, distinguished by the richness of urban landscapes and the desire for autonomy of elements[4] within the global structure of the city. Contrary to what has too often been said, there was nothing aristocratic about nineteenth-century urban art.

Even in its conception of the town centre, it rejected the single axis of the palace prospect and, on the idealized model of the antique forum, created a juxtaposition of equally potent elements in a dialogue that constituted its moving force. The exceedingly beautiful Marktplatz of Karlsruhe, designed and executed by Friedrich Weinbrenner from 1804 to 1824, was, from that standpoint, one of the most highly synthesized monuments of Europe. The great axis of the Via Triumphalis, the perspective of which is closed by the castle in the background, broadens out into

a double square framed by the differentiated but equivalent masses of the church and the town hall, somewhat in the manner of the Roman *capitolia*. As H.R. Hitchcock has pointed out,[5] the composition consists of a terraced arrangement of separate blocks culminating in a small-scale monument, a public fountain, whose perfect pyramidal form focuses the interest of the empty space that envelops it.
Secondly, whereas the city of former times functioned through accumulation and increasing density until space was totally saturated, the neoclassical city sought to preserve vast open spaces, rigorously disposed, which were as much promenades as thoroughfares. Instead of the traditional dialogue between vernacular and monumental architecture, the neoclassical city preferred the mineral/plant opposition, incorporating nearly two centuries of experience in landscape gardening. Lastly, it opposed the symbol-monument by the public building, possessing a social or functional purpose: town hall, church, school, theatre or market, if not garden or shopping arcade.
So, in pre-Haussmann Paris, the strongholds of social life were the theatres and gardens, in that unforeseen association which, by the mediation of the café, reorganized worldly pursuits on the theme of leisure. It was there that the shopping arcades and galleries were built and pedestrian passages converged.

4. Bath: The Royal Crescent, 1767-1776.
Architect: John Wood the Younger.
Watercolour by Thomas Malton, 1769.

1. Paris: Palais-Royal, restoration of 1814-1831. Architect: Pierre-François-Léonard Fontaine. *Paris et ses environs reproduits par le daguerréotype*, 1840.

2.3. Paris: Rue de Rivoli, planned in 1801. Architects: Percier and Fontaine. Paris: Rue de Castiglione, planned in 1802. Architect: Jacques-Charles Bonnard. *Paris and its Environs*, 1829.

The Palais-Royal is the prime example. Diverted from its aristocratic use, it was transformed into a public space; the garden became a place for popular walks, one frequented by prostitutes, wealthy marchionesses and marriageable young women, in the most improbable of cohabitations. The Palais-Royal was at the same time a theatre; it was also, and above all, a collection of galleries, whose outstanding architectural quality was further enriched, in 1829, by the construction of the beautiful glazed Galerie d'Orléans.

In the same way, the Terrasse des Feuillants, which overlooks the Tuileries gardens, took its place as early as 1801 in the monumental group of the Rue de Rivoli, in the designs of Percier and Fontaine. Before its extension under Napoelon III, the Rue de Rivoli, filled with cafés, was useless for traffic, since it stopped at the Louvre; but as a promenade it was a magnificent space, where the powerful architecture of arcades joined that of gardens. The success of the whole was due to the purity and simplicity of the implemented forms, as well as to their falling in with a major function of urban life–the provision of space for public walks and trade.

There are many examples of these great urban alignments, which served to structure the townscape and generally occurred along with vast promenades–planted malls, quays or terraces–to be found in the quarters of Lyons built under Louis XVI; in neoclassical Geneva, where the Corraterie and the Quai des Bergues are two characteristic examples; or in so many other more or less successfully completed provincial schemes (Louis Bruyère at Le Mans, Pierre Besnard at Pontivy).

Yet in was England, the first of the great industrial countries, which perfected this urban landscape aesthetic based on the relationship between landscaped monumental thoroughfare and leisure parks. The London venture of John Nash included both the digging of Regent Street and, further north, the laying out of Regent's Park, encircled by buildings arranged in terraces, like the edifices of Bath. Cutting through an already constituted urban structure, the new avenue adapted its form to the accidents it met along the way, to interruptions, gaps, alignment in curves, expansions around a particular centre of interest, thereby turning each sequence into an independent element. The strength of the overall design was never compromised, while the continuous modulation of forms, scale and

4

3

4. Geneva: Rue de la Corraterie, 1827-1834. Architect: Samuel Vaucher. Adviser: Dufour. Lithograph by Jean Du Bois, c. 1830.

5. Geneva: Quai des Bergues, 1833-1838. The Port and the Ile Rousseau, detail. Three-colour lithograph, before 1850.

5

direction made possible the integration of functions extremely differentiated according to the nature of the district travelled through. To treat the shops of Piccadilly, the monuments of Portland Place or the residential buildings of Regent's Park with the same architectonic resources was a gamble which John Nash took and won.

The comparison between the sumptuous middle-class city that was neoclassical London and the Parisian operations of Napoleon's architects is, moreover, eloquent. Beside its English rival the Rue de Rivoli lacks both variety and allure. The fine outline of the Rue de Castiglione, disposing the former Place Royale around the Vendôme Column, has a monumental solemnity that is a trifle severe, and about which one ultimately wonders whether its heavy emphasis makes any sense. It is understandable that Courbet later

1.2. London: Chester Terrace, Regent's Park, 1825.
Cornwall Terrace, Regent's Park, 1821.
Architect: John Nash.
Metropolitan Improvements; or London in the Nineteenth Century, 1827.

3. London: Plan of a new street from Charing Cross to Portland Place, 1814.
Architect: John Nash.

1

2

applied himself to the destruction of that political symbol, the imperial column!

Town planning, elaborated under Louis XVI (with the Paris ordinance of 1784, which would serve as a model for all Europe, and which specified a standard outline directly derived from the vertical section of the buildings of the Place Vendôme), was perfected under Louis XVIII by a systematic policy of alignment aimed at regularizing and straightening the routes of urban transit. This vast regulatory apparatus [6] sought to combat the defects of the urban agglomeration by defining principles of municipal jurisdiction to ensure its economic and social effectiveness.

It was under French jurisdiction that this preoccupation became most widely known, when the prefect Chabrol drew up the distribution of administrative responsibilities for the imperial city of Pontivy–town hall, prefecture, barracks, law courts and prison, all of which were buildings of government; but also inn, market,

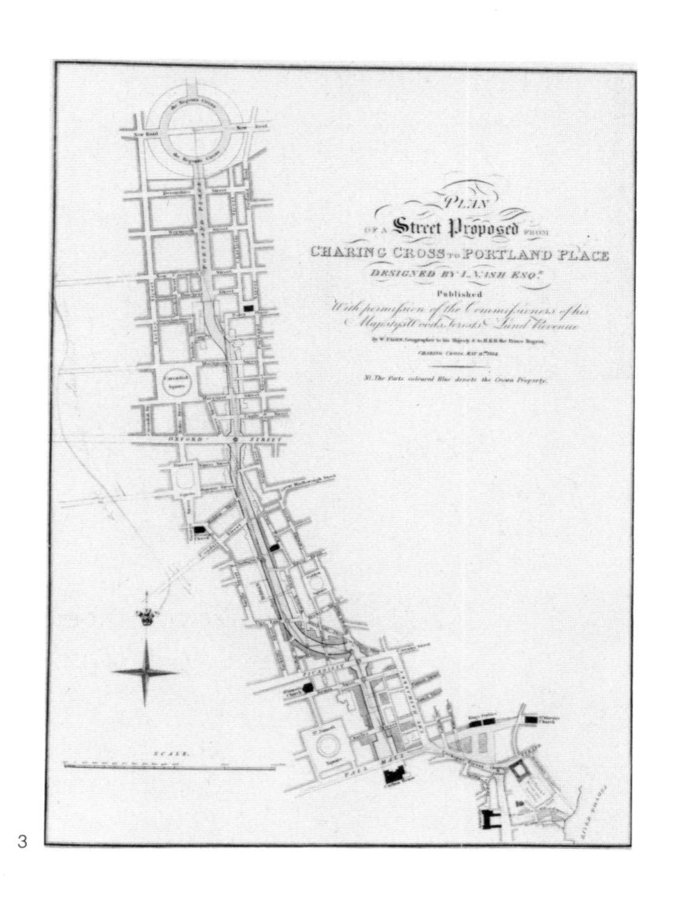

3

4. London: Cumberland Terrace, Regent's Park, 1826.
Architect: John Nash.

4

hospital, school, church or theatre, whose presence made the reality of social life secure in this new community.[7]
Once he had become Prefect of the Seine in 1812, Chabrol placed in the forefront of his concerns the problem of wholesale and retail markets; in other words, the organization of collective subsistence. And, in due course, his successors would create, within the new boundary divisions of the Restoration, the first examples of a policy of community centres, organized around the town hall, the church and the school (for example, at La Villette)–a policy of which Haussmannism took advantage under the Second Empire.
From the very beginning of the neoclassical period, urban renewal was the order of the day. It aimed at remedying the most crying defects of the traditional city, such as crowding, unsanitary conditions, insufficient leisure spaces and amenities. The social aims of the Haussmann policy were the end result of a striving for betterment dating back in reality to the eighteenth century. For, as

Vue de la maison du Jardinier, à l'entrée du Parc de la Garenne
à Clisson, sur la route de Chollet.

1

industrialization proceeded, this adaptation of urban space to its economic function became more and more necessary (and more urgent with the dangers of a social flare-up).
But at the beginning of the nineteenth century, what made itself felt most was the effort to achieve an overall harmony of the landscape. To combat urban mineralization or, conversely, to landscape the countryside, were complementary missions, both of them aiming at re-establishing a complementarity. Similarly, to challenge the pre-eminence of the single monument by a diversified ensemble was a means to restore a balance–as valid for the relation between the castle and the rural world as that between the church or palace and the town. The neoclassical ideal of perfect unity necessitated this profoundly utopian move in a global effort to restructure human activity, its space and its art.
The effort was clearly seen in the new domain of suburbia, the "town in the country" dreamed by the nineteenth century in the face of the destructive effects of that developing urban concentration which is the product of industrial necessities.[8] The anti-urban enterprise of the suburb then appears as a total rejection of the model imposed by economic necessities; the artist's activity as a continuous correction of the blunders of society.
There was something tragic, as well as an immense conviction, in this undertaking doomed to failure by the sole fact that it defied

Clisson, near Nantes: La Garenne Lemot

1. View of the Gardener's House, at the entrance of the Parc de la Garenne at Clisson, on the road to Chollet. *Voyage pittoresque dans le bocage de la Vendée*, 1817.
2. The so-called Gardener's House. Square tower and park enclosure, c. 1809.
3. Lemot House, 1824-1866. Front. Architects: Mathurin Crucy, François-Frédéric Lemot, Jules-Frédéric Bouchet.

2

3

4

5

4. View of the Colonne Milliaire (milestone) in the Parc de la Garenne at Clisson. *Voyage pittoresque dans le bocage de la Vendée*, 1817.
5. Temple of Vesta, 1819-1823. Architect: Mathurin Crucy.

economic reality. And besides, the suburb, in so far as it was the product of urban destruction caused by industrial machinery, caricatured the rural Eden of that Arcadia, peopled with Tuscan memories, which had haunted the storehouse of the artistic imagination: it was a far cry to the Paris suburbs from La Garenne Lemot![9]

That artists' colony, grouped around François-Frédéric Lemot (the brother-in-law of David and himself a noted sculptor), looked on the banks of the Sèvre Nantaise with a purely aesthetic eye, one so steeped in classical references that it even recognized there the landscapes of Poussin. The result was the creation there of a purely

1

Tuscan architecture: a marvellous vision of a landscape idealized to the point of assuming the forms of another age, of another world; of transforming a whole village, an entire valley, into a kind of immense park, dotted with picturesque buildings.
The romantic dream of Clisson had many precedents, whether or not they were classical in their references. We may liken it to an English creation of the eighteenth century, Inveraray Castle, in Scotland, rebuilt for the Duke of Argyll by Roger Morris from 1743 to 1761 and complemented by the creation of a new town, completed in 1801.[10] The importance of Inveraray as an innovative

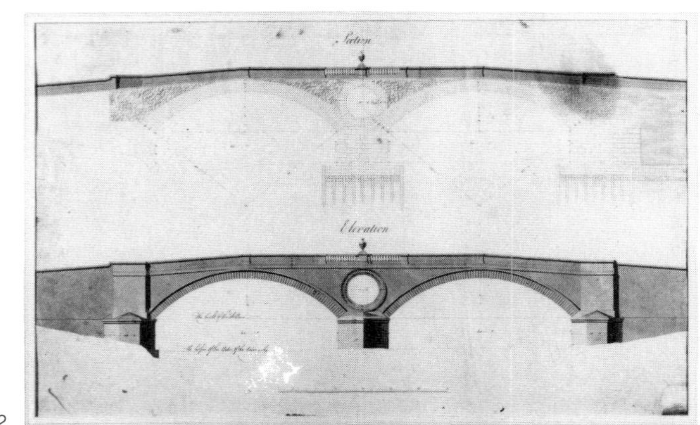

2

Inveraray, Argyllshire, Scotland
1. Aray Bridge, present state.
2. Drawing of Aray Bridge by Robert Mylne, before 1811.
3. Inveraray Church. Drawing by Robert Mylne, 1800.

3

4. The Town of Inveraray.
   Lithograph after L. Clark, 1824.
5. Inveraray Castle, 1743-1761.
   Present state.
   Architect: Roger Morris.

scheme lies in this double reconstruction, accompanied by a displacement of site. Instead of the overlapping of town and castle which distinguished the former medieval construction, the third Duke of Argyll preferred a more functional composition in which town and castle, divided by a park, adjoined each other along both sides of a basket-handle curve on the banks of Loch Fyne. The scheme included the construction of bridges, roads, canals, public buildings and even some of the houses, out of the Duke's finances. On the other hand, the application of the decrees of 1746, abolishing hereditary jurisdictions and the clan system, placed in the hands of the Duke an immense territorial patrimony, which he set out to exploit as a landowner and no longer as a lord; for in any case, living in London off the income of his estates, he no longer had any of the attributes of a clan chieftain.

Industrialization of the agricultural domain

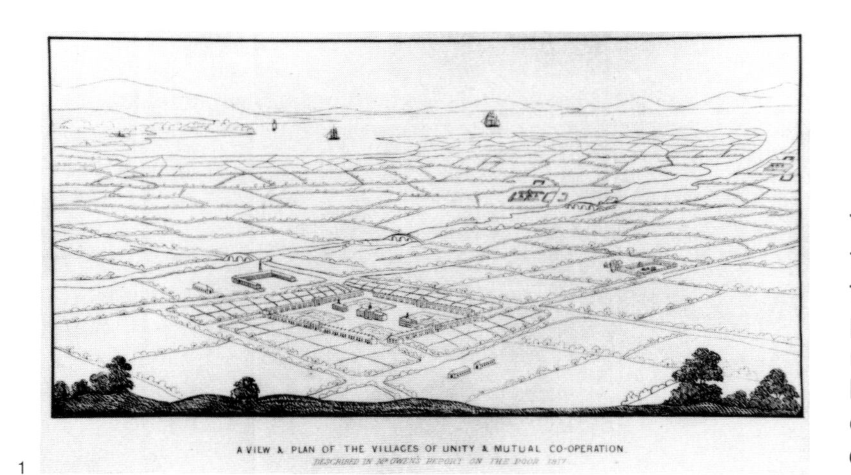

A VIEW & PLAN OF THE VILLAGES OF UNITY & MUTUAL CO-OPERATION

That well-known phenomenon of the destruction of ancient rural structures was the first step towards a purely capitalist exploitation of the agricultural domain, on models of which (and not by chance) Palladian Italy had already furnished an example in the second half of the sixteenth century.[11] It went hand in hand with the transformation of the rural landscape, the result of new methods of exploitation, and with the reconstruction and regrouping of living quarters in new village communities, far removed from the model of traditional sharecropping. Under the watchful eye of the municipal court and the dual church (English and Gaelic), placed along the medial axis, were aligned the terraced houses of agricultural workers, fishermen, labourers or tradespeople, whose aggregate constituted this new urban entity. When the Duke of Argyll built a model farm at Maam Barn, in 1784, he omitted the construction of a house for the farmer. In the midst of this vast domain the tiller of the soil became no more than an interchangeable employee, and the sundering of the physical link between work and dwelling-place had more than symbolic significance: it expressed the destruction of the relations of human complementarity which had united the community of former times in favour of the strictly financial logic of profit.

It was this logic which governed the schemes spawned by the nineteenth century to remodel the rural domain. A principal device for the instrumentation of the agricultural domain, at which all transformations aimed, the laying out of parks in the English style promoted the elimination of fences, which hindered the mechanization of farming. At the same time it eliminated the purely prestige elements–the formal park with its burdensome maintenance staff–by restoring them to the domain under cultivation. There too, rationalization was in command, closely linked with the development of agricultural mechanization after the end of the eighteenth century. Those practices were, besides, the fruit of reflection for more than half a century by the members of learned societies intensely concerned with giving prominence to agriculture and with modernizing its methods of exploitation.

Landscape model and architectural model went hand in hand. The concentration of agricultural workers in villages gave rise to a serial architecture composed of repetitive units, whose purely formal variations did not succeed in disguising its anonymous, elementary character. More and more, the house became assimilated to a production tool; nothing any longer distinguished the house of a worker on the land from that of an artisan in a room or a factory worker, all subject to a common classification and the same proletarian statute.

The ultimate stage of this levelling tendency in habitat architecture was provided by theorists who, in the manner of Robert Owen, proposed groupings of several thousand inhabitants in a rural

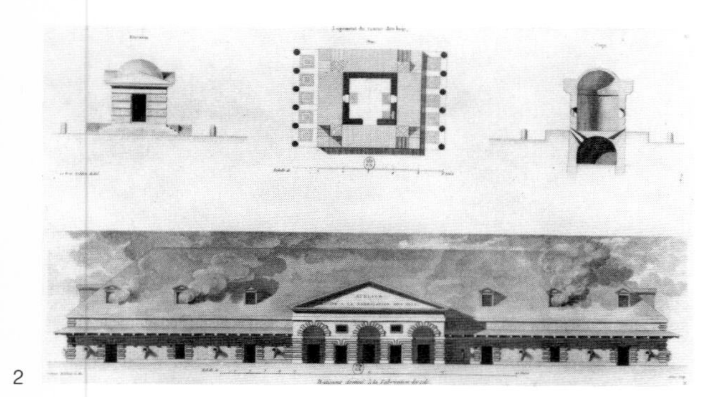

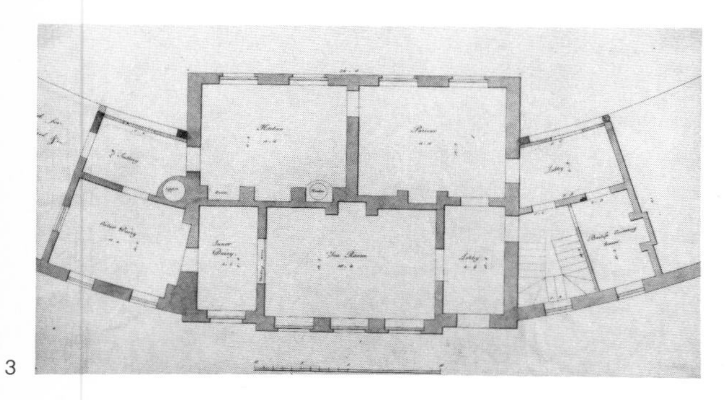

1. View of a group of associated Owenite villages, 1817. *A Supplementary Appendix to the First Volume of the Life of Robert Owen*, 1858.
2. Arc-et-Senans, near Besançon: The Chaux Salt Factory. Front elevation. Architect: Claude-Nicolas Ledoux.
3. Inveraray: Plan of the Maam Barn farm, 1784. Architect: Robert Mylne.

zone, around manufacturing structures derived directly from the industrial models suggested a little earlier at Arc-et-Senans by Claude-Nicolas Ledoux—except that the salt factory and the manager's house at the centre of this Roman encampment were replaced by commercial farm buildings or by public edifices.
Rather than topographical or historical accident, the Utopians preferred the abstract model of a perfect geometric form–the regular plane–implying a regulated behaviour. The nineteenth century was a society not of authority but of order,[12] as its architectural enterprise never failed to show. And however coercive it may appear in the light of facts, there was nothing wilfully oppressive in its vision of space; on the contrary it stands as a liberation in the face of the authoritarianism of former rule and its disorders springing from too long a history. Symbolically, the

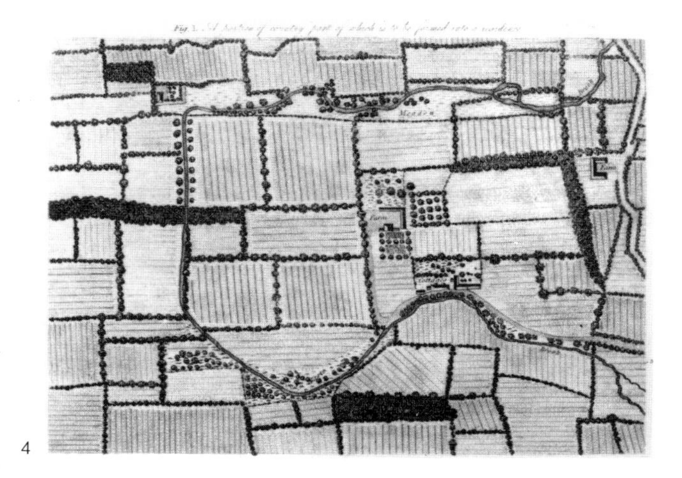

4

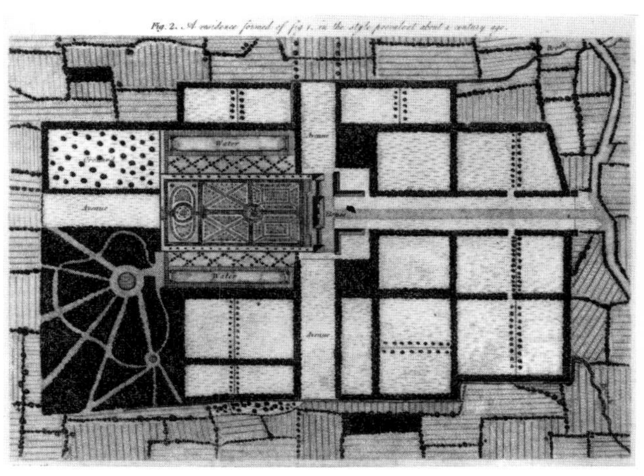

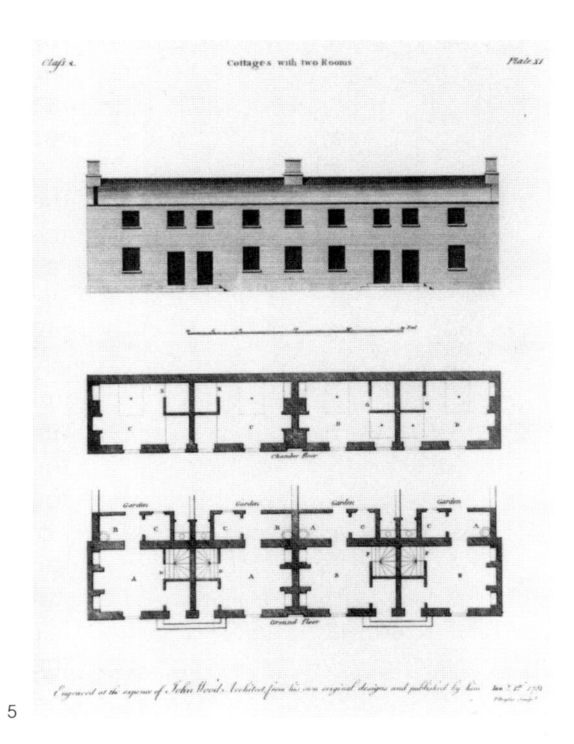

5

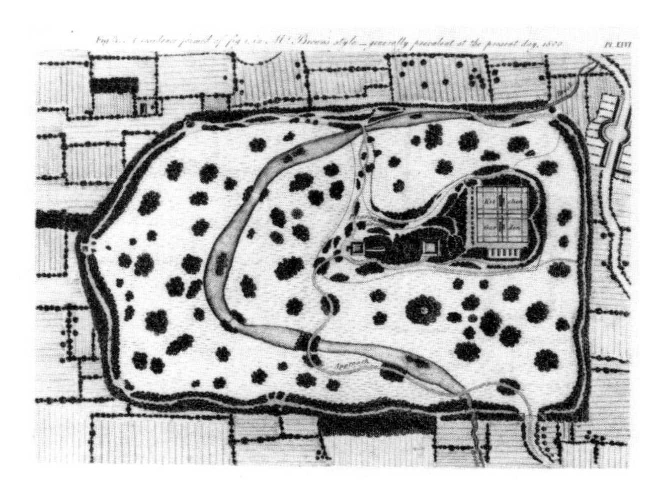

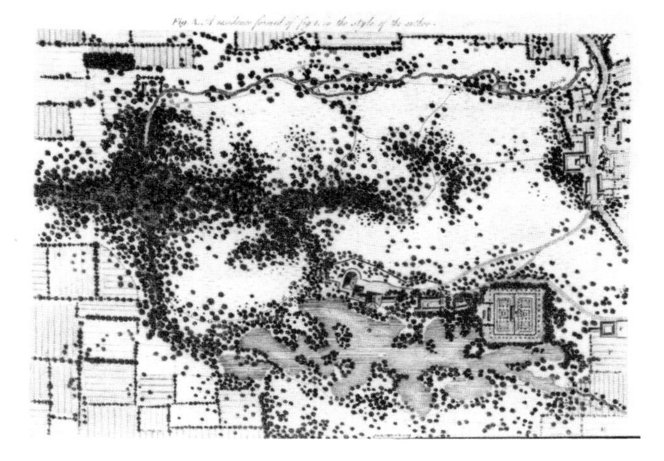

4. Four illustrations from *A Treatise on Forming, Improving, and Managing Country Residences*, by John Loudon, 1806.
5. Second-class cottage, four-family house. *A Series of Plans for Cottages or Habitations of the Labourer* by John Wood the Younger, 1781.

1

2

3

1.2. Scenes of Flax-growing and the Linen Trade, St Gall, Switzerland. Paintings of the later 17th century.

3. St Gall: Cloth-drying Tower. Later 18th century.

French Revolution chose the metre, a product of the mathematical division of the earth's circumference, over the traditional measuring units of the foot or the inch.

With the eighteenth century was born the industrial landscape, [13] an industry which for the time being did not leave the rural setting. Strong bonds of complementarity held it there besides, in terms of both employment–the worker-peasant being an everyday reality–and raw materials: the resources of mines, water or forests were to be found in the country, like flax, hemp or wheat. Traditional industry was based on mills or limekilns, which had haunted the rural landscape since the Middle Ages. The metallurgical industry, by bringing in the blast furnace fuelled by mineral coal, and the cotton textile industry, with its drying towers and immense multistoreyed workshops, introduced new models which quickly acquired considerable importance, from the end of the eighteenth century in England, and after 1830 in France.

Before the emergence of a manufacturing architecture it was above all the vision of the metallurgical works which struck the sensibility of artists: Philip James de Loutherbourg painted the site of Coalbrookdale at night, in the glow of a stream of molten iron issuing from the blast furnaces. Industry as yet was still the impressive spectacle of Vulcan's forge, the torrent of metal in fusion, the clouds of white and black smoke, the incandescence of matter. But, outside these visions of nocturnal hell, nature still belonged to Ceres and Pomona.

It was thus not the factory which left a deep mark on this planned landscape, in a world where agriculture remained the principal source of activity and incomes. The rationalizing effort bore upon the human agglomeration, whether urban or rural, in a twin transformation of the dialectical relation between monument and environment (diversification of programme themes, challenge to the hierarchy of habitat and monument).

4. Landscape with Limekiln, 1702.
Drawing by Jan van der Meer the Younger.

5. Coalbrookdale by Night, 1801.
Painting by Philip James de Loutherbourg.

4

Rationalization of transport: roads and canals

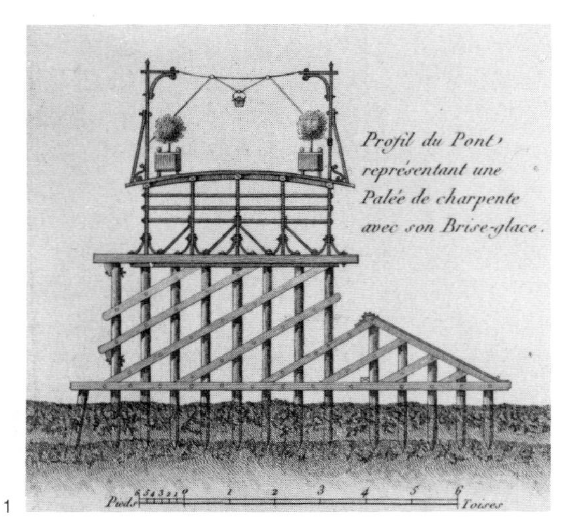

The challenge to the traditional hierarchy expressed in church and castle, those two monuments of authority, had as its corollary the birth of new urban programmes: the theatre, the promenade or the café, whose conjunction formed the new poles of interest of the city. Similarly, the road, the bridge, the canal or its lock were the salient features of the rural landscape, which they restructured according to a dynamic tied to the value of trade. To the model farm of Maam Barn mentioned above (page 22), the Duke of Argyll did not neglect to add a bridge and a port, because industry came into being on the foundation of trading facilities, and therefore imposed as a prerequisite the setting up of an infrastructure of communications.

Once again, the initiative came from the eighteenth century. It was the regime of Louis XV which formed the Civil Engineers Corps in France and gave it a power it has not lost to our day. The civil engineer replaced the military engineer, a smooth transition extending over a whole century, from Vauban to Louis-Alexandre de Cessart.

For the landscape was dominated by opening it up for communications, albeit military. In creating, from the end of the eighteenth century to the reign of Louis-Philippe, a network of roads and canals covering the entire country, France set up the infrastructure required for industrial development. This effort integrated not only the complete cartographic study of the terrain–cadastre, General Staff maps and hydrographic charts, over which two generations of surveyors and navigators had laboured–but also the census of resources in men, equipment and raw material, a census in which the old "enumeration" of the population made way for statistical analysis.

The result of recorded economic observation, the building of roads and canals had as its explicit objective an economic rationalization, while yet availing itself of the methods of refined architectural expression, notably in the domain of the iron bridge, the first attempts at which dated back to the end of the eighteenth century. The symbol of a new economic and social state, the cast-iron bridge concentrated around its design and execution an exceptional inventiveness, as witnessed by the distance which separated the attempts of Louis-Alexandre de Cessart,[14] under the reign of Louis XVI, from the works of Thomas Telford in the early nineteenth century.

The contradictions which, from the start of the nineteenth century, brought the planning of engineers into opposition with the somewhat nostalgic ideals of artists or with urban lifestyle–based, as yet unconsciously, on the cult of consumption and its totems–revealed the discrepancy between the philosophical design, wholly permeated by artistic idealism, and the orientation imparted to things by a capitalism developing in full swing. Henceforth the split between culture and the economy would only grow wider.

Paris: Pont des Arts, 1801-1803. Demolished.
Engineers: Louis-Alexandre de Cessart. Jacques Dillon.

1. Section of the bridge. *Description des travaux hydrauliques d'Alexandre de Cessart*, 1806-1808.
4. Drawings for the initial project for an iron bridge.
2. Plan for the laying out of a road. *Dictionnaire des Ponts et Chaussées*, 1787.

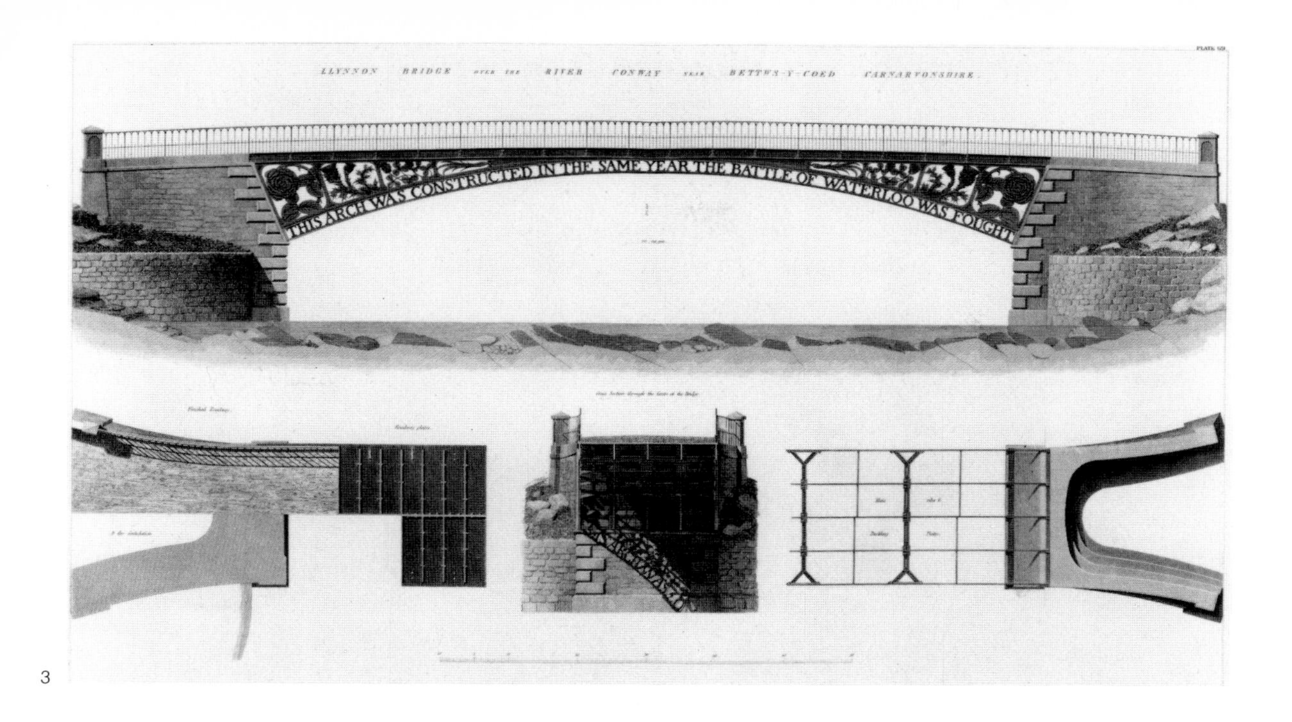

3

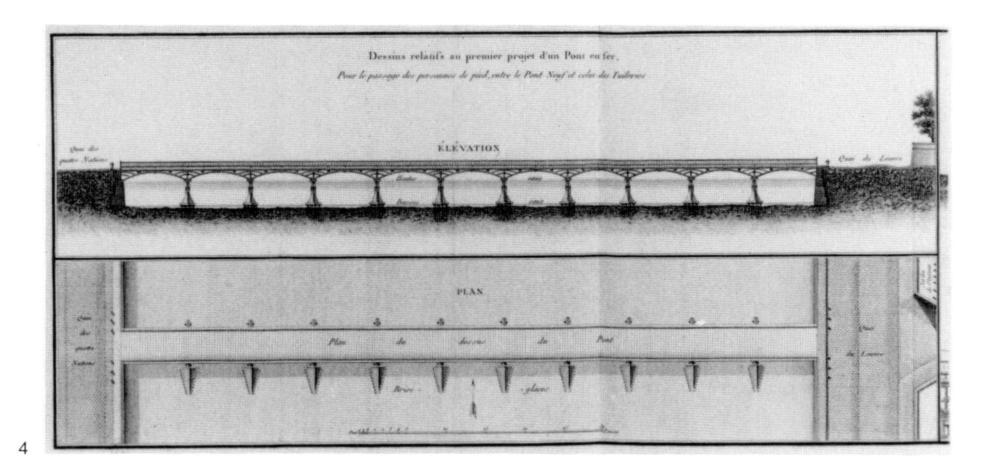

4

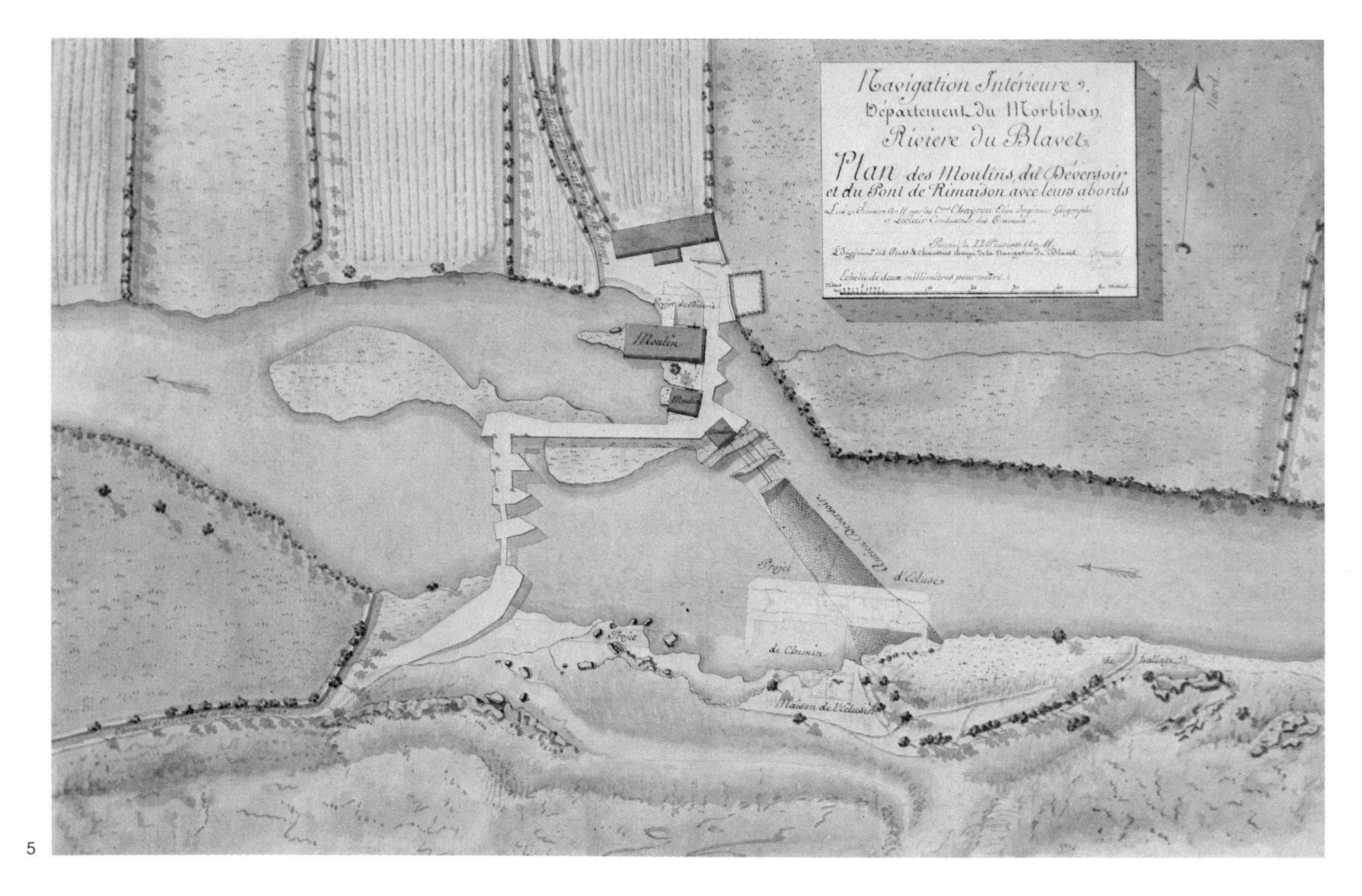

5

3. Bettws-y-Coed (Carnarvonshire): Llynnon Bridge, known as Waterloo Bridge, 1815. Engineer: Thomas Telford. *Atlas to the Life of Telford.*
5. Plan for a lock on the Blavet (Brittany), 1803. Engineer: Bouessel.

The representation of the secular power

1

Because political and religious values were no longer the only ones to which it referred, Neoclassicism created the museum. Starting at the end of the eighteenth century, Etienne-Louis Boullée[15] defined in his graphic work a series of building programmes which, added to the Metropolis and the Sovereign's Palace, expressed the symbolic needs of a new architecture: the Municipal Building or the Law Courts are of less importance there than Newton's Cenotaph, the Museum or the National Library. For neoclassical idealism, culture was the dominant fact of civilization: the expression of its importance took precedence over all other social needs.
That is why, even more than the Library, the Museum was symbolic: this immense central-plan construction, surrounded by porticos, was a temple of memory, of Fame. Access to it was by four great staircases that were like the tiered steps of an immense altar, in the crypt-like space of a long vaulted tunnel. At the rear, a colossal dome admitted–in the manner of the Pantheon of Rome–a cone of harsh light, which enveloped the void of a central crown of colonnades. This monument to culture thus ended on an empty centre, a place for meditation at the meeting of earth and sky.
In a more concrete form, the idea of the Museum, free and open to all, was at the heart of the cultural concerns of the French Revolution. By transforming the royal collections into public ones, the Convention opened the way for the creation of museums in all the large cities in France, an initiative which had much favourable influence abroad. If Boullée's edifice never saw the light of day, the Cour Carrée of the Louvre, a synthesis of national classicism, filled its place; it was joined to the Institut, the temple of Mind, by a fragile iron bridge, the Pont des Arts, the symbol of the new times.

2

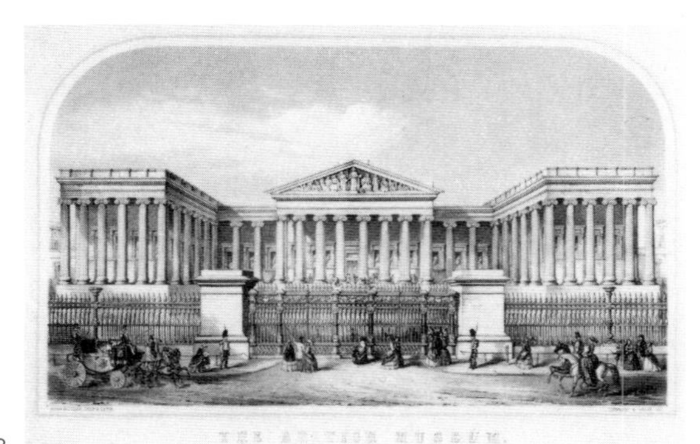

3

4

1. Interior view of a Museum.
Drawing by Etienne-Louis Boullée.
Late 18th century. *Detail p. 10.*
2. Berlin: Altes Museum, 1823-1830.
Architect: Karl Friedrich Schinkel.
3. London: British Museum, 1842-1847.
Architect: Sir Robert Smirke.
Lithograph by Augustus Butler, 1853.
4. Edinburgh: The Scottish National Gallery, 1850-1857.
Architect: William Henry Playfair.
Watercolour design by Playfair, c. 1845.

5

5. Munich: The Glyptothek, 1816-1830.
Architect: Leo von Klenze.
Watercolour design by Klenze, 1815.

1

That the museum to us looks like a Criminal Courts Building is a regrettable accident of history. Both temple and portico at the same time, the neoclassical museum took its place at the summit of the hierarchy of public buildings, in keeping with a formula that would later be diverted to more institutional purposes. The mighty Ionic temple raised by Leo von Klenze in Munich for the Glyptothek (Sculpture Gallery), begun in 1816, had its equivalent in the admirable façade of the Altes Museum of Karl Friedrich Schinkel in Berlin (1823-1830). From the fusion of these two models would come those porticoed ensembles, culminating in a large-scale pediment, of which the British Museum is the characteristic example.

Beyond the symbolic aspect of the building, the interior arrangement was more difficult. If the Louvre here had the advantage of a completely successful model, the great glazed gallery of Hubert Robert (the revolutionary principle of which was overhead lighting), there remained the compositional difficulty of the accumulation of art works whose conflicting visual voices rivalled the internal architectural layout, when they were not competing with each other!

The form of presentation yielding the best result, therefore, turned out to be that of the collector's private gallery, based on secret elective affinities between the assembled works; and the finest museums were thus the least didactic. The unity of thought and feeling broke down into two distinct modes of response: the intellectual effort of identification and classification, with its criterion of rationality, diverged from an aesthetic sensibility reposing on more and more sensitive foundations. The jumble of works of art assembled by Alexandre Lenoir in his Musée des Monuments Français was the first of the Romantic museums. Art and Science ceased their dialogue and locked themselves into opposed behavioural patterns: the ambivalence of modern thought was born.

2

3

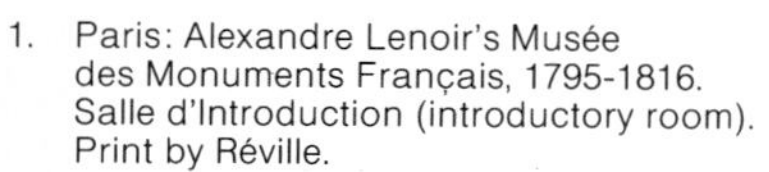

1. Paris: Alexandre Lenoir's Musée des Monuments Français, 1795-1816. Salle d'Introduction (introductory room). Print by Réville.
2. Berlin: Altes Museum, Rotunda. Architect: Karl Friedrich Schinkel. Drawing by Carl Emanuel Conrad.
3. Paris: Palais du Louvre, Musée Royal des Antiques. Salle de la Médée and Corridor de Pan, 1800-1803. Architects: Percier and Fontaine. Print after a drawing by Civeton.
4. London: Sir John Soane's House and Museum, 1812-1813. Architect: Sir John Soane. Watercolour, 1825.

66
aug. 16. 1825
View towards the Chimney Side of the Monk's Room
looking up into the Picture Room.—

4

Bank architecture

The development of capitalism was to give birth to a new type of architectural programme: that of the bank building, the prototype of the office building as the nineteenth century conceived it. Alongside the farmer, the artisan or the middle-class citizen, the employee came each day to occupy a more important place–which does not mean that an appropriate architecture sprang up to meet his needs. For a long while the employee, like the artisan, continued to work in a non-specific space, whether it was a room in his lodgings converted into an office, or the entire lodgings themselves, diverted from their original use.

The appearance of office architecture was the expression of a need for social representation. Functionally speaking, to sit down to write does not call for specific constructions (except that one must be able to keep warm and enjoy a bit of quiet). As a general rule, working space has scant representation in architecture: the agricultural hangar, the workshop or factory are even anti-architectonic by vocation, for it is their adaptability which takes precedence over any kind of symbol.

It was thus as a Monument of Money that office architecture developed. As a public edifice, the bank had to find an appropriate architectural formulation, on the same basis as the market or the church, that is, as a place of passage and of trade. It therefore sought its models in classical antiquity, which provided the examples of Trajan's market or the Roman public baths: large covered volumes, heated and abundantly lighted from above (skylighting being the most uniform, the most suitable for writing). In its form, the bank also had many similarities with the library. In the 1790s John Soane established, for the Bank Stock Office of London, a model of space, light and graceful mouldings whose perfection has since scarcely been equalled, and which has been put into general use for many other buildings.

2

3

London: Bank of England, 1791-1833.
Demolished.
Architect: Sir John Soane.

1. Bank Stock Office, 1791-1792. Watercolour.
2. Old Colonial or 5% Office, 1818. Watercolour by Joseph Michael Pandy.
3. Old Dividend or 4% Office, 1818.

4. Consols Office, 1797.
Watercolour of 1799-1800
by a pupil of Sir John Soane.

Trade and shopping centres

1

One of the first efforts of planning to which the nineteenth century devoted itself was the construction of corn exchanges, with the aim of regularizing the grain market, which was subject to sudden scarcities due to the irregularity of harvests. The great Parisian Halle au Blé of Nicolas Lecamus de Mézières, built under Louis XV, would be transformed in the early nineteenth century by the raising of a vast glazed dome, first in wood, then in iron (it remains one of the oldest examples of this type, despite the transformations it underwent at the end of the nineteenth century). From a granary the corn exchange had been insensibly transformed into a stock exchange, with the vast floorspace of the glazed rotunda being used for trading. The lightness and vastness of the metallic structure drew the admiration of the public of the day, while technicians retained its principle of construction "à la Delorme," an easy conversion from wood into iron.
To utilitarian public buildings, such as market halls, fountains and wash-houses, the neoclassical period assigned a fundamental role in urban projects. Acting on the principle that the flow of food supplies needed to be regularized, the administration assumed the supervision of markets (a supervision that was both financial and sanitary). The prefect De Chabrol, after the end of the Empire, had a series of markets built in Paris, the most remarkable of which was that of Saint-Germain (J.B. Blondel and A.L. Lusson, 1816), a vast covered portico whose timbered lantern took its inspiration from the theoretical model designed by Vitruvius for the basilica of Fano. The absolute architectural starkness of the building, the single-minded attention to bringing out the strength of its construction (notably in the principle of tying applied to the king-post timbers), showed that Neoclassicism was not in the slightest degree decorative: conceptual rigour largely overshadowed the sense of ornamentation. It is true that this work was imbued with the doctrine of J.N.L. Durand.

2

3

1. Paris: Palais-Royal, Galerie d'Orléans, 1829-1831. Demolished in 1934.
   Architect: Pierre-François-Léonard Fontaine.
   Lithograph after Carlo Gilio.
2. Paris: New Market of Saint-Germain, Interior view.
   Architects: Jean-Baptiste Blondel.
   Adrien-Louis Lusson.
   Plan, coupe, élévation, et détails du Nouveau Marché Saint-Germain, 1816.

4

Paris: Dome of the old Corn Exchange (Halle au Blé, now Bourse du Commerce), 1806-1811.
Architect: François-Joseph Bélanger.
Engineer: F. Brunet.

3. Arcaded interior.
L. Bruyère, *Etudes relatives à l'art des constructions*, 1823-1828.
4. The dome in its present state.

1

2

3

Neoclassical purism, dreaming of perfect monuments, was perhaps nevertheless a compensation for the reality of the times. Commercial architecture, as opposed to public architecture, did not cumber itself with concepts, but sought to respond to the demand for luxury of the aristocratic clientele of a great capital. Combining the major experiments of its day in the handling of space, it devised the covered passage, [16] an offshoot of the Grande Galerie of the Louvre, whose mighty ceiling span and overhead lighting may be found repeated in the beautiful Galerie Vivienne (by F.J. Delannoy, 1823) or in a lighter, more transparent form in the arching roof of the Passage Choiseul (by M. Tavernier, 1825-1827) or of the Passage du Bourg-l'Abbé (by A.L. Lusson, 1827-1828). The perfection as a public building here has less importance than the spectacular effect of the glazed roofing and the sumptuous appearance of a highly elaborated architectonic décor, making the passage more akin to the palace than to the boutique, of which it is nevertheless the support.
Breaking with neoclassical purity, prestige construction, enriched with all the hallmarks of luxury, made its reappearance in the second quarter of the nineteenth century, the period of Balzac's Paris. The passages, associated with the great theatres (the Opera, Choiseul, les Italiens...), filled the place of the gardens of the Empire or the Revolution. They revealed the transformation that had taken place, as the effect of economic development, in that period of intense speculation which the economic crisis of 1827 would bring to an abrupt, but temporary halt.
Restoration Paris [17] provided a foretaste of the Paris of the Second Empire, when industrial development brought with it bourgeois prosperity. And, besides, the model of the passage, although it fell into disuse in the Paris of Haussmann, would achieve outstanding success in other cities: the Galeries Saint-Hubert (by J.-P. Cluysenaar, 1846-1847) stand witness in Brussels, as does the Passage Pommeraye in Nantes (by J.-B. Buron and H. Durand-Gosselin, 1840-1843).

1. Paris: Passage Choiseul, 1825-1827.
   Architect: M. Tavernier.
2. Brussels: Galeries Saint-Hubert,
   Galerie du Roi, 1846-1847.
   Architect: Jean-Pierre Cluysenaar.
3. Paris: Galerie Vivienne, 1823.
   Architect: François Jacques Delannoy.
4. Nantes: Passage Pommeraye, 1840-1843.
   Architects: Jean-Baptiste Buron
   Hippolyte Durand-Gosselin.

4

LOCOMOTIVE A MARCHANDISES
Chemin de Fer d'Orléans (Système C. Polonceau)
COUPE
DESSINÉ ET GRAVÉ PAR J. PETITCOLIN.
Paris, chez l'Auteur, rue St André des Arts, 33.
Imp. par Drouart, rue du

The Industrial Revolution, whose effects were felt in France after 1830 (but in England, sixty years earlier), was a phenomenon of such amplitude that it may be compared to the great changes which have left their mark on the different phases of human civilization since its origins: there would be an "industrial age" as there had been a stone age or an iron age. It would, of course, be vain to try to ascribe a precise date to this revolution, which determined the image of the nineteenth century as a whole, within its most extended limits, from the French Revolution to the First World War. And it is therefore not vain to look as far back as medieval history for the first fruits of industrial production (just as it is correct to insist on the appearance of capitalism as early as the fourteenth century). The fact remains that around 1830 there occurred a crystallization of this series of consonant trends, the operative factor being the invention of the railway: before it was industrial, the revolution was social (starting with Le Chapelier's law in 1791), then mechanical.
The year 1830 saw the forfeiture of the revolution in France, but also the birth of Belgium, the first nationalist movements in Germany, Austria and Italy. A liberal wind was blowing across Europe, challenging the philosophical ideals of the late eighteenth century in favour of a more pragmatic mentality, opposing aesthetic pleasure to intellectual beauty, and feeling to the idea. What characterized the mentality called Romantic (to generalize a term used by literary historians), was its total rejection of dogmatism; hence its challenge to prevailing Neoclassicism as the only system of explaining and organizing the world.
In fact, eclectic thought is the true characteristic of the July Monarchy in France (and not of the generation that succeeded it). Eclecticism meant the freedom to choose, the independence

The mechanical revolution 1830-1850

of personal judgement outside any pre-established norm–any system or any religion. One must not see in it that hodgepodge and confusion which a purely negative approach gave to the term later (especially in that mistaken opinion, so unjust to nineteenth-century artists, which takes eclecticism to be the mixing of genres and styles, a practice the epoch never ceased to abhor).
Because the generation of 1830 accepted the independence of personal choice, the equivalence of different tastes and cultures, it could suddenly become receptive to multiple historical visions of other cultures. The discovery of the Middle Ages (which was at the same time the discovery of the Romanesque, Gothic, Carolingian and other styles) was paralleled by that of the East or the Far East. India, China or the Arab world thus entered European culture, on the same footing with the civilization of antiquity, and this at the very moment when it was being realized that Athens and Rome were not indistinguishably fused in a single culture. Archaeology, by turning its interest to Assyria, Egypt, Armenia or Iran, was breaking out of its cultural circle; it, too, was relativizing its terms of reference.
Thus the philosophy of relativism slowly entered European thought. It would challenge the pre-eminence of Platonic idealism, by reducing Neoclassicism, in the artistic field, to a choice among others. The nineteenth century, because it was living through a brutal change in civilization, woke up to the fact that cultures had become mortal. In the sudden obsolescence of its own referential system, nothing remained but to launch into the uncontrollable enterprise of creating a "new art." [1] From the reign of Louis-Philippe on, this problem was at the heart of the cultural debate. Stated differently, if the Industrial Revolution seemed to have no immediate impact on artistic creation, in reality it shook it profoundly; where classical thought for nearly three centuries had affirmed the complete, untouchable superiority of antique culture, the Industrial Revolution made possible the awareness of art in all the variety of many times and places.

Birth of artificial transport

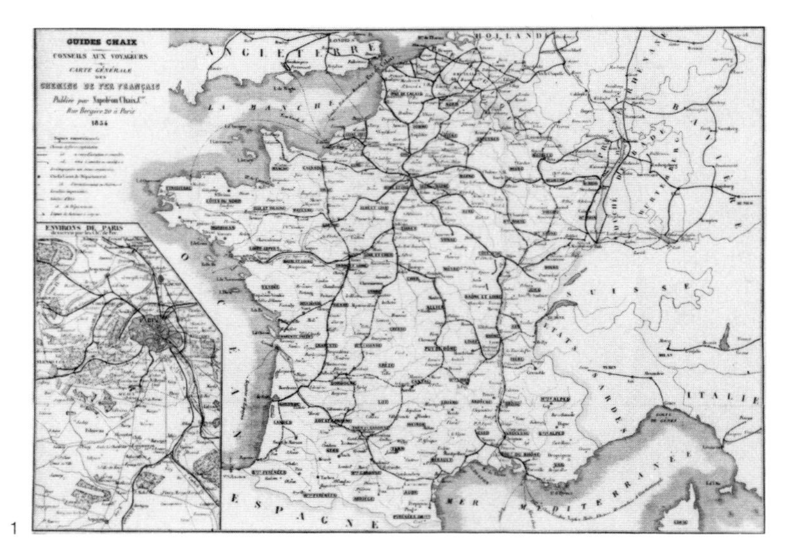

The birth of the railway is a long story, from the first wooden rails of the seventeenth century to the finishing touches put on the steam locomotive, by Marc Seguin and George Stephenson, in 1827-1829. Capable of pulling a train of thirteen tonnes at a speed of 24 km./h.–in other words, the speed of a horse at an ordinary gallop–Stephenson's locomotive transformed the data on the transport of heavy materials. It made finally possible the exchanges of raw materials that were indispensable for the creation of industries. It became operational, moreover, at exactly the same time that the Saint-Etienne line was opened, in 1827, by the Seguin brothers. In 1832, on the Saint-Etienne–Roanne line, the steam locomotive replaced the horse-drawn vehicle for good.
The following year the first law was passed authorizing railway building in France, while the first Belgian, English and American lines were begun; and it was nine years later, in 1842, that the charter was promulgated under which the French national rail network was constituted. By the end of the Second Empire (1870), all Europe would be linked by rail. This transformation was all the more remarkable in that the preceding generation had already accepted the immense effort represented by the creation of a network of roads and canals on a national scale. The birth of industry was possible only thanks to this powerful infrastructure.
The creation of the railway was also the occasion for engineers to place in question the technologies developed under the Empire for the construction of bridges. The vibrations set up by the passage of trains were so violent that the cast-iron bridges, built using the technique of assembled voussoirs (inspired by construction on stone beds), failed to stand the strain. It was therefore to a new technique, that of the "wire" suspension bridge, that engineers would henceforth devote themselves. The road bridges of Marc Seguin at Tournon (1824) or of Thomas Telford over the Menai Straits (1826) or at Conway (1828) would serve as models, alongside experimental research in masonry construction (leading to that admirable structure, the Morlaix viaduct, built in 1864 by the engineer Victor Fénoux), as well as in steel construction (the Britannia tubular bridge by Robert Stephenson over the Menai Straits, 1846-1850). The evolution here was constant, each enterprise enabling techniques to be perfected, implementation procedures to be simplified, economies to be made in materials, or performances to be improved.
Finally, the creation of the railway must be considered together with another initiative, the impact of which would revolutionize urban life: the opening in Paris, in 1828, of a horse-drawn omnibus service between the Porte Saint-Martin and the Madeleine. Public transport–which the Duchesse de Berry called, with cynical humour, "the poor man's carriage"–was born. It broke with a tradition several millennia old of matching city size to pedestrian

1. Map of the French railway network. *Guide-Chaix, Conseils aux voyageurs en chemins de fer*, 1854.
2. Suspension bridge over the Rhône between Tain and Tournon, 1824. Engineer: Marc Seguin.

3

3. Suspension bridge over the Menai Straits (Wales), 1818-1826.
Engineer: Thomas Telford.
Britannia tubular bridge over the Menai Straits, 1846-1850.
Engineer: Robert Stephenson.
The Wonders of the Menai, in its Suspension and Tubular Bridges, colour lithograph.

5

4

4. Conway suspension bridge (Wales), 1826-1828.
Engineer: Thomas Telford.
Lithograph by P. Gauci from a sketch by G. Pickering.

5. Early horse-omnibus in Paris, running from the Porte Saint-Martin to the Madeleine, 1828.
Print by Loeillot.

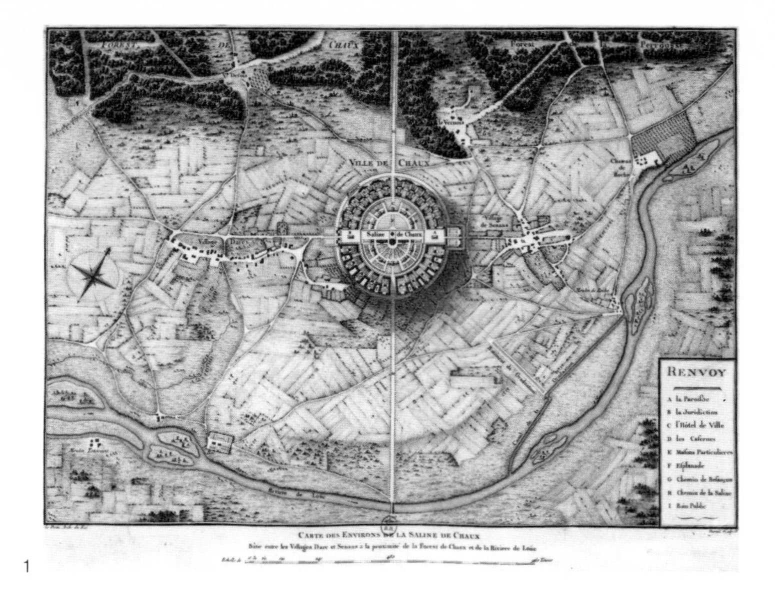

1

1. Arc-et-Senans, near Besançon: Map of the Chaux saltworks and the surrounding area, 1775-1779. Architect: Claude-Nicolas Ledoux.
2. Le Grand Hornu (Belgium): Central courtyard of the industrial works. *La Belgique Industrielle*, 1852.

travel. The bursting out of city centres into suburbs was immediate, and it provided the means of achieving the urban expansion imposed by industrial concentration.

From that perspective, factory architecture was of small importance. First of all, building programmes were rarely carried out according to a freely determined architectural design: the case of the Grand Hornu in Belgium was the exception that proved the rule. Here the neoclassical architect Bruno Renard, taking his inspiration from the model set up by Claude-Nicolas Ledoux in the previous century, created an imposing industrial plant between 1820 and 1832. It must still be observed that, if the form remains perfect, the aim is essentially practical. The conception of the factory is dictated by functional imperatives to which the architecture submits, without monumental proportions and above all without useless expense (down to and including the repetitious system of standardized arcades).

More usually, the architecture of the first factories was the product of a recovery operation: the old royal glassworks at Le Creusot (which the Schneider family would later turn into their château) or the many medieval monasteries, sold as national property and converted to industrial use.

2

3

3. Le Grand Hornu (Belgium), 1820-1832: The central courtyard. Architect: Bruno Renard.
4. Le Creusot (Saône-et-Loire): Château de la Verrerie (former glassworks), present state.
5. Jumet, near Charleroi (Belgium): The Amercœur Collieries. *La Belgique Industrielle*, 1852.

4

5

1

The only type of architecture to come out of this first phase of industrial history was that of the multistorey factory, the first examples of which in England date back to the 1780s. Construction in stories was not imposed, as might be thought, by land prices in metropolitan areas, but by a technical facility: the gear transmission of mechanical energy from the steam engine to the workshops. The drive shaft and its transmissions (fixed to the ceilings) were connected by belts to pulleys which operated the looms. The vertical disposition of the workshops facilitated this transmission, even if it complicated the construction. Moreover, the floors were made more resistant by replacing the timberwork by iron bars, on cast-iron piers, inside a strong containing wall of masonry. The Philip & Lee cotton mill at Salford, Manchester, was the first factory built according to this system, in 1801, by the Boulton & Watt foundry of Soho. [2]

1. Gleiwitz (Upper Silesia): The Royal Ironworks. Colour lithograph, c. 1850.
2. Scotland: Lanark Cotton Mills. Engraving by J. Denholm Delt, c. 1794.

2

3

3. Mulhouse (Alsace): Koechlin Cotton Mills. Print, early 19th century.
4. Cromford near Matlock (Derbyshire): Arkwright's Cotton Mill by Moonlight. Painting by Joseph Wright of Derby, c. 1793.
5. Manchester: Cotton Factories, Union Street. Engraving from *Lancashire Illustrated*, 1831.

4

5

The social restructuring of the city

1

The fact remained that the industrial building paid scant heed to ordonnance–it took root where it could, and where conditions were technically most favourable to it–whereas urban architecture, for its part, was entering a period in which the composition of the built-up landscape became more important every day. The generation of 1830 would attempt, daringly but without success, to replace the anarchic city that was forming under its eyes by an organized city, coherent in its choices and forms.

In the industrial society being born, the city was at stake: the city of the rich and that of the poor challenged each other, opening the way to permanent urban reconquest. In reality the opposition between rich and poor promoted speculation, for it brought with it a constant falling into disuse of former construction in favour of new districts; in this regular turnover of privileged areas there were numerous opportunities for financial intervention, yielding substantial gains in appreciation of property values when reconstructions were undertaken. The city was thus no longer a patrimony but a market-place: like securities, real estate had its stock exchange.

This financial logic had a profound impact on the building sector. It became the driving force of urban transformation, bringing as a consequence a very rapid acceleration in the downgrading of buildings. A complete contradiction existed between the continuous beautifying of the city to which speculation gave rise in the rich neighbourhoods, and the depreciation it caused elsewhere. The architects were the victims of this situation, which, while offering them far wider means of realizing their projects, each day produced a little further deterioration in the equilibrium of the urban structure.

The publication of *Paris Moderne*, by Normand in 1837, brought to an end the generation of the Empire and the Restoration, from the Rue de Rivoli to the church of Saint-Vincent-de-Paul and the beautiful square that set it off, at the upper end of the Rue d'Hauteville. Louis-Philippe architecture, in the 1840s, would be "ornate," a profusion of decorative scenes stamped in relief or moulded, of which the repetitive technique of production derived directly from industrial processes. On plaster façades, stucco or terracotta adornments competed with ornamental cast iron to please the eye. The phenomenon was not confined to France: it reached as far as the new Athens, which reinvented the process of terracotta moulding for the decoration of capitals, for acroteria and even for statues in the round. [3]

The ornamental fantasy of Greek neo-antique (utilizing the grammatical elements of classical style, but in an entirely different perspective) had its equivalent in the brushing-up of repertories by neo-Renaissance or neo-Gothic houses elsewhere. The taste ran to luxury, a luxury expressed by profusion. Only a practised eye,

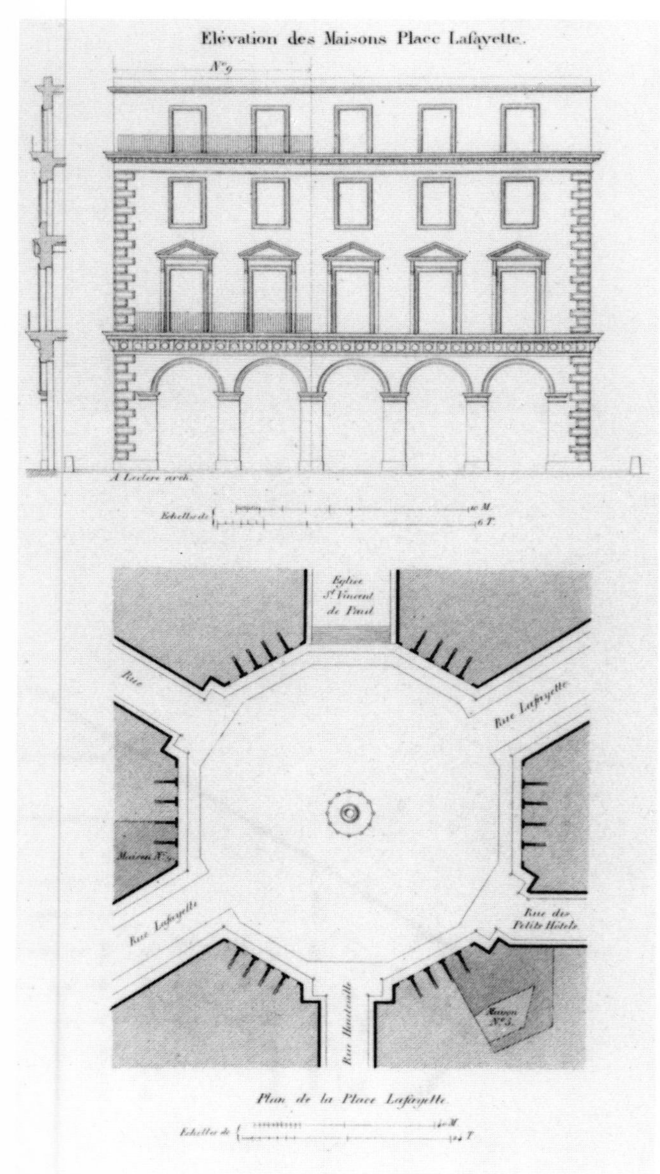

2

versed in the technique of construction, could tell whether that luxury was authentic or not. For in appearance nothing distinguished the stucco, moulded ornament on a plaster façade from the same ornament carved in stone. The bourgeois architecture of the rising classes craving social recognition played for the time being on that ambiguous relation between poverty and wealth set up by spontaneously assimilating richness in ornament to riches in money. Succeeding generations would be less naïve.
The urban landscape of the poor quarters was quite different. The influx of population caused by the development of the railway in the big cities and the constant growth of industries had as its consequence a practically unbearable saturation of urban space. For population density increased first in the city centres. To the already unpleasant crowded conditions of the old housing was added the maximum exploitation of land by a totally anarchic

1. Frontispiece of *Paris Moderne, ou Choix de maisons construites dans les nouveaux quartiers de la capitale et dans ses environs; levées et dessinées par Normand fils*, 1837.
2. Paris: Elevation of the houses in the Place Lafayette and plan of the Place Lafayette. Architect: A. Leclerc. *Paris Moderne*, 1837.
3. Paris: Avenue Frochot, Nos. 4 and 6, c. 1830-1840. Architect unknown.

4. Paris: Place Saint-Georges, No. 26, c. 1840-1842. Architect: E. Renaud. Sculptures by Desbœufs and Garraud.

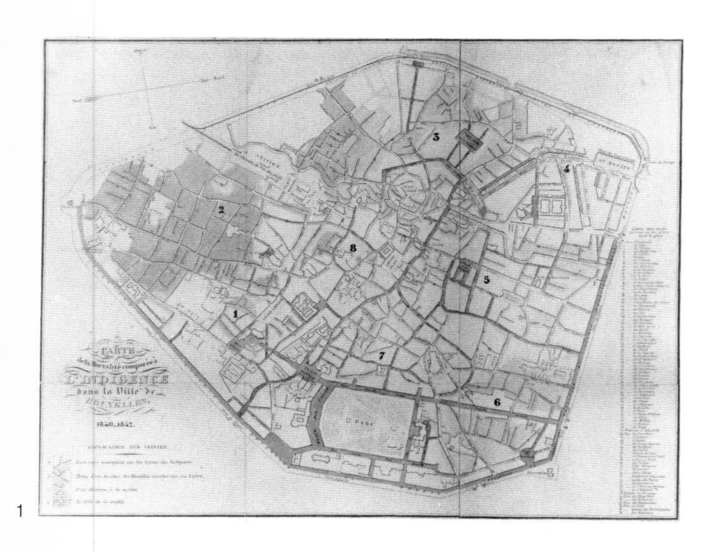

1. Map showing neighbourhood mortality rates in Brussels, 1840-1842.
De la mortalité à Bruxelles, comparée à celle des autres grandes villes by E. Ducpétiaux, 1844.
2. View of a Phalanstery.
Lithograph after a drawing by C.F. Daubigny.

construction: the filling of parcels of land by successive blocks opening onto courtyards on sites meant for gardens; systematic over-elevation by which cities grew from two to six stories high in less than a generation. In agglomerations that had neither sewers nor water mains, sanitary conditions became disastrous, bringing in their wake numerous epidemics which were the sign of a deep crisis of urban structure. The pauperism of this early period was not yet that of the "zone," but rather that of "unsanitary blocks," whose former habitat was undergoing a growth so violent that it was a threat to health and safety alike.

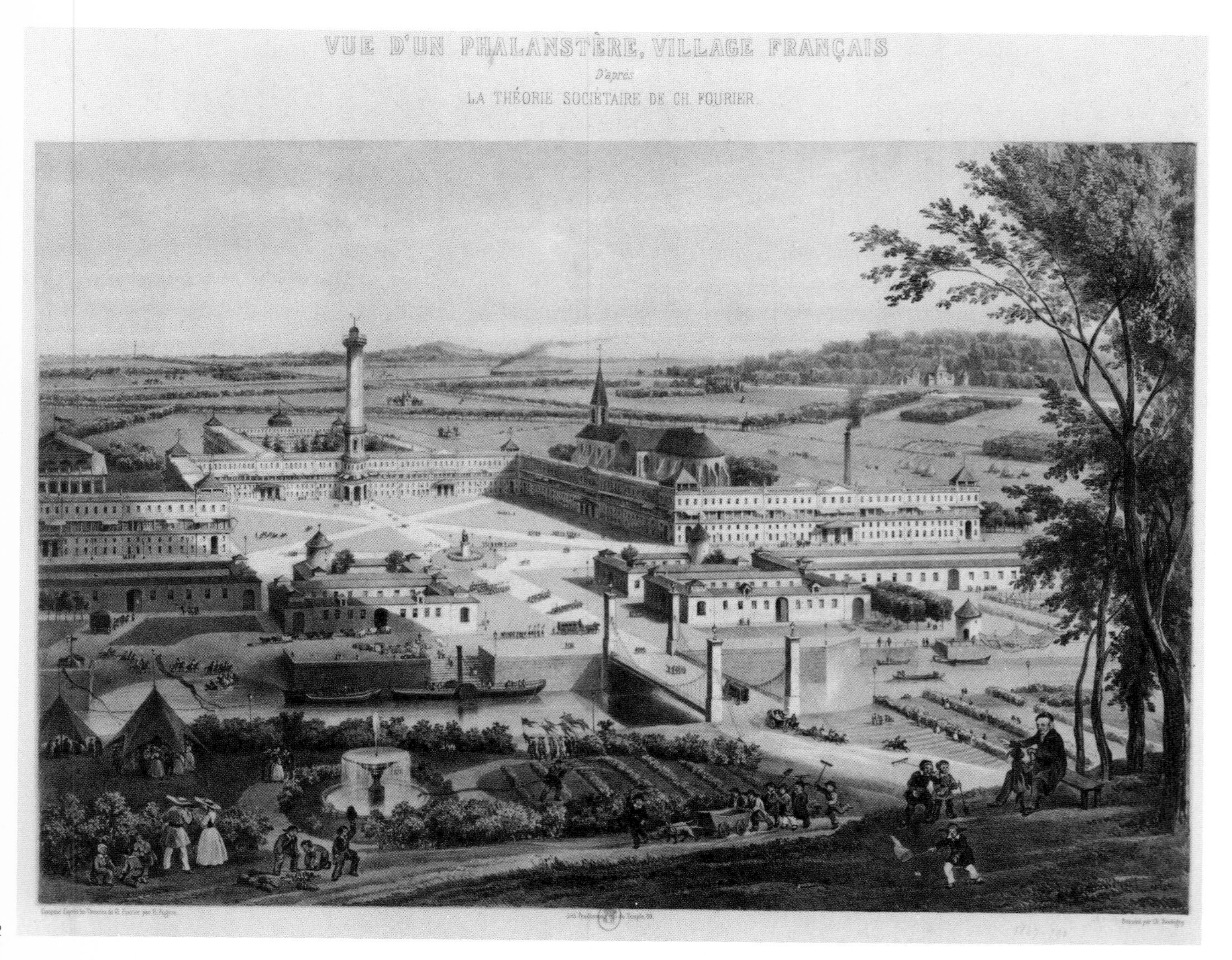

3

The bloody incidents of the Rue Transnonain in Paris in 1834, or of the silk-workers' revolt in Lyons three years before, showed that the squalor of town centres had become explosive. The cholera epidemic of 1832 (which struck down even the Prime Minister of France) had sounded another alarm. From then on the medical hygienists would be listened to: it was from their analyses that the notion of insalubrity was born, starting with maps like the one drawn by Dr Ducpétiaux in Brussels, linking the death rate with the number of indigent citizens by neighbourhood. The criticism of the city had begun. It had as its consequences both the escape into phalansterian utopias (as proposed by the Fourierites) and the rejection of the present; hence the escape into History, as proposed by Ruskin or especially Pugin, in one of the most cruel (but also most revealing) comparisons between the modern and the medieval city. The destructuring of the city was notorious, calling for immediate intervention.

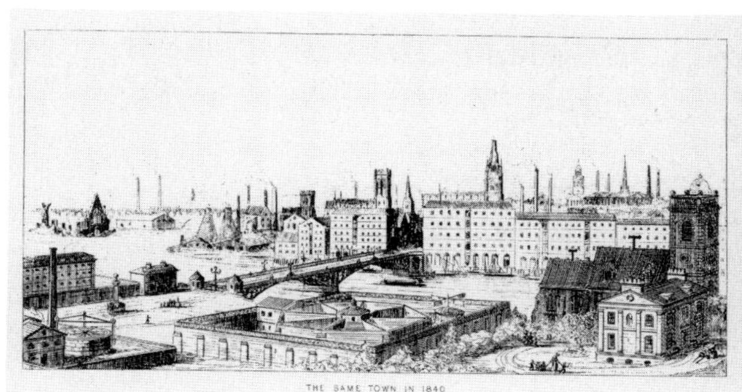

5

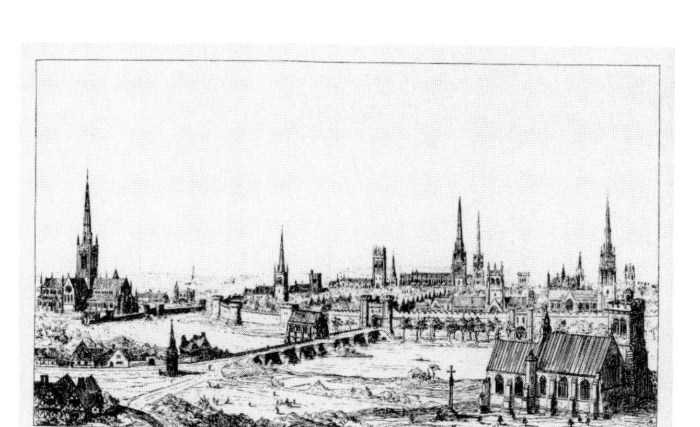

4

3. Paris: The Rue des Saules, Montmartre, in 1887.
4.5. Catholic Town in 1440.
The Same Town in 1840.
A. Welby Pugin, *Contrasts: or, A Parallel between the Noble Edifices of the Middle Ages and Corresponding Buildings of the Present Day*, 1841.

The refusal of industrialization

After 1830 the divorce between the neo-classical utopia and capitalist reality had become so glaring that it was impossible not to take account of it. The model of classical culture became relative through the failure of its programme of intellectual planning, faced with the destructive effects of new forms of economic organization. The proselytism of classical thought had seen in the perfect harmony of the system of laws–political or artistic–the answer to the conflicts of its century; it did not survive the profound structural changes that were taking place before its eyes.

There was consequently nothing surprising in the tendency to look for models of behaviour in other times and other places: art would transpose them into visual terms. The educative function of artistic expression had never been so specifically in demand, since art was henceforth entrusted with the reform of manners, and there was introduced into the notion of "style" a pedagogical, if not moral character. The historical gaze is true kin to the social-utopian: like the latter, it reveals the rejection of economic or political reality, the total crisis of the institution; it seeks the remedy.

There is thus no conflict, as has been too often asserted, between two rival schools–Reason and Feeling, the Classical and the Romantic (or, to give full measure, the Gothic)–for there is as much feeling in the Classical of the Ecole des Beaux-Arts as there is reason in the Gothic of the diocesan architects. In both cases there is even too much: the Ecole des Beaux-Arts sins through excess of aesthetic sensibility, the Gothics by a rationalism too assertive and too barren, the positions being indeed often paradoxical! The problem lies elsewhere.

In the first of the great works marking the history of European neo-Gothic,[4] the country house of Horace Walpole at Strawberry Hill (remodelled from 1750 on), the fundamentally moral, at the same time as political, character of the new style was already obvious. Horace Walpole's enterprise was not just architectural; it had a critical content manifested in the symbols or the inscriptions by which the architecture was accompanied. Idealism was sometimes turned to account there, but in terms of other values, notably patriotism.

In any case, the ideas remained ambiguous, for as soon as an eclecticism comes into being, the formal opposition it sets up between several different languages is of a kind that encourages transpositions into political terms (as the end of the sixteenth century had already clearly shown). But this transposition is only a cultural reading of the form; it does not belong to that form and is therefore liable to the most confusing somersaults of meaning. Thus there is nothing to prevent seeing in neo-Gothic the expression of a libertarian patriotism, as well as the manifestation of a reactionary frame of mind, hostile to progress. In reality, in neo-Gothic as well as the neoclassical, divergences of intention

1. Paris: View of Notre-Dame and the portico decoration erected for the christening of H.R.H. the Duke of Bordeaux on 1 May 1821. Portico designed by: J.I. Hittorff, J.F. Lecointe. Print by Hibon.
2. Paris: Sainte-Clotilde, 1846-1857. Architects: Franz Christian Gau, Théodore Ballu. Drawing by M.A. Blanchot.

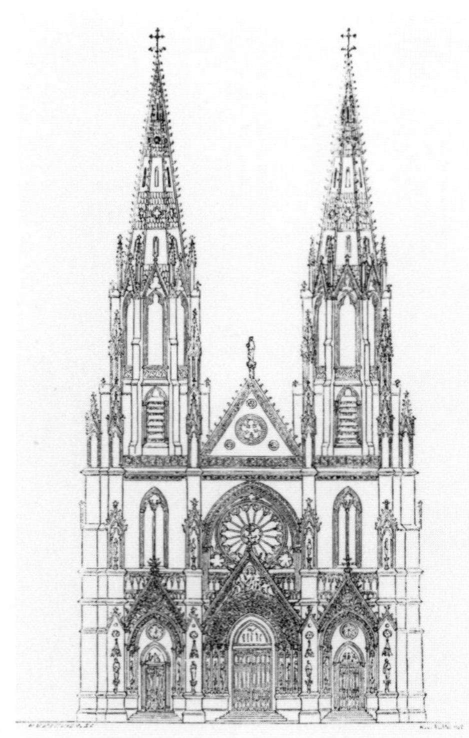

appear: they are often clarified by the differences of form, but many ambiguities and confusions nevertheless make their reading uneasy.
That is demonstrated quite well by the utilization of neo-Gothic as the "legitimist" style in a characteristic setting–the baptismal festivities of the Duc de Bordeaux, by Hittorff (1821)–in parallel with the use Schinkel made of it for the sets of *The Maid of Orleans* (1818), a nationalist epic of diametrically opposed significance. The forms are the same; the message is not (the same thing was still true in the twentieth century, in the contradictory uses made of the classical reference).
The ambiguity of the neo-Gothic architects (more serious still than that of the neoclassicists, whose divergent tendencies began nevertheless to appear at the same time) cleared up only after 1830, when for circumstantial reasons Gothic became identified with modernity, and classicism with academicism.

3. Berlin, Royal Opera House: Stage set by Karl Friedrich Schinkel for Schiller's *Die Jungfrau von Orleans* (IV, 1), 1818. Gouache.

3

1

2

3

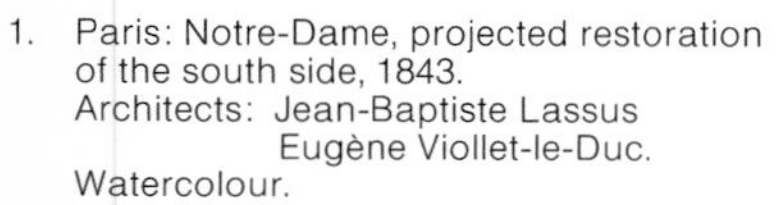

1. Paris: Notre-Dame, projected restoration of the south side, 1843.
   Architects: Jean-Baptiste Lassus
   Eugène Viollet-le-Duc.
   Watercolour.
2. Paris: Notre-Dame, south side during restoration.
   Photograph by Hippolyte Bayard, 1847.
3. The Banks of the Rhine at Cologne, c. 1840.
   Print by M.J. Starling after a drawing by W.L. Leitch.

This transformation went hand in hand with a new self-awareness of which archaeology was the conveyor. The critical restoration of the troubadour decorative style was the product of historical culture which a generation of archaeologists and collectors had managed to compile throughout Europe. From then on, neo-Gothic ceased to be theatrical exoticism or an art of nostalgia; the cast-off garments of the past became a patrimony; it was that patrimony which provided the support for the national consciousness of the new middle class. A de facto identification was thus established between neo-Gothic and middle-class by the roundabout route of archaeological culture. This assertion still needs to be qualified, for there were at least three ways of conceiving the neo-Gothic, depending on whether one was a priest, an architect or an aristocrat!

The Gothic of the priests placed religious sentiment foremost. It demanded little as regards the quality of the form, still less the purity of its references; but it set a high value on the character of spectacle. Architecture was the setting for prayer; it had to produce that "ravishment" which was basic to the mystical experience and to which liturgy had wholly devoted its efforts for three centuries. If the Gothic of Sainte-Clotilde was at once plagiarized and inconsistent, that had small importance in relation to the effect produced by the setting, to the feelings it aroused. In the Temple of the Church, the money-lenders of Saint-Sulpice had the freedom of the city, provided that they contributed to the moral good of the people.
The architects' Gothic was partly archaeological. With the knowledge of its patrimony it applied itself to the restoration of edifices, as well as to making them complete. The didactic thought of the nineteenth century liked complete, illustrative examples. It

4. Cologne Cathedral at the beginning of the 16th century.
5. Cologne Cathedral on its completion in the 19th century.
Histoire et description de la Cathédrale de Cologne by Sulpice Boisserée, 1843.

5

4

tended to crystallize knowledge around a few monument-symbols, enriching them and, if need be, filling in what was missing to make them more articulate. "Reactivated" Gothic (to parody a phrase of Mies van der Rohe) was its formal ideal.
The patriotic enterprise of the completion of the cathedral of Cologne (of which only the choir had survived) slowly adapted itself to this preoccupation with scientific exemplarity, the rationality of which was in absolute contradiction with the all-pervading sentimentalism of the epoch. Here the idea alone no longer sufficed; it needed the warrant of History to be taken seriously. The discovery of the plans of Cologne cathedral by Georg Moller and Sulpice Boisserée, in 1814-1816, would furnish at once the instrument of the project and the proof of its accuracy; from 1833 to 1842 the architect Ernst Friedrich Zwirmer devoted his energies to

unifying the contradictory data of archaeological observation and archival documentation to achieve a synthetic design erasing all professional doubts and imperfections. It was only at the conclusion of this effort to overcome historical contradictions, and so attain a purely didactic unity, that work could begin on the construction site!

The same was true of that Gothic historical structure shaped by the efforts of French archaeologists around a few Parisian monuments from the time of St Louis: Lassus and Viollet-le-Duc, in restoring the Sainte-Chapelle and Notre-Dame, made them national examples. If the unity of the building presented no problem in the first case, it

1

2

1. Arras: High altar of the Old Cathedral. Drawing by Jean-Baptiste Lassus. *Annales archéologiques*, 1849.
2. Moulins: Saint-Nicolas du Sacré-Cœur, 1850-1855. Front elevation. Drawing by J.-B. Lassus and Esmonnot, 1849.

was an entirely different matter in the second: although Viollet-le-Duc was aware of the complexity of Notre-Dame de Paris, [5] and strove to demonstrate it through fine analysis, his restoration of it partly wiped out that diversity in favour of a global image which his intervention sought continuously to strengthen.

It was normal that this line of thought should have resulted in the construction of edifices synthesizing all the aspirations of the nineteenth century in its reading of history. By insisting, in the construction of Saint-Nicolas at Nantes (started in 1840), on the rationality of Gothic structure, on its logic of design and the economy it made possible on the building site, Jean-Baptiste Lassus [6] was not simply finding circumstantial arguments: he was seeing what was essential in the Gothic message. The demonstration was clear. The emotional qualities of medieval space allied themselves to the rationality of structure and implementation; the duality of feeling and reason thereby disappeared, without either the bad taste of pastiche or the sterility of academicism: a double victory!

3. Nantes: Saint-Nicolas, 1840-1850.
Architect: Jean-Baptiste Lassus.

This vision, however, scarcely coincided with that of the aristocrats, the builders of châteaux. There once more the content of neo-Gothic was complex. The temple of the German nation–another Valhalla–created by Schinkel at the time of the restoration of Stolzenfels (1836) was a far cry in its intentions from the enterprise attempted by Jacques-Félix Duban at Blois (1845-1866), in a spirit whose archaeological rigour was qualified by a taste for the picturesque. Finally, for the construction of their châteaux, the legitimist aristocrats, reinstalled in the French provinces since the coming to power of Louis-Philippe in 1830, adopted a conventional Gothic style,[7] perfectly "troubadour," which was at the opposite extreme from that budding cult of archaeology.

Built by Châteignier,[8] between 1845 and 1848, the Château de Comacre (unfortunately demolished in 1962) was nothing but a vast Palladian villa, "castellated" by means of a large number of turrets or pinnacles, and "laced" by a rich openwork decoration. The same fairy-tale Gothic is found in the immense construction of Challain-la-Potherie, put up in 1848 by René Hodé for the Comte de La Rochefoucauld-Bayers. The image of the château was taken from *Les Très Riches Heures du duc de Berry*; its plan and layout had a wholly classical rigour. That Gothic was a surface Gothic, a

Burg Stolzenfels on the Rhine.
Architect: Karl Friedrich Schinkel.
1. View of the castle ruins from the Rhine.
2. Schinkel's restoration project, 1836.
Watercolour drawings.
3. Château de Blois, Louis XII wing.
Inner front before the restoration of 1845-1866.
Architect: Félix Duban.
Drawing.

1

2

3

political poster of opposition to the Orleanist regime (at the same time as a nostalgic reminder of the old noble extraction of its proprietors). But that detracts nothing from the efficiency of the management of the rural domain: inspired by the English model, it strove to regroup the estates and make them profitable.

The second quarter of the nineteenth century thus saw France and England becoming dotted with churches and châteaux in numbers that are astonishing for a time of industrial concentration. Notwithstanding their divergent characters, which made the all-embracing neo-Gothic a many-branched tree, all these buildings had a specific trait in common: rebellion against the present. The "rejection front"[9] dominated artistic culture, from the proclamations of Ruskin to the most modest church or country house. A whole generation, facing the upheavals in its existence created by a galloping industrialization, could only witness the ravages, while putting forward a retrospective model as an alternative.

5

4

4. Château de Challain-la-Potherie (Anjou). Parkside front, 1848. Architect: René Hodé. Lithograph by A. Maugendre.
5. Château de Mehun-sur-Yèvre, near Bourges. Miniature by the Limbourg Brothers, c. 1415, in the *Très Riches Heures du duc de Berry.*

Monuments of the machine

1

Far more than the factory, the railway station [10] is the symbol of industrial architecture, for two reasons: it is the place where machines are displayed to the public at large, and it is also the place to which the materials produced by industry quite naturally find their way soonest. It must be said that this dual aspect came out only rather slowly, through experiments of a variety matched only by their utter originality; there was no reference model in classical European culture for the construction of railway stations.
That was why the very earliest stations, like Euston in London (in 1838), retained only a highly lifelike idea of railway transport, in true neoclassical tradition: that of the City Gate, as the symbol of going a journey. The monumental portico of Euston Station, a magnificent Doric pronaos with two columns "in antis," recalled in its arrangement the Brandenburg Gate in Berlin or those Propylaea which Leo von Klenze built a few years later at the entrance to Munich. The technical side had less importance than the idea. For the thematic orientation here was based entirely on the notion of departure or arrival, not on that of machine worship.
The station in a railway cutting, like Edge Hill in Liverpool or the old Saint-Lazare "landing pier" in Paris, was another variety, of which the design (like the name "gare" itself, in French) derived from canal architecture. The fluvial metaphor brought with it a whole repertory of retaining walls, bridges, quays or embankments, perfectly adaptable to the new building programme. For in reality the railway, contrary to the road, shares with the canal the common technical requirement of construction with a very low gradient, imposing monumental engineering works, as well as a complete remodelling of the landscape.

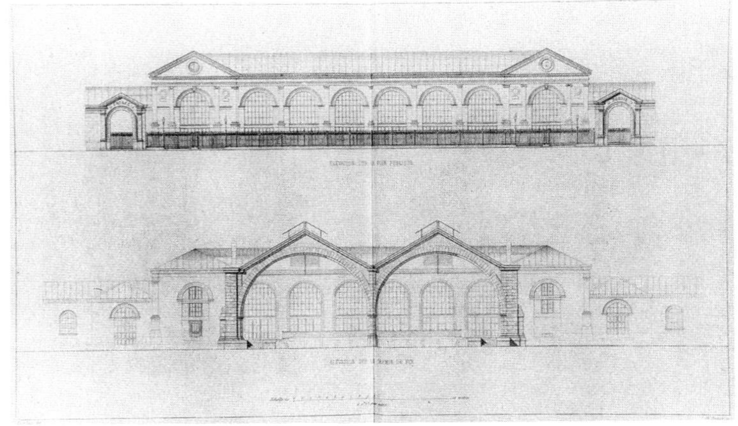

2

3

4

1. The Propylaea in Munich.
   Oil painting by Leo von Klenze, 1848.
2. Paris: The first Gare du Nord, 1846.
   Demolished in 1861.
   Architect: Léonce Reynaud.
   Revue Générale de l'Architecture et des Travaux Publics, 1845-1846.
3. London: Entrance to Euston Station, 1838.
   Architect: Philip Hardwick.
   Lithograph by T. Allom, 1837.
5. Detail of Euston Station.
4. Liverpool: Opening of Edge Hill Station on 15 September 1830.
   Drawn and engraved by F. Shaw, Jr.

5

1

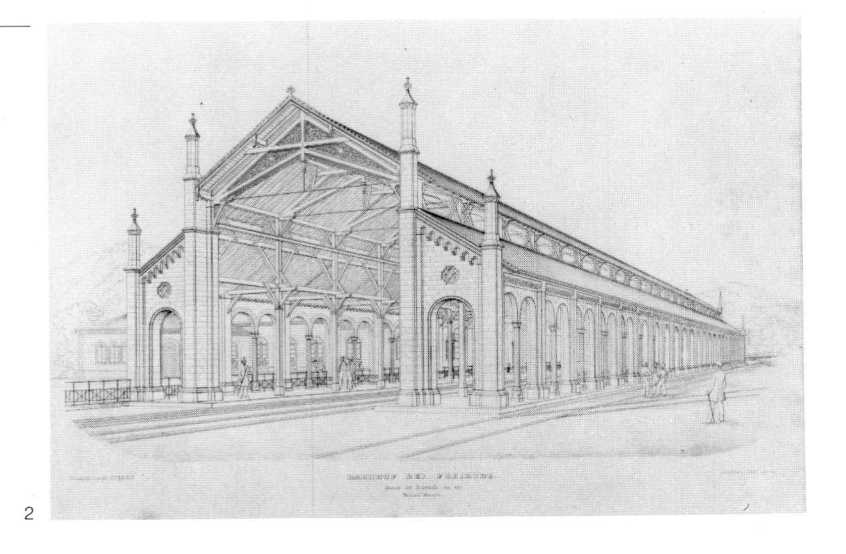

2

Nevertheless, railway station architecture was to show itself, as a programme, in the construction of vast covered halls permitting sheltered access to trains. The very form of this long construction imposed historical reminiscences, whether in the narrow Lombardic basilica of the station of Freiburg im Breisgau (a project executed in 1845), in which the side aisles covered the platforms and the nave covered the trains, or in its great Renaissance sister station in Florence, conceived in 1847 by Thomas Henry Wyatt, in a rather surprising Palermitan vein (it is true that it was a competition project). A similar design, the single great hall, also in timberwork, could have drawn its inspiration from recent examples (the Customs hall at the Octroi of Paris, Rue Chauchat, by A.L. Lusson in 1822), as in the case of the Munich station built in 1849; or transposed the English framework of the Gothic period on a colossal scale, as in the strange nave of the first Temple Meads Station in Bristol, in 1840.
Nevertheless, the timber framework–especially using the Delorme system, in planks, the only one permitting long spans–had the disadvantage of deteriorating through the effects of exposure to the steam of locomotives. The solution which had the greatest future, therefore, was cast-iron and iron construction, with light coverings made spacious by glazed lanterns. Together with its monumental architecture, Euston Station in London offered one of the finest examples of the genre, built from the plans of the engineer Robert Stephenson. With its double nave separating the arrival and departure tracks by a row of columns, this model enjoyed lasting popularity for terminals, as for example, in Paris, the first Gare du Nord (Léonce Reynaud, 1845, demolished) or the second Gare Saint-Lazare (A. Armand & E. Flachat, 1852), whose two halls still exist, incorporated in the present station, rebuilt under the Third Republic.

3

4

Florence: Station of Santa Maria Antonia, 1847.
Architect: Thomas Henry Wyatt, 1847.
1. Print of 1848.
5. Watercolour by Sir Matthew Digby Wyatt.
2. Freiburg im Breisgau: The Railway Station, 1845.
Architect: Friedrich Eisenlohr.
F. Eisenlohr, *Ausgeführte und zur Ausführung bestimmte Entwürfe.*
3. Munich: The Railway Station, 1849.
Innenansicht der Bahnsteighalle des Münchner Hauptbahnhofes.
4. London: Euston Station, 1835-1839.
Architect: Philip Hardwick.
Engineer: Robert Stephenson.
From a drawing by T.T. Berry, 1837.

5

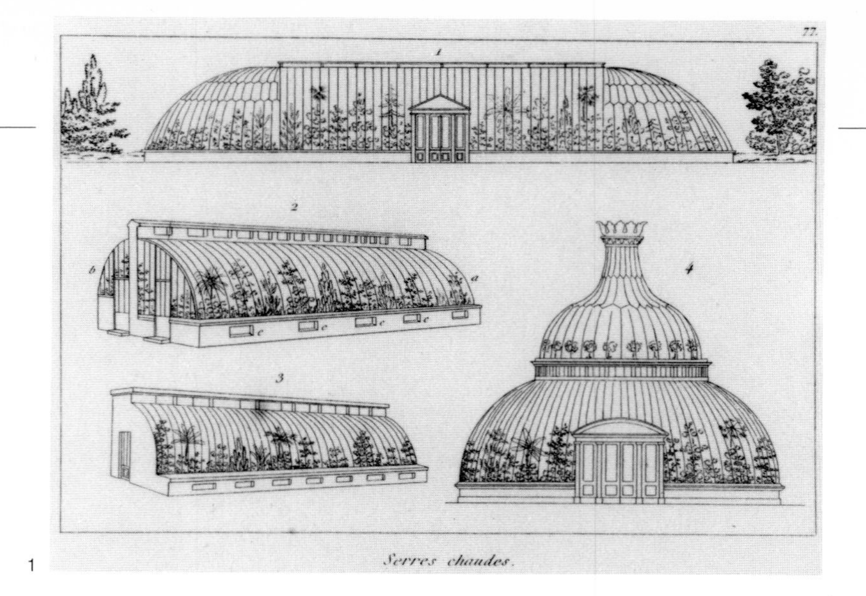

Pavilions of enchantment

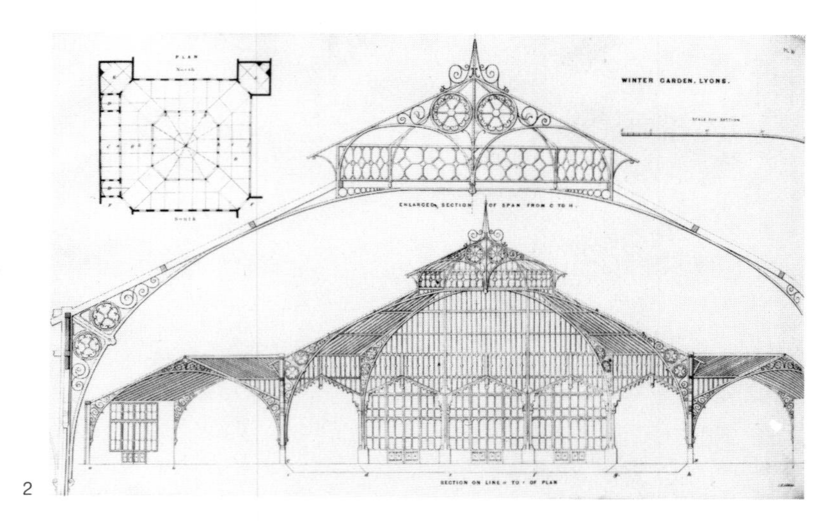

What the commercial galleries had been during the first third of the century, the greenhouses and garden pavilions were after them. Edifices of leisure–theatres, circuses, ballrooms or cafés–these constructions were generally mixed, closely interwoven with the gardens in which they were implanted. More than luxury, it was change of scene that made their charm; for the greenhouse, more than any other place, was the home of the unusual, the most gripping architectural paradox that could be imagined, and which modern technology made it thereafter possible to create. Hence its immense success.

For just imagine a heated place invaded by exotic plants, bathed in cascades of natural light or enriched by the flickerings of multiple gaslights. Imagine that this place is vast enough for several hundred people to gather there. And finally, imagine that the walls of this magic space are made of fine sheets of glass inserted in a lattice of wood and cast iron. You will then perceive the magical character of these constructions, which caught up the most cautious architects, first among them Hector Horeau,[11] in wild futuristic dreams.

The winter garden of Lyons, built by Horeau in 1847, was doubtless not the greatest work of the nineteenth century. Nevertheless, it succeeded in uniting all these characteristics, by reassembling closely related experiments carried out in the architecture of the garden greenhouse properly so called (like the ornate models of M. Boitard or the great greenhouses of Charles Rohault de Fleury in the Jardin des Plantes in Paris) as well as in that of the pleasure pavilion (of which the most magnificent example in the world is still the Royal Pavilion of Brighton,[12] built in 1818 by John Nash in a fanciful oriental style). Finally, Horeau's plan for greenhouses once more adopted the design for panoramas or circuses which had been in fashion since the Empire (notably the Cirque National of 1841, built by Hittorff on the Champs-Elysées). "Pavilion of enchantment," the greenhouse crystallized many aspirations of the time, to the extent that Horeau subsequently spent his whole life trying to turn it into a kind of total spectacle, immersed in social utopia.

1. Hothouses.
M. Boitard, *L'art de composer et décorer les jardins*, c. 1835.
2. Lyons: Winter Garden, plan and section, 1847.
Architect: Hector Horeau.
The Civil Engineer and Architect's Journal, 1851.
3. Paris: National Circus (later called Circus of the Empress), 1839-1841.
Architect: Jacques-Ignace Hittorff.
Lithograph by Provost.

4

4. Brighton: The Royal Pavilion, 1818.
Architect: John Nash.

5. Beauties of Brighton, 1826.
Etching by George Cruikshank.

5

1

Greenhouse architecture could take less extreme forms, with more ordinary contents. It remained nonetheless a symbolic edifice, on which architectural and technical interest focused: like the railway station, it lent itself in effect to technological display. The materials used in its construction were glass, wood and iron. For the growth of the vegetation it contained it had to be entirely transparent. Thus, once the techniques of artificial heating by slow-combustion stove had been mastered (in 1834 Rohault de Fleury went to England to learn about these new methods for the construction of greenhouses in Paris), it became possible to free the greenhouse almost entirely from its containing walls, the iron and cast-iron work making possible a structure as light as it was resistant.
The traditional greenhouse, whose barrel roof was supported by a base wall (used as a reflector of light and heat), therefore came to be insulated in pavilions on the principle of Kew Gardens, in Surrey, or of the Jardin des Plantes in Paris. At Kew the square pavilion was capped by a double storey of curved glazings, while in Paris the skylight roof rested on great columns rising from the bottom and, on the outside, on a wall of glass, rhythmed by cast-iron piles. [13] The first model was the more elegant in design; the second was destined for a great future, for it was the archetype of the central market halls that Baltard was to build twenty years later in Paris.

2

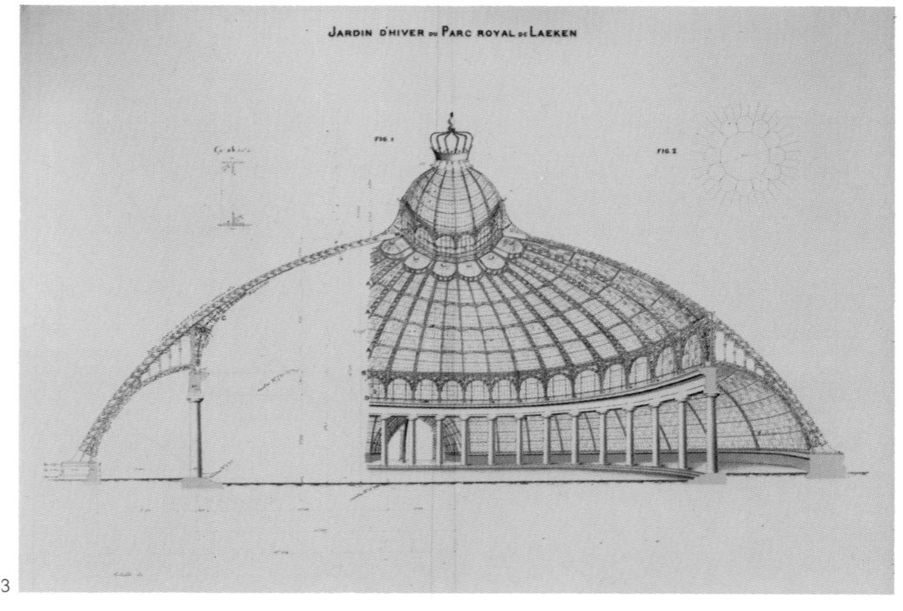

3

1. Kew Gardens (Surrey): Palm House, 1844-1848. Restored in the 1950s. Architect: Decimus Burton. Engineer: Richard Turner.
2. Paris: Jardin des Plantes (Botanical Garden). *Paris et ses environs reproduits par le daguerréotype*, 1840.
3. Brussels: Royal Greenhouses of Laeken Castle. Perspective-section of the Winter Garden, 1880. Architect: Alphonse Balat. Engineer: Arthur Vierendeel. A. Vierendeel, *La construction architecturale en fonte, fer et acier*, 1893.

4

Paris: Jardin des Plantes, greenhouse of the Natural History Museum, 1833. Destroyed in 1870, rebuilt in 1874, 1907 and 1934.
Architect: Charles Rohault de Fleury.

4. View in its present state.
5. Cross-section, watercolour drawing, 1855.

5

Refusal and doubt

CIMETIÈRE DU PÈRE LA CHAISE.

1

In the face of the hard everyday realities of the law of profit, introduced by industrial capitalism to the detriment of the whole social and cultural structure inherited from preceding centuries, art tended more and more to play a compensatory role, in which the characteristic element was the escape into history. Escape into the past, escape into fairyland, escape into myth: the themes run in parallel, even if the formulas do not reinforce each other.

Alongside château or church architecture, that of the commemorative monument, imprisoned in a heavy allegorical tradition coming from Neoclassicism, found a new expression thanks to a double transformation of its artistic resources. Figurative sculpture, leaving metaphor aside, tended towards heightened realism in the expression of body, face, costume or environment (armchair, objects); conversely, it gave the architecture of setting an enhanced emphasizing role, by recourse to a far more imposing construction–the miniature temple shaped like a ciborium, the frame or the ornamented niche took on more importance than the sculpture itself.

In this proliferating architectonic repertory, Gothic occupied a leading place. The fanciful mausoleum of Heloise and Abelard, conceived under the Empire by Alexandre Lenoir (transferred to the Père-Lachaise cemetery in 1816), with the fragments of authentic Gothic sculptures, became the prototype of a series of commemorative monuments featuring miniature chapels, except that the composition became standardized on the model of the Scaliger monument in Verona. George Gilbert Scott took it as his inspiration for the Albert Memorial in London; Viollet-le-Duc, for the Duke of Brunswick monument in Geneva.

The escape was not without nostalgia: the realism of the personage contradicted the monumentality of the setting. The celebration of the institution (necessary to its survival) no longer fitted with that untender gaze levelled by statuary at the individual. This split between the social and the interior personality is one of the marks of bourgeois civilization: the cowl makes the monk, but what does the monk think of his cowl? The sign is there of a grave turbulence of institutions. The insistent reference to the social role, and that complementary guarantee furnished by the historical alibi, are the tokens of the incertitude of present times.

1. Paris: Père Lachaise Cemetery, 1804. Architect: Alexandre-Théodore Brongniart. Print by Civeton, 1829.
2. Paris: The 14th-Century Room at the Musée des Monuments Français. B. de Roquefort, *Vues pittoresques et perspectives des salles du Musée des Monuments Français*, 1816.
3. Paris: Tomb of Heloise and Abelard. Frontispiece of F.M. Marchant de Beaumont, *Le Conducteur au Cimetière de l'Est, ou du Père La Chaise*, 1820.
4. Geneva: Tomb of the Duke of Brunswick, 1875. Architect: Jean Franel. Adviser: Eugène Viollet-le-Duc.
5. London: Albert Memorial, Hyde Park, 1863-1872. Architect: Sir George Gilbert Scott.

VUE DE LA SALLE DU QUATORZIÈME SIÈCLE.

2

3

4

5

II
ECLECTICISM

That other Renaissance formed by the French Second Empire or the reign of Queen Victoria in England did not leave so honoured a memory as the one of the sixteenth century. The social type on which the nineteenth century reposed was that of the bourgeois upstart, on whom every form of ridicule has been heaped. Even if it is true that the imperial society of the great courts of Europe smacked somewhat of a Labiche comedy, [1] the period between 1850 and 1870 was marked by a social and cultural expansion, reflecting the blossoming of the new middle classes. This situation had its underwriter: the working-class misery of the great industrial towns was no empty phrase. From the silk-workers of Lyons to the Commune of Paris, social warfare [2] was a daily fact of life for two generations, in the continuous uncertainty of riots and in the horror of bloody repressions carried out by the army.
The social and human consequences of the change wrought by the Industrial Revolution deepened after the 1830s, and especially after the railway, in its development across all Europe, began to cause the most spectacular urban transformation in European history: the rural exodus began, emptying the population overflow from tracts of countryside into those immense suburbs which sprang up around the metropolises. From this migration, entailing a complete severance from the roots of a thousand-year-old rural culture, the proletariat was born. By way of compensation the first ethnographic research appeared: anthologies of popular music or verse, [3] peasant novels, collections of objects. It is certain that the working class suffered, along with material squalor, a form of cultural alienation, forced on it by its uprooted condition, which its new status scarcely allowed it to compensate.

Industry in its splendour 1850-1870

The case was different for the bourgeoisie who, subjected to the same change, were equipped to give themselves a new image by taking over scholarly culture for their own use. The paradox arose from the fact that this cultural transplant was impossible. The culture which fell into the hands of the rising classes was dead; classical ideology had had its day; idealist philosophy had lost its credibility, as had the aristocratic principle. On the other hand, bourgeois morality, based on order and work, was thoroughly alive; it demanded uniformity and identity of conduct, tending towards an absolute conformism.
The sense of bourgeois respectability should have given a new lease of life to the neoclassical tradition if, in parallel, the awareness of a total liberation–produced by continuous accumulation of wealth, the accelerated development of business enterprises and the opening up of a vast consumer market–had not touched off a sort of cultural "fireworks" lasting throughout the Second Empire from Offenbach to Charles Garnier. It was an era of fêtes, of balls and inaugurations marking each step forward in the quickened march of expansion.
The image of luxury was spread by the commercial production of the manufactured object, replacing the traditional handicrafts, which it copied by cheap mechanical processes. "Bad taste" (which was but the copy of the "great" taste of preceding generations) invaded the market for the object, giving it a place it had never known in history. Henceforth daily life was to be marked by that ubiquitousness of the object which characterizes industrial society.
Competition, contradiction: bourgeois culture was dominated by the ambivalence of conduct, between conformity and debauch. Its effects were felt by art, which suffered from a kind of insidious doubt peeping through the noisiest manifestations of its vitality and clear conscience. Uncertainty or lack of conviction, the latent malaise expressed itself through secret deviations, curious incoherences or incongruities for which ignorance was no excuse. On the contrary, in archaeological culture the distortion increased! We are not far from thinking that an anti-classicism was being secretly set up beneath the outward appearances of the most fundamentalist academicism. [4]

The industrial phantasm

1

The expansion of the third quarter of the nineteenth century was all the greater in that the equipment in infrastructures had been in progress for half a century, giving now to industry its means of production. From the extraction of raw materials to the marketing of the finished product, all the links in the chain of production were henceforth in place in France, England and Belgium, and soon would be in Austria and Germany.
A triple network of roads, canals and railways assured the transport of goods, whether exchanges of iron and mineral coal, in the Ruhr and northern France, or the distribution of textiles down to the smallest village shop. Great national or regional markets provided the necessary economic and financial relays for the sale of products, including those of the agricultural market, the economy of which was thrown into upheaval.[5]
Industrial activity, outside the centres of raw material extraction, tended to desert the rural milieu and draw closer to its customers, on the outskirts of the big cities. The steam engine made this possible. No longer was it necessary to have a specific site available in order to start a manufacturing industry;[6] for the resources of motor energy were no longer those of water or firewood, but that of mineral coal transported by rail. Industry put forth its branches close to the railway stations, which were soon surrounded by workers' housing.

2

Industrial architecture proved to be that of those millions of brick chimneys, "industrial minarets,"[7] which the nineteenth century built wherever it needed them. The city skyline was no longer dominated by the neighbourhood church steeples, but surrounded by a belt of chimneys whose smoke blackened the houses and blotted out the sky.
The traditional square chimney was replaced by the cylindrical smokestack, much more resistant to the assaults of the wind and the heat of fire. It became a pretext for decorative fantasies,[8] licensed by the natural polychrome of the brick. The most modest stack bore the date of its construction or the initials of the factory owner; the most lavish was ornamented with twists, zigzags or crosses, turning it into a kind of ornamental column, the giant sister of the urban candelabra.
The generation of the Second Empire was not yet that of great industrial architecture, for the factory was still conceived of only as a means of production, whose anarchic development would be a function of needs; only the chimney bore a few ornaments, tending to make it into an emblem. The rest was no more than wooden

posts, brick enclosing walls and a tile roof–a vast shed! The activity of the founding fathers of the great industrial dynasties, such as Krupp and Schneider, was oriented entirely towards the consolidation of their business and the solution of the most crying social problems–overpopulation, delinquency, illiteracy. Industry did without art; the working classes did not even have access to it.
If architecture did develop it was elsewhere, in the representational space of the great trade fairs. The first exhibition of industrial products had been held in Prague in 1791, and the idea was taken over in Paris in the form of a plan for annual exhibitions in the Cour

3

4

3. View of Manchester, 1851.
Watercolour by William Wyld.

1. Brick factory chimneys.
J. Lacroux, *La brique ordinaire au point de vue décoratif*, 1878.

2.4. Essen (Ruhr): Statue of Alfred Krupp.
The Krupp steel works in 1852.
Krupp 1812-1912, 1912.

Carrée of the Louvre. From 1798 to 1849 France organized eleven national exhibitions, the number of exhibitors increasing from 110 to 4,532, in direct proportion to the development of industry.[9] But it was with the Great Exhibition of 1851 in London that the "world's fair" was truly born, each country trying to demonstrate its industrial vitality and gain access to foreign markets by presenting its national production.

Here architecture was invited in at the start of the project. It was to be the guarantor of the prestige of the exhibition, the provider of its image of distinction around a symbolic monument: the Crystal Palace in 1851, the Eiffel Tower and the Galerie des Machines in 1889, the Grand Palais and the Petit Palais in 1900. And it was a highly specialized architecture: that of great covered market halls needed to display machines, or of national pavilions, the self-styled bearers of the culture of a whole country.

1

Undertaking great exhibitions was a festival on a worldwide scale. In London, in 1851, on a surface of twenty acres, the exhibition received six million visitors; in Paris, in 1900, on a surface of 114 acres, 50 million people came. The event was of such importance that whole neighbourhoods were built up, whose infrastructure would remain after the exhibition, like the Champ-de-Mars, urbanized for the Paris exhibition of 1867.

1. London: Hall proposed for the 1851 Exhibition. Design by Hector Horeau, 1849. *L'Illustration*, 1851.

2

London: Crystal Palace, Hyde Park, erected for the Great Exhibition of 1851. Architect: Joseph Paxton.

2. View of the Crystal Palace from Kensington Gardens. Lithograph, 1851.
3. South transept of the Crystal Palace. Photograph by William Henry Fox Talbot, 1851.

3

The Great Exhibition of 1851 in London, the triumph of Victoria and Albert, was centred on a monument the memory of which remained in all minds: the Crystal Palace, a gigantic hall of glass and iron for which the French architect Hector Horeau had supplied the original idea. Joseph Paxton, an English specialist in the construction of greenhouses, was to give Horeau's dream a durable form: the Crystal Palace was an impressive assemblage of cast-iron pillars, girders in trelliswork, and skylights, whose main feature was that they could be dismantled. From the outset, industrial construction asserted its prefabricative character, linked with the idea of mobility; and in fact the Crystal Palace was to be reconstructed immediately afterwards at Sydenham, in the suburbs of London (to be accidentally burned down in 1936).

What was prodigious about the Crystal Palace was its transparency. It expanded Robert Stephenson's prototype at Euston Station on a monumental scale, combining the theme of metallic construction with the spatial formula of the greenhouse–a striking summing up of the ambitions of the age. But it was a summing up doubtless too simple. In 1855 the Palais de l'Industrie on the Champs-Elysées in Paris ennobled Paxton's model by giving it the space and volume of a Palladian basilica, with its immense arching roof and its envelope of stone vaulted galleries. And to this programme it added the indispensable complement to any architectural representation: the monumental gateway, whose giant arch, inspired by the Belvedere in Rome, was stuck onto one of its façades. Nothing could be more ambiguous than this *collage* of culture on industrial products.

4

Paris: Exposition Universelle of 1855.
Palace of Industry.
4. Main entrance.
Architect: J.M.V. Viel.
Paris dans sa splendeur, 1861.
5. Glass and iron hall (Galerie des Machines) of the Palace of Industry (photographed during the Salon of 1896).
Engineer: Alexis Barrault.

5

1. London: King's Cross Station, 1851-1852.
Architect: Lewis Cubitt.
Print showing Queen Victoria arriving for the York Races train.

Hymn to Industry or City Gate, the two contradictory formulas had already clashed in the thematic material of the railway station. But the problem became still more complex. When an entire section of a city had to be handled, as was the case in Paris in 1867, or when a culture had to be synthesized (as in the Paris exhibition of 1889, which was something of a fair of nationalities), the conflict between the language of art and that of industry became glaring.
The problem is plainly seen in the theme of the railway station, decidedly very close to that of the exhibition. In 1851 King's Cross Station in London affirmed with extreme purity the principle of the double hall. Opening on the exterior through a porticoed shell and dominated by the clock tower marking the axis of its mighty pylon, the station was no more than an immense place of exchange, at once colossal and solemn, whose architecture recalled that of the great market halls.
Fifteen years later, in 1868, the most sumptuous of London stations was St Pancras. With a span of 73 metres, its glass roof remained for a long time the largest in the world. And yet this train-shed on a vast scale, in which locomotives became Lilliputian, was entirely clothed in a construction inspired by Italian Gothic, designed by Sir George Gilbert Scott. The point was that urban architecture–that of façades turned towards the outer world–had to be continuous with its environment; and it also had to carry a message different from the much too simple one of industrial technology. One may choose to be scandalized by a conflict like this between the glass roof and the building shell. Architecturally, it produced an effect striking by the total discordance of elements, each taken to the limit of its expressive capacities. Daring was needed to carry such a contradiction to its logical conclusion!

Surrounded by buildings, the station front could assert itself in different ways. The simplest was the exploitation of the great arch of the glass roof and the hall-portico dialogue. François-Alexandre Duquesney applied the principle in the first Gare de l'Est in Paris (1847-1852). At the end of the Boulevard de Strasbourg the glazed spandrel of the basilica announced the long nave of the station, on the lines of that decidedly Palladian model [10] with which the French Beaux-Arts tradition was so impregnated that it carried it over from the theatre to the exhibition palace, and from the palace to the railway station.

3

2

2. London: St Pancras Station, 1868-1869.
Metal train-shed.
Engineers: W.H. Barlow
R.M. Ordish.

3. London: Grosvenor Hotel, Pimlico (Victoria Station), 1860-1861.
Architect: Sir James T. Knowles.
The Builder, 1861.

4. London: St Pancras Station and Midland Grand Hotel, 1868-1876.
Architect: Sir George Gilbert Scott.
The Building News, 1874.

4

1

It was possible, too, as Jacques-Ignace Hittorff did at the Gare du Nord, to deny oneself the conveniences of the vaulted covering and construct nothing but an immense glazed saddle roof, whose steel truss rested on alignments of cast-iron pillars at a dizzying height. And in this case it was logical that the façade should bear a resemblance to that of Horeau's grand design for the Crystal Palace–a play of diminishing vaults punctuated by pylons. Nevertheless, before attaining this simplicity, Hittorff himself had hesitated for a long while between several typologies. The first plans insisted on the palatial expression of the façade, hiding the glass roof by a large construction with offsets; or they took as inspiration the Roman scheme for the façade of the baths, with giant opposed vaults commensurate with one of the stories of the rest of the building.
Hittorff's hesitations were revealing, even if they strongly displeased the prefect Haussmann (who reproached the architect with having destroyed the unity of the square in front of the station by discarding the ordonnanced building shell in favour of large arches). A long tradition of structural rationality forbade the French to accept the divorce implied by the contradictory requirements of the covered structure and of its urban environment. Sir Charles Barry, on the other hand, was able to assume that contradiction and to make it plastically interesting, in the same manner by which he succeeded in grafting an Italian Gothic ornamentation onto a five-storey building structure unknown in the Middle Ages!

Paris: Gare de l'Est (originally called Embarcadère de Strasbourg), 1847-1852.
Architect: François-Alexandre Duquesney.
Engineer: Pierre Cabanel de Sermet.
1. Detail of the front.
2. Exterior view of the station.
E. Textier, *Tableau de Paris*, 1852-1853.

2

The proclamation of Gothic style in a railway station had symbolic value, even if English nationalism might have been somewhat put out by a syntax taken from Italy. After all, it was but one contradiction the more, assumed as adroitly as the others. If the Gothic in question was not archaeological, if it was slapped onto a building whose needs had nothing to do with medieval models, all that was of small importance. The essential thing was to have risked the rapprochement and to have given it a plastic solution. From 1851, with the report of Comte de Laborde on the Great Exhibition of London, the nineteenth century was conscious of not possessing its own style, and of living off borrowings from the past. But it utilized those borrowings with a daring liberty, a scorn of pastiche equalled only by its incessant desire for invention. In fact nothing was a truer expression of the nineteenth century than those hybrid graftings of sources onto the forms of another language.

Paris: Gare du Nord, 1861-1864.
Architect: Jacques-Ignace Hittorff.
3. Preliminary design, watercolour, 1859-1861.
4. Design for the main front, 1861.

3

4

Establishing a hierarchy of urban space

1

The will to face up to the cultural crisis, as to all the crises born of the industrial upheaval, stamped the thinking of the nineteenth century as a whole. After its early utopian phase, the behaviour of the men of the second generation of the industrial era was essentially pragmatic. The theoretical debate shifted its ground, as much in direct revolutionary struggle, political commitment or social action as in the effective taking over of the levers of economic intervention. Saint-Simonian philosophy inspired some of the greatest bankers or industrialists of the Second Empire; its reflection can be seen in the French national railway network, in the baking institutions, or even in the establishment of the programme for the Paris exhibition of 1867.

It is true that the picture of the city, revealed by the studies of public health specialists, was scarcely satisfactory. The ordered beauty of the docks was counterbalanced by the saturation of the town centres, the degradation of working-class suburbs, the rejection of the poorest onto the fringes of society. Overrun by self-built housing, the outskirts of the cities were almost immediately saturated with miserable, anarchic hovels, which were the starting point of future unsanitary blocks. Those who could not find a place there were reduced to indigence: professional instability, vagrancy, solitude, for which the only feasible remedies lay in improving the sanitation of the places of shelter. Broken up, the working-class family was composed of isolated beings who found a night's sleep only in the wretched refuge of former stables or disused sheds in which they huddled together. In the face of the continuous influx of migrants, the charitable societies could offer only a bit of nourishment and a bed in a roomful of people.

The crisis of the urban structure was obvious to everyone. The Paris riots of the July Monarchy were the catalyst of that "transformation" of the city which everyone was demanding and for which plans filled the newspapers. The opening of the Boulevard de Strasbourg and the extension of the Rue de Rivoli in 1847 began the policy of restructuring which has been called Haussmannism–because the great prefect took it to its conclusion–but which came into being long before (Haussmann was to become Prefect of the Seine only in 1853).

The transformation of the city was accomplished by taking into account its totality, as well as by imposing a strict order on the diverse elements of the urban organism. The policy of opening new streets was only one aspect, even if it was the most spectacular. More important was the global restructuring of the urban form and its architectural representation.

Among Haussmann's predecessors the idea was doubtless not as clear. The twofold Strasbourg-Rivoli operation, that of the "crossroad of Paris," had a triple objective. The easiest to perceive

2

Two woodcuts by Gustave Doré illustrating *Londres* by Louis Enault, 1876:
1. "Travellers will come and sit on the ruins beside the Thames."
5. "London, view over the roofs from a train."
2. The London docks. J. Gailhabaud, *Monuments anciens et modernes*, 1850.

ARRIVAL OF THE WORKMEN'S PENNY TRAIN AT THE VICTORIA STATION.—SEE PRECEDING PAGE.

3

4

3. London: Arrival of the workmen's penny train at the Victoria Station. *The Illustrated London News*, 1865.
4. The Distress in East London: Labour yard of the Bethnal Green Employment Association. *The Illustrated London News*, 1868.

5

1

2

3

4

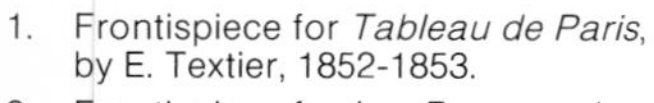

1. Frontispiece for *Tableau de Paris*, by E. Textier, 1852-1853.
2. Frontispiece for *Les Promenades de Paris* by A. Alphand, 1867-1873.
3. Frontispiece for *Le Nouveau Paris*, 1861. Woodcut by Gustave Doré.
4. Paris in 1860: Bird's-eye view with Notre-Dame and the Cité (left) and the church of Saint-Gervais (lower right).
Paris dans sa splendeur, 1861.

was the creation of an outlet from the future Gare de l'Est then under construction, for the railway was the first driving force behind the transformation of the city. Afterwards came an ordering principle. By having two main thoroughfares cross each other, it was hoped to clarify the reading of an urban form totally confused by the growth, over twenty years, of a vast suburb around the former ring of the Fermiers Généraux tax offices.
Finally, urban renewal selected as its target the most dangerous sector: that of the Central Markets (Les Halles), [11] the theatre of all the riots and successive revolutions since 1830. The demolition of the buildings of the old city centre disembowelled the den of the workers and hastened their departure towards the periphery of the town. This last pattern was of major importance: all the projects for the transformation of Paris attacked and destroyed its medieval nucleus.
But Haussmann's ambition went much further. The imperial project set out to salvage the east end of Paris by compensating the asymmetrical development of the two parts of the city–the poor at

Belleville, the rich at Chaillot. The great new space-making avenues created out of thin air a major infrastructure eastwards of vast planted thoroughfares: the Place de la République and its two boulevards, whose function was to innervate the south-east quadrant of Paris. Similarly, the thrust northward–for over twenty years construction had invaded the slopes of Montmartre and overflowed in a pincer movement towards the Batignolles or the Goutte d'Or–was balanced by a systematic programme of reinforcement of the subsoils of the Left Bank (the south ring of Paris being undermined by the thousand-year-old presence of stone quarries beyond the Luxembourg). It was a pity that the skirting of the Montagne Sainte-Geneviève by the Rue Monge and the creation of the Boulevard Raspail to the west were not later followed by complementary operations outward from Paris.
The imperial sights were set high. In 1860 Haussmann proclaimed the annexation of the Paris suburbs and the simultaneous creation of ten outer arrondissements. In those vast, underdeveloped

5

5. Paris: Avenue d'Eylau (now Avenue Foch) and Avenue de l'Impératrice (now Avenue Victor Hugo) seen from the Arc de Triomphe, c. 1858. Stereoscopic view.

6. Paris: Opening up the Boulevard Henri IV (from the Rue de Sully), c. 1866. Photograph by Charles Marville.

6

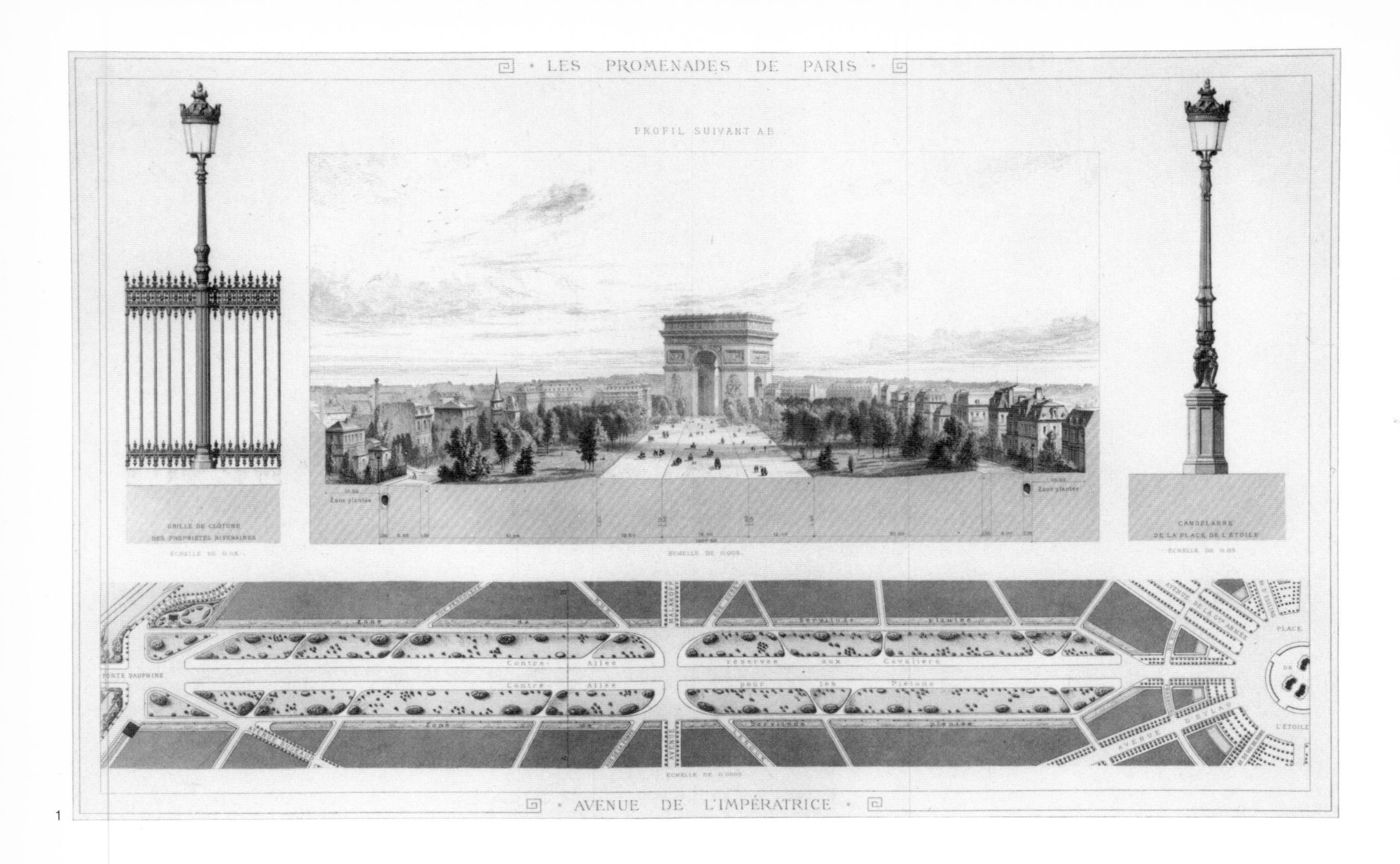

1

sectors, urbanizing intervention had as its object an overall rearrangement, achieved by the creation of main axes and the constitution of new centres for each of the new arrondissements. Instead of relying on the structure of the old villages of the periphery, the Parisian town-planners decided to organize new centres around the town hall of each arrondissement and a series of nearby facilities (church, school, market, square and, later, post office or high school) attracting demand and increasing the population density of the hinterland between the former centres.

Haussmannian voluntarism found its logical extension in urban ordonnance. By laying down wide planted thoroughfares more than 18 metres from façade to façade, it introduced an additional category into the hierarchy of urban spaces–axis and boundary at the same time–by which all the secondary sectors were delimited within the new grid. Very quickly Haussmann realized that the scale of 25 metres was not enough in itself. Not only did he build roads 50 metres wide (and even, as in Avenue Foch, 100 metres); he also introduced a new regulation promoting the increase in the "envelope" of buildings situated along wide thoroughfares. The majestic quality of the great building rows was thus opposed to the de-emphasized scale of secondary thoroughfares.

2

1. Paris: Avenue de l'Impératrice (now Avenue Victor Hugo). A. Alphand, *Les Promenades de Paris*, 1867-1873.
2. Paris: Avenue du Bois de Boulogne. Late 19th-century postcard.

The success of Haussmannism was due to this holistic vision of space, in which the mosaic of individual neighbourhoods participated, by its very diversity, in the clarification of a comprehensive urban order.[12] Every large French city strove to follow the example of Paris by restructuring its population centre around the opening of a few grand avenues. Certain examples are especially interesting: Lyons, Lille, Marseilles or Poitiers; others were less important or less successful, as in the case of Rennes, where left-bank urbanization was a failure.

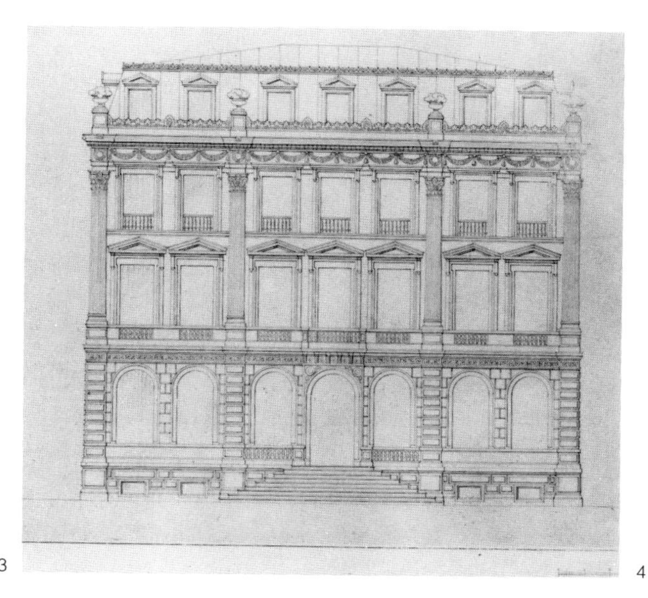

3

4

3. Paris: Façade design by Jacques-Ignace Hittorff for a house in the Place de l'Etoile, c. 1853.
4. Lyons: Grand Hotel (now No. 16, Avenue de la République), 1857-1858. Architect: Benoît Poncet.
5. Lyons: Rue de la République (the former Rue Impériale).

5

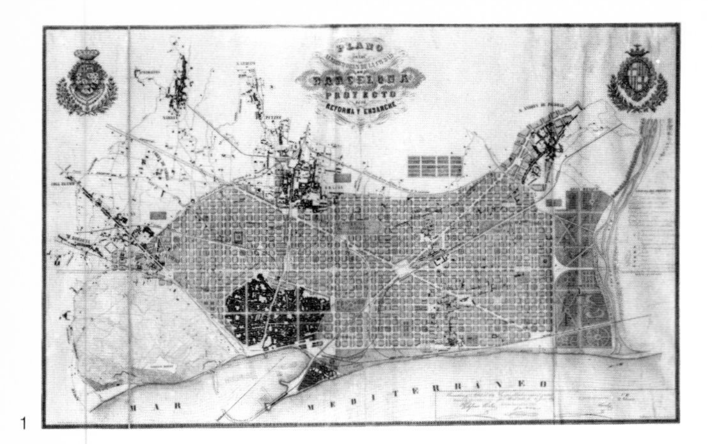

The French example was of such importance that it inspired many foreign realizations. If the Ring in Vienna deserves something of a special place (it consisted in taking advantage of the demolition of the old town ramparts in order to create a belt of green spaces and boulevards in the very heart of the city), the examples of Barcelona or of Brussels were characteristic. In Barcelona, the growth of the city had been determined by a systematic chequerboard structure, favouring the creation of modest-sized blocks, with a central courtyard. Their repetition, in the monotonous sweep of a wide plain, would have produced an abominable effect if the city had not been structured along the famous "diagonal," a major landmark whose oblique passage across that grid layout created a succession of remarkable "accidents." The dialogue between grid and diagonal, in which lay all the originality of Cerda's plan, made it easier to see the city in its dual character of general uniformity (what gives a city its atmosphere is the constant repetition of a

1. Barcelona: Project for the improvement and extension of the city, 1859. Engineer: Ildefonso Cerdá.
2. Brussels: Plan showing the new boulevards laid out in the centre, 1865. Architect: Léon-Pierre Suys.
3. Brussels: Place de la Bourse and Boulevard Anspach. Postcard of about 1900.

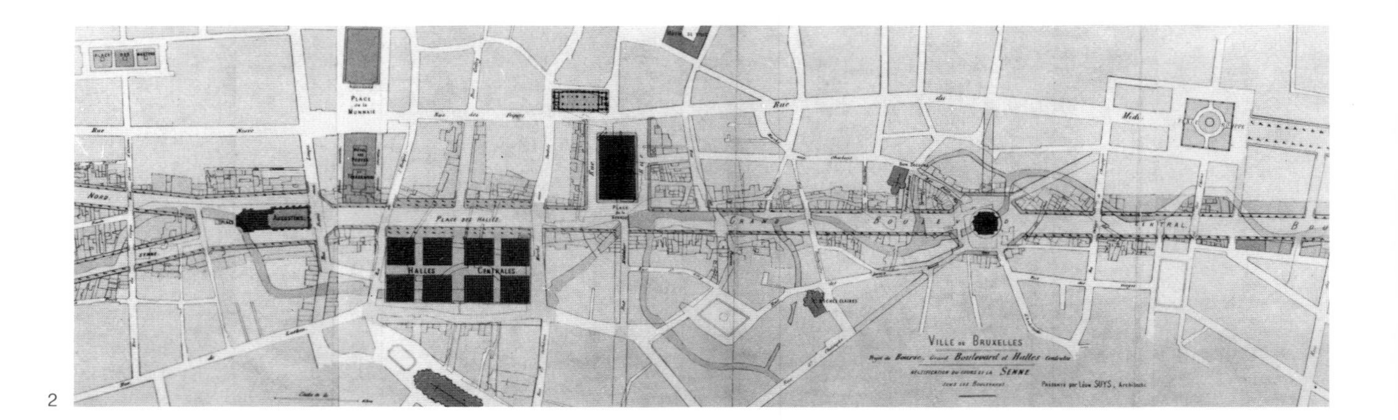

4

4. Brussels: The Bourse (Stock Exchange).
Architect: Léon-Pierre Suys.
Watercolour of 1871.

model of space and an associated architectural form) as well as of specific originality–*abnormal* places, which are like so many landmarks in the city's confused extent.

In Brussels,[13] the Haussmannian procedure was more directly Parisian (the more so in that the boulevards had been created by Parisians attracted to Belgium by the French national crisis after 1869). In the Brussels project the creation of the grand boulevards was linked with the improvement in sanitation of the lower town by the curving of the Senne (whose irregular course made that whole sector insalubrious). Exploiting the geography of the site, at the foot of the steep slopes of the Montagne-de-la-Cour and the Palais de Justice, the new boulevards made the urban image clearer by centring it on the Place de Brouckère and the Place de la Bourse. Moreover, somewhat curiously, they imported into Belgium a characteristically French typology: that of the Haussmannian apartment building, totally foreign to the lifestyles of the populations of the flatlands.

The Haussmannian model, the definition of which owed much to the previous experiences of England (and especially to the London of John Nash), was inconceivable without bringing green spaces into the heart of the urban organism. Not only was the royal tradition of the planted boulevard revived and adapted to the expansion of the urban hierarchy of thoroughfares, but the figure of the "square" was introduced, in multiple forms whose own hierarchy corresponded to the general ordering of space.

As the Emperor conceived them, the "squares" were private workingmen's gardens in the English manner, rearranged so as to bring light and air into the apartment blocks while promoting the subsistence of the workers through the advantage of kitchen gardens. In practice, the Parisian square became something quite different: a public garden deriving from the pleasure gardens of aristocratic private homes and shifted outside the block into the middle of the organism of traffic routes, in which it participated. Enclosed by low fences protecting it from traffic, the square was a place for walks, punctuated by benches, vistas shaped by clumps of shrubs or groves of trees, and peopled by ornamental sculptures. It was in daily use, unlike wooded commons, which were less regularly frequented; it was on a neighbourhood scale, the scale adapted to mothers of families, to pensioners or people on fixed incomes, for whom it provided a favourite place to walk.

2

1

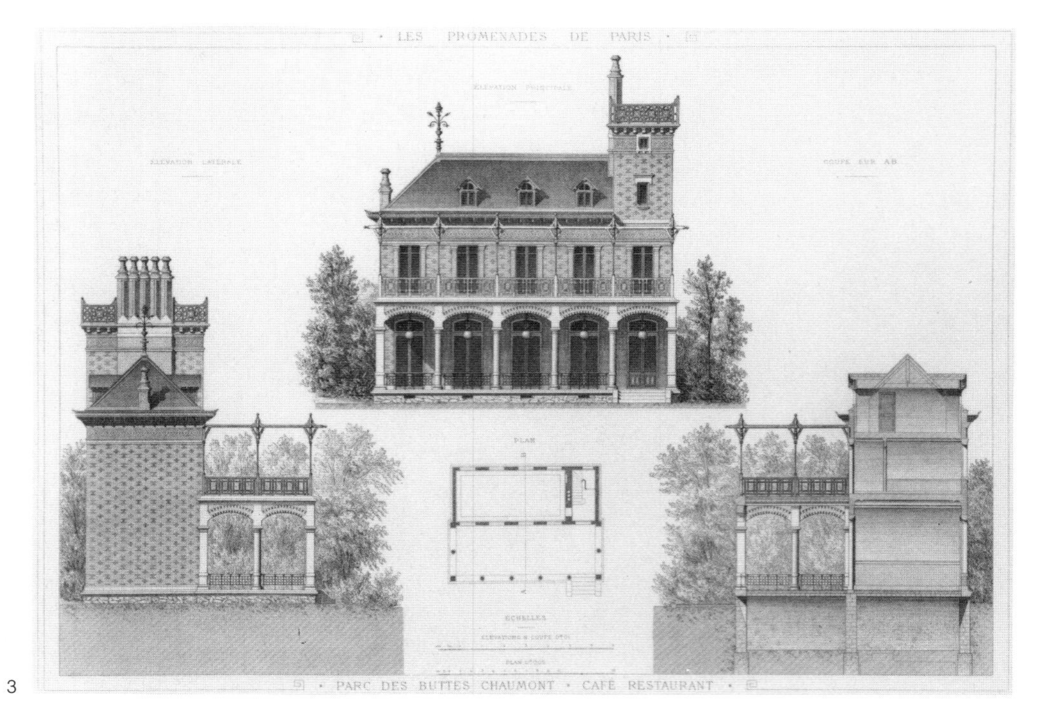

3

1. Paris: Gardener's House (above) and Lodge (below)
   J. Lacroux, *La brique ordinaire au point de vue décoratif*, 1878.
2. Paris: Square Montholon and Square de la Trinité.
   A. Alphand, *Les Promenades de Paris*, 1867-1873.
3. Paris: Café Restaurant in the Parc des Buttes-Chaumont.
   A. Alphand, *Les Promenades de Paris*, 1867-1873.

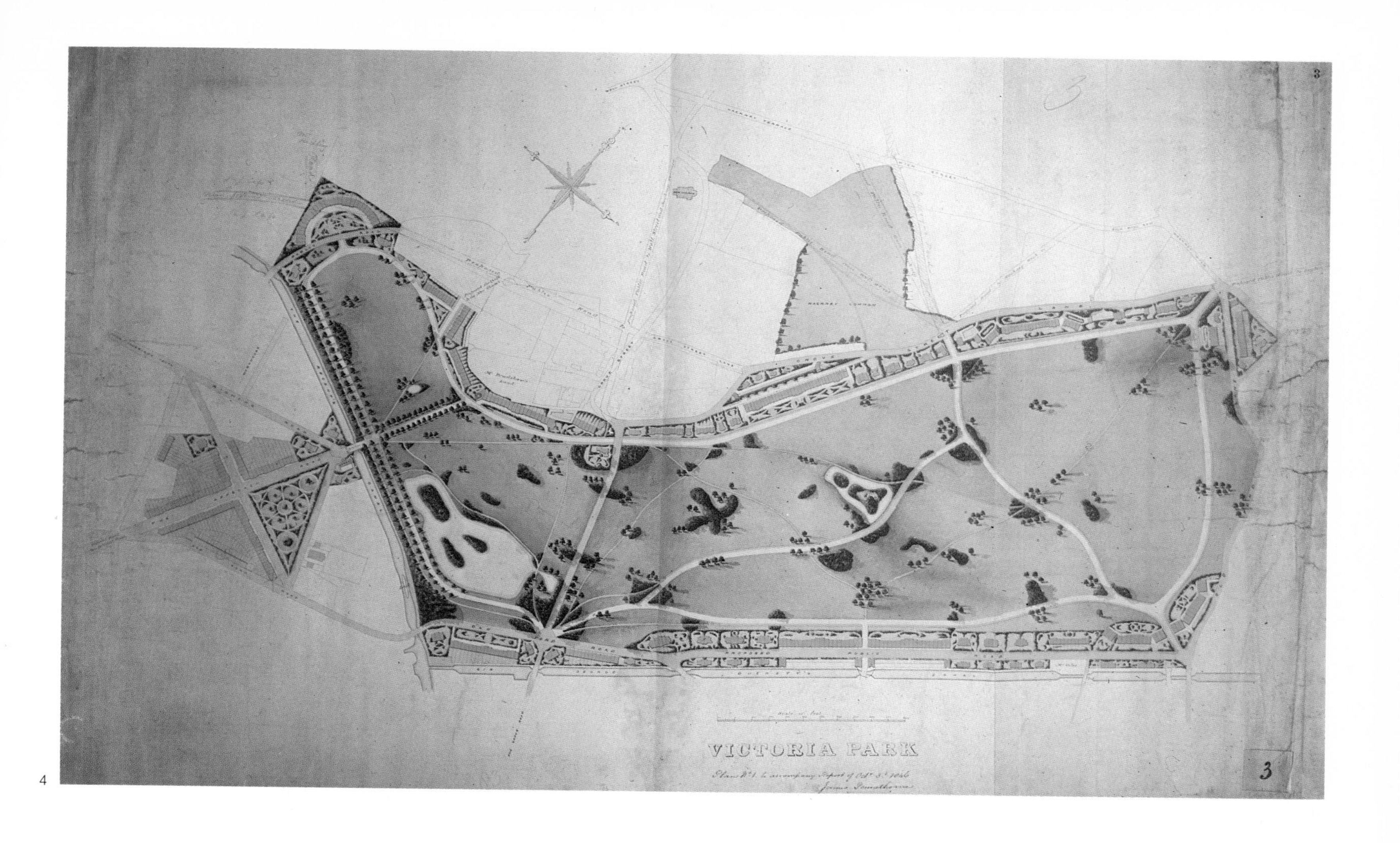

The urban park, of distinctly larger size, or the two great wooded areas that framed the capital, formed higher degrees in the spatial hierarchy; they were, in their way, monumental. That fact was perfectly understood by certain great provincial or foreign landscape architects. The Buhler brothers, for the Tête-d'Or park in Lyons or the Thabor park in Rennes, and Joseph Paxton in Liverpool, James Pennethorne in London (Victoria Park) or Frederick Olmstead in New York, very soon furnished major examples of landscaping in the treatment of urban parks.
It was there that suburban architecture, at its birth, found its models. A. Olive at Le Vésinet, beginning in 1856, or Unwin and Parker at Hampstead Garden Suburb, at the start of the twentieth century, all took advantage of the final touches placed in the mid-nineteenth century on the model of the urban park, surrounded by houses or aristocratic residences. In a more general way, the period invented a new type of urban arrangement, starting in the 1830s: the suburban parcelling out of building lots–a kind of park city, of which the most characteristic expressions in Second Empire France were the great Parisian "villas" or Le Vésinet and, a little later, Maisons-Lafitte, with Hampstead or Bedford Park as their counterparts in Greater London.

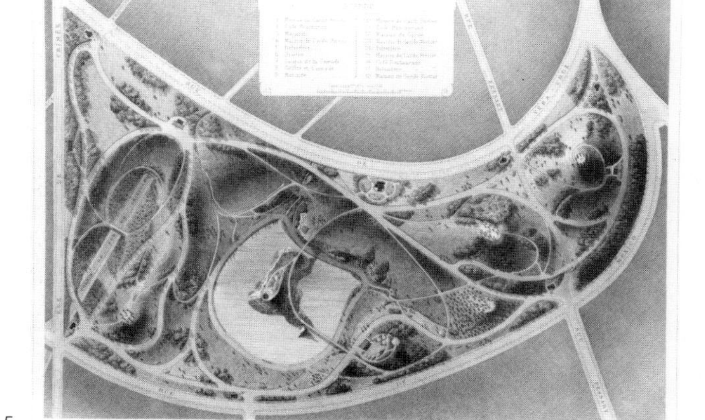

4. London: Plan of Victoria Park, 1846. Watercolour drawing by Sir James Pennethorne.
5. Paris: Plan of the Parc des Buttes-Chaumont. A. Alphand, *Les Promenades de Paris*, 1867-1873.

Representing the civil power

1

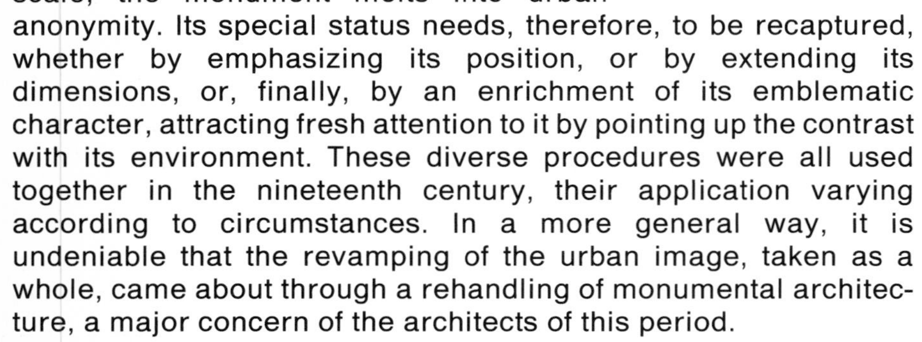

The last element in the restructuring of the urban organism, the escalation in the architectural envelope of private buildings, necessitated a revision of the place occupied by the monument in urban space. In classical tradition the monument was characterized first of all by the quality of its construction, in mason's stone, then by its richness of ornamentation and, finally, by its uncommon size. But when a type of apartment building becomes widespread that utilizes these three features on a grand scale, the monument melts into urban anonymity. Its special status needs, therefore, to be recaptured, whether by emphasizing its position, or by extending its dimensions, or, finally, by an enrichment of its emblematic character, attracting fresh attention to it by pointing up the contrast with its environment. These diverse procedures were all used together in the nineteenth century, their application varying according to circumstances. In a more general way, it is undeniable that the revamping of the urban image, taken as a whole, came about through a rehandling of monumental architecture, a major concern of the architects of this period.

The highlighting of large monuments was greatly facilitated in the Haussmannian city by the opening of new avenues, abutting on "target monuments," the most impressive of which was without doubt the Paris Opera. Contrary to the Emperor, who was interested only in the practical aspects of the new thoroughfares being created, Haussmann concerned himself with their perspectives. The course of the Boulevard Saint-Michel was slightly inflected at its lower end to be brought into relation with the spire of the Sainte-Chapelle; the Boulevard Henri-IV, starting from the column of the Bastille, set its course by the Panthéon; finally, the Boulevard de Sébastopol was given a new focal point by the construction of a specific monument at its southern end, that so strange-looking dome which overtops the Tribunal de Commerce, shifting it off centre.

Along the great north-south Paris axis, the crossing of the Seine by the Boulevard du Palais was framed at its two extremities by a monumental composition: to the north, the twin theatres of Le Châtelet; to the south the great monumental fountain, inspired by the Fountain of Trevi, which Davioud[14] erected against the buildings at the bottom of the Boulevard Saint-Michel. The scale of the Left Bank monument being smaller than that of the two great theatres on the Right Bank, the hierarchy of importance of the different spaces of the city was clearly indicated.

In more difficult locations, like the Haussmann-Malesherbes intersection, the boulevards met on an obliquely positioned monument, the enormous church of Saint-Augustin by Victor Baltard, whose Florentine dome capped the apartment building

1. Frontispiece for *Les Théâtres de la place du Châtelet: Théâtre du Châtelet – Théâtre Lyrique*, by C. Daly and G. Davioud, 1860-1862.
2. Paris: Théâtre du Châtelet in the Place du Châtelet, 1862. Architect: Gabriel Davioud.
3. Paris: Church of Saint-Augustin, 1860-1871. Architect: Victor Baltard. Photograph of about 1900.

2

rooftops. In itself the church was curious, as if it had been stuck together by accident. Baltard had wanted the different restrictions of the side–contour of terrain, approaches, visibility on different scales–to be transcribed into the architectural form and into the very difficulties of that form, too complex to yield a satisfactory result. He thereby expressed to perfection the architectural ambiguity of the academic style.

That complexity became improbability in the Paris Opera, where the height of the arches equalled that of Notre-Dame–three times the height of the tallest buildings! Charles Garnier carried it off with exceptional skill, by exploiting the perspective of the Avenue de l'Opéra (even before its creation) so as to raise up from afar the three tiered masses of the great foyer fronting the street, the rotunda of the auditorium and the roofing of the arches.

The formal composition turned attention away from the incoherence of scale of the three visible components, just as it masked the architectural heart of the edifice: the great staircase sandwiched between the foyer and the auditorium. A stroke of genius, this disguising of one of the programme elements created surprise within the building when, the entrance having been passed, suddenly there was discovered this sumptuous staircase.

3

1

The exploitation of the site to set off a monument may also be conceived on the scale of the whole urban landscape, on that beautiful model provided by the Ottoman tradition of Turkey: the situation of the mosques of Istanbul on the Golden Horn remains one of the most stirring urban spectacles in the world. Nineteenth-century Europe well understood it, and crowned its most elevated sites with gigantic monuments visible for dozens of miles. Here the palm must go to Belgium and to Joseph Poelaert,[15] the builder of the Palais de Justice of Brussels (1866-1883). Dominating the escarpments of the upper town, the edifice was a kind of distillate of classical architectural history: there can be found the lordly line of the roofs of the Louvre colonnade, the mass of the Castel Sant'Angelo and something of St Paul's dome in London. But this monstrous and, as is well known, wholly inconvenient Law Courts building possesses one outstanding feature: the extraordinary

2

1. Paris: Avenue de l'Opéra with the Opera House at the far end. Late 19th-century postcard.
2. Paris: Opera House, 1862-1875. Architect: Charles Garnier. Partial view of the façade.

effect of mass of its silhouette, prolonging and giving dynamism to the city skyline with that Herculean power which evokes at once the palaces of Assyria and the prisons of Piranesi.
Such consideration of site, no doubt on a more moderate scale, can be found as easily at Notre-Dame de la Garde in Marseilles or at Montmartre as in the gigantic extensions to the Louvre or the reconstruction of the Houses of Parliament in Westminster. The site may be different. Still, at the Louvre as at Westminster, it was the expanse of the river that provided the necessary detachment to set off the building, and that imposed its silhouette–the frizz of the Louvre roofs or that so forceful compositional accent supplied by the massive tower of Big Ben.

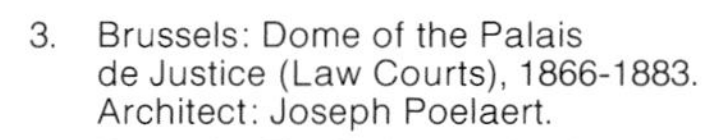

3. Brussels: Dome of the Palais de Justice (Law Courts), 1866-1883. Architect: Joseph Poelaert.
4. Brussels: The Palais de Justice and work on the North-South junction line. Etching by R. van de Sande.

3

4

2

1

The Louvre and Westminster equally had this in common, that they relied on a pre-existing construction, of which they only set themselves up to be the extension. Those parts of Westminster that had not burned down, as well as the Abbey immediately nearby, provided the starting points for shaping the final form, in the same way as the presence of the Old Louvre and its extension by the Grande Galerie, in Paris.

This was the last point on which the monument based its distinctiveness: the use of an individualized emblematic system, clearly distinguishing it from its environment. A dialectical opposition came into play between the architecture of the monument and that of the city, the condition of which was that monumental architecture should not be confused with that of its surroundings. Hence the need to resort to eclecticism as a way of distinguishing forms. The Gothic of the Houses of Parliament, as well as that of St Pancras which we have mentioned, was a political Gothic–its vocation was to express English nationhood–but it was also a Gothic of situation, if I may call it so: its dissimilarity to the dominant environment, drawn in a neoclassical hand, was what gave it its functional value. In Paris there was the neo-Baroque of Lefuel to contrast with the strict alignments of Haussmannian perspectives, in the unbroken flight of their balconies and cornices,

London: The Houses of Parliament, 1840-1850.
Architects: Sir Charles Barry, A. Welby Pugin.

1. Victoria Tower, Westminster. J. Fergusson, *History of the Modern Styles of Architecture*, 1862.
2. The River Front under construction. *The Illustrated London News*, 1842.
3. The North Front. Adopted design of Sir Charles Barry, 1836.

3

4. Paris: Quai des Tuileries, c. 1890. Photograph.

whose flattened rooftops were barely to be distinguished. The reciprocal relationship thereby established between the monumental and the vernacular thus found itself fortified by a style chosen for its unusual character. In the event it made little difference whether the pretext was political, cultural, historicist or quite simply exotic.
In the restructuring of the city which the mid-nineteenth century undertook to meet the new conditions of industrial civilization, the overall ordering of space and its clarification–in the face of runaway urban anarchy which spontaneously set in–had largely to do with the question of the monument. The edifices of the second half of the nineteenth century were, moreover, precisely those that are today among the most famous and most visited in the world.

The palaces of eclecticism

1

Because economic and social reality had become incommensurate with the world of imagination among artists and their patrons, from the mid-nineteenth century art began to play a permanent role of compensation. Its function was not to exalt the real, to give it grandiloquence or a harmonious image, but to run away from it. Classical ideology was stone dead: the monument no longer had as its prime function the transcription in physical space of intuited structures.
Did monument and civil power turn away from each other? Not exactly. For the effort which aimed at the "transformation of the city" included the rehandling of the monument and the re-establishment of a clear hierarchy of social or institutional representation. And–inasmuch as the construction of the rural château or the church reasserted the power of socially important people, a power which, driven as they were out of the great urban centres, they were seeking to recapture–so the reconstructions of church or château were in the first place political gestures, of an inspiration that was notoriously reactionary.
Yet, beyond the explicit content of the undertaking, a latent language began to be seen. In the immensity of the constructions, in their complete absence of realism or necessity (very often the fortunes of their owners were engulfed in financial chasms), nineteenth-century reconstructions of châteaux missed their aim. There was a total contradiction between the economic scheme of rural resettlement and the literary phantasm, at once sentimental and theatrical, that was reflected in the architectural execution.
Each social actor plays his assigned role: the steward is not the architect. One is asked to present accounts; the other, dreams–even if there is no dream without accounts. The architect knows it very well, and always seeks to satisfy his client within the means allotted to him. And it happened that, with the general accumulation of wealth, the epoch was propitious for grand schemes: there is no recoiling from immense undertakings when money keeps pouring in.
Ever since Etienne-Louis Boullée, the training of architects had not ceased to develop their imaginary worlds. In the romantic projects of the painter-architects, of whom Karl Friedrich Schinkel must be counted in the first rank, the generation of 1850 found the bases of its lyrical expression; its ties were close, besides, with the impassioned outpourings of operatic theatre, from Bellini or Weber to Berlioz, Wagner or Verdi.
Once again, it would be a mistake to think that the question of style had any importance: Schinkel's admirable designs for Orianda, in 1838, were alternately classical or Gothic–Hellenic or Scottish, if one prefers. Twenty years after, the castles of Ludwig II of Bavaria would be in Louis XIV or Teutonic style, on request. As interpreter of the dreams of his client (who was, besides, mad), the architect Georg von Dollmann took the precaution of enlisting the aid of a great theatrical designer, Fritz von Seitz, the director of the State Theatre of Munich. Architecture became the setting for a kind of waking dream–outside time, because the times had become decidedly too hard for those capable of contemplating them! At Neuschwanstein, first Eduard Riedel, then Georg von Dollmann and his collaborator Julius Hoffmann, gave a real architectural dimension to these fabulous settings that Ludwig II wished to have around him.

2

1. Crimea: Palace of Orianda.
Unexecuted project of Karl Friedrich Schinkel for the Czar's summer residence.
Watercolour by Schinkel, 1838.

2. Bavaria: Castle of Falkenstein.
Unexecuted project of Christian Jank for King Ludwig II of Bavaria.
Gouache by Jank, 1883.

3

4

3.4. Bavaria: Castle of Neuschwanstein, 1869-1886.
Architects: Eduard Riedel, designs 1867
Georg von Dollmann, 1874-1884
Julius Hoffmann, 1884-1886.

1

The aching emotion which coursed through the fragile sensibility of the mad prince can scarcely be compared with the luxury of the great Victorian residences of the second half of the nineteenth century. At first glance their monumental proportions seem to express only the complacency of wealth. Nevertheless, the immense construction which the Earl of Carnarvon commissioned Sir Charles Barry to carry out at Highclere Castle, between 1840 and 1850, was the most bewildering of transformations. Out of a grand neoclassical residence Barry made a Renaissance château, with its angle towers and great square keep, somewhat recalling Longleat. Nothing was left of the original construction, completely redesigned and inordinately enlarged, to the point where the interior arrangement could be carried out only by the next generation, after 1860.
This tendency was asserted still more strongly in the neo-Gothic restoration made by William Burges between 1868 and 1885 of the old Cardiff Castle for a millionaire client, Lord Bute. The castle keep which he fitted out for him as a bachelor flat was a construction of unheard-of luxury, enriched with a profusion of painted or sculpted works and culminating in a vast smoking-room in Italian style under the roof of the building.

2

Highclere Castle, near Newbury, Hampshire, 1840-1850.
Architect: Sir Charles Barry.
1. Watercolour by Barry, 1840.
2. The entrance hall.

Cardiff Castle, Glamorganshire, Wales, 1868-1885.
Architect: William Burges.
3. The towers from the park.
4. Design by Burges for the Clock Tower, c. 1868 (not as built).

3

CARDIFF CASTLE
NEW TOWER:
No 9
— GALLERY —
— SUMMER —
SMOKING — ROOM —
SERVANTS — ROOM —
— CLOCK — ROOM —

4

1

In his architectural repertory William Burges was manifestly influenced by the worksite of Pierrefonds, where, for Napoleon III, Viollet-le-Duc had reconstituted the sumptuous dream of a great fourteenth–century château. A strange dream for one of the greatest rationalists of the nineteenth century: the archaeological résumé offered by Viollet-le-Duc at Pierrefonds was a sort of adventure story in which each architectural detail was once more placed on stage in the life of a great lord of the Middle Ages–that life with which Viollet-le-Duc painted the walls of the Emperor's bedchamber.
Pierrefonds yields two resolutely contradictory readings.[16] On one hand, following Viollet-le-Duc to the letter, it is possible to see it as a sort of dreamland, a fantasy world, an architectural waking dream easily the equal of that of Ludwig II. But it is also possible to affirm, proofs in hand, that Pierrefonds is a demonstration of rationalism, and that its whole architectural repertory paves the way for the Art Nouveau style, of which it is the veritable founder. The most curious thing is that these two points of view are equally indisputable: by the end of the Second Empire the ambiguity of architectural content was plainly revealed to anyone who took the trouble to interpret it.

2

3

4

Château de Pierrefonds (Oise).
Restoration begun in 1858 (and completed in 1885 by Maurice Ouradou).
Architect: Eugène Viollet-le-Duc.

1. View of the ruined medieval château, 1818. Lithograph by F. Delpech.
2. Flanking turret and gate. *Encyclopédie d'Architecture*, 1876.
3. Gate in the surrounding wall.
4. East front. Drawing by Viollet-le-Duc, 1869.
5. The Hall of Noble Ladies with Napoleon III's collection of armour. Painting by Charles Giraud, 1867.
6. The Hall of Noble Ladies (Salle des Preuses).

5

6

The town house

1

The dramatic intention behind monumental construction was missing in the architecture of the urban habitat: its purpose was more modest, aiming directly at the expression of social standing. Some may see a contradiction in this. We prefer to assert this opposition as a dialectic; habitat architecture, even luxurious, is not to be confused with that of the monument. Where the eighteenth century had tended to unify the two programmes of town house and château, the nineteenth century re-established a complete break between them. The fact that the château was a residence then counted less; it was above all a symbol. Conversely, the town house was and had to be a residence only: any excessive assertion of its monumentality would seem a fault in taste. That was why the most luxurious of Parisian town houses made but a poor show in relation to the financial resources brought to bear. The six million francs which the Marquise de Païva put into building her house in the Champs-Elysées [17] would have amply sufficed to build Pierrefonds–which was no more expensive! Yet the façade stands firmly as a construction on a modest scale, of a taste refined yet unobtrusive. All the effort was concentrated on the sumptuousness of the interior decoration and furniture, for which Pierre Manguin, the architect, called in some of the leading artists of his generation–Baudry, Carrier-Belleuse, Dalou, Picault, Delaplanche, the cabinetmaker Kneib and the ceramist Deck. The choice of architect was good. The architectural team of the Hôtel Païva, which took over ten years to build, from 1856 to 1868, was one of the best of the Second Empire. Most of the artists who composed it, moreover, were to meet again on the building site of the Garnier's opera house.

2

3

Paris: Hôtel Païva, 1856-1868.
Architect: Pierre Manguin.

1. Small drawing-room on the first floor.
2. Fireplace in the dining-room.
   Sculptures by J. Dalou and Jaquemart.
3. Bathroom decorated with Deck earthenware.
4. Onyx staircase in the main entrance-hall.

4

The apartment house

1

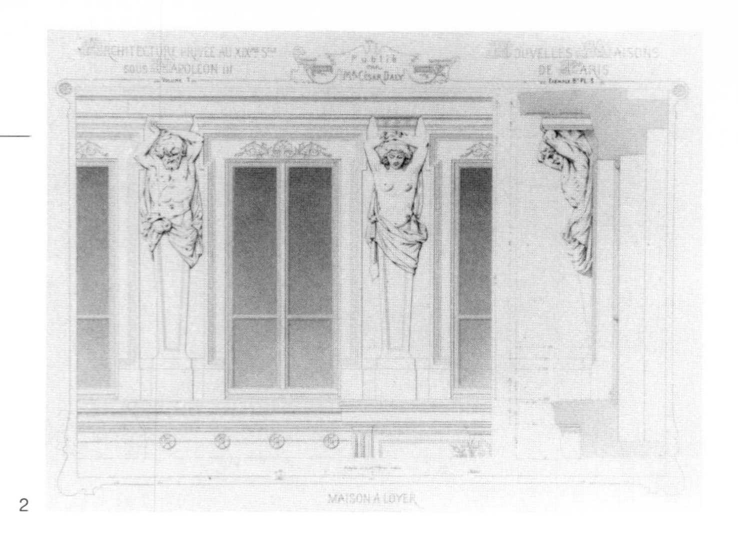

2

The same considerations of propriety made apartment house architecture an anonymous art in which the activity of the greatest names blended into a high standard of production. Who could pick out the buildings of Viollet-le-Duc at the corner of the Rue Lafayette, those of Garnier on the Boulevard Sébastopol, or of Davioud on the Boulevard Saint-Michel, if the architectural reviews of the period did not supply the names of the master builders? A curious banality, when palace architecture was that of formal frenzies: the only explanation lies in the desire by which architects were constrained for total equivalence between programme and form. The perpetual shuttle set up between the effort at rationality and the kind of superabundance or *laisser-aller* to which certain works bear witness, reminds us once again of the fundamental ambiguity of nineteenth-century architecture.

The Second Empire classified apartment buildings and houses in the same way as railway carriages: there were first, second or third-class buildings, depending on their cost of construction, urban position, decoration and the going rent. All this was clearly explained in the architectural journals and compiled in César Daly's great publication: *L'architecture privée au XIXe siècle sous Napoléon III* (Paris 1864).

And it is true that, on closer inspection, the buildings presented, within the same system of architectural outline and style, a detailed hierarchy of ornament, from the most luxurious sculptured decorations down to the mechanically repetitive mouldings of simply profiled balcony platforms, and from rich wrought-iron balconies to simple cross-patterned grilles.

Behind the hierarchy of wealth, bourgeois architecture affirmed its deep-seated unity. Whereas the 1830s, through mechanization of methods, had created total confusion in standards, the generation of the mid-century re-established clear definitions related to precise social standings. The effort was all the more striking in that the change in existing conditions had been recent, and spectacular.

3

4

4. Paris: Apartment house, second class.
   Nos. 2 and 4, Boulevard de Sébastopol.
   Elevation.
   Architect: Gabriel Davioud.
5. Paris: Three apartment houses, third class.
   Nos. 36, 38 and 40, Boulevard Beaumarchais.
   Front elevations.
   Architect: François Rolland.
   1-5 from C. Daly, *L'architecture privée au XIXe siècle sous Napoléon III*, 1864.
6. Paris: Place Sébastopol.
   Perspective view, detail.
   Watercolour by Gabriel Davioud, 1856.

5

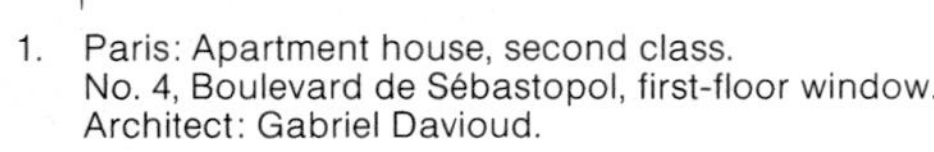

1. Paris: Apartment house, second class.
   No. 4, Boulevard de Sébastopol, first-floor window.
   Architect: Gabriel Davioud.

   Paris: Apartment house, first class.
   No. 125, Avenue des Champs-Elysées.
   Architect: Levicomte.
2. Details of the front.
3. Elevation.

6

Workers' housing

1

Public housing, the last panel in the triptych of voluntarist reconquest of flowering industrial civilization, could not meet with indifference from those who were trying to resolve the problems of the century. After the purely theoretical analyses and utopian solutions proposed by the founders of socialism, a great number of experiments were tried, after 1860, on very opposed lines. [18]

The first experiments were English: the types of "Private architecture of English proletarians" published in Paris by the *Revue Générale de l'Architecture et des Travaux Publics* at the end of the July Monarchy derived from the first night shelters in their barracks-like appearance–large blocks, long and narrow, partitioned into dormitories without any self-contained accommodation. The same model was found besides in most of the charitable institutions, the buildings of which belonged more to hospital than to house architecture: a chain of cells in series, not always individual, in association with a group of shared catering and maintenance services. It is true that these centres of accommodation–which were only institutional homes, in the sense we would use today–did not absolutely try to provide an answer to the question of family housing. The worker was treated as an asocial, that is, an isolated being.

Beneath a comparable outward appearance, the workers' cooperative at Guise, [19] inspired by the ideas of Victor Considérant, had a much wider scope. Built in twenty years, from 1859 to 1879, by J.B.A. Godin, this "social palace" did indeed possess those features of monumentality and isolation that characterized the barracks or the hospital. But although it looked more like a castle than a town, it gave working-class family life the right to existence: each family disposed of its own lodging (and, an exceptional phenomenon, the size of the lodging was related to that of the family, not to the hierarchical rank of the employee). The ensemble of dwellings was grouped around a vast covered courtyard: the yard symbolized (and authorized) the unity of the group, its constitution in a democratic phalanstery. The accent placed on communal life and on group unity did not, nevertheless, jeopardize the right to private life. In that respect the collectivism of Godin remained very moderate.

2

3

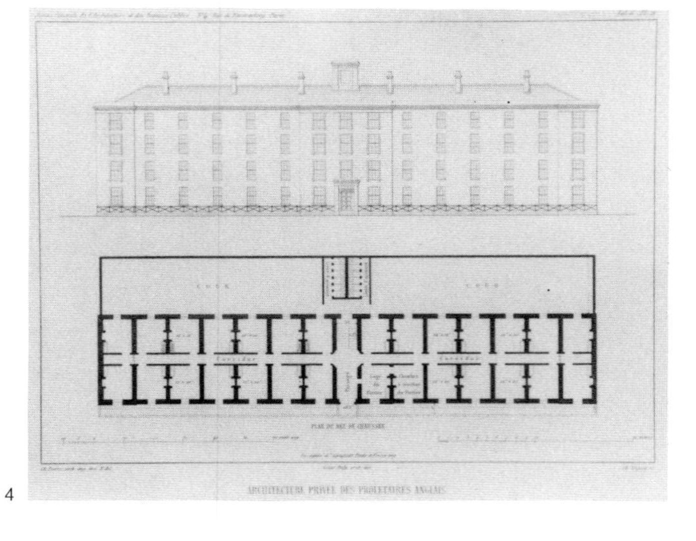
4

1.5. Guise (Aisne): *Familistère* or community settlement founded by J.B.A. Godin in 1865. Detail showing metal framework of the building on the left.

2. London: New ward for casual poor at Marylebone Workhouse. *The Illustrated London News*, 1867.

3. London: Model Lodging-Houses, Columbia Square, Bethnal Green, erected by Miss Angela Burdett-Coutts, 1859-1862. Architect: Henry Darbishire. *The Illustrated London News*, 1862.

4. "Private architecture of English proletarians": Lodging-house for English working-men containing 112 separate rooms. *Revue Générale de l'Architecture et des Travaux Publics*, 1845-1846.

5

1

This proposal was at the opposite extreme from those by which a number of Christian employers set great store: the construction of isolated individualized houses, on suburban lots. For the partisans of Frédéric Le Play, the moralization of the working class could be achieved only through reconstituting the autonomous family unit and pulling it out of the enforced collectivity of the working-class world–the promiscuity of night shelters or overcrowded living quarters, the daily frequentation of the bistro, breeding alcoholism, prostitution or revolt.

The petty bourgeois model of the small suburban house[20] was born of the rejection of the working-class condition for reasons both of morality and of vested interest. The pavilion, the one-family house reduced to its simplest expression, offered a living room, one or two bedrooms, an outside sanitary unit and a small individual garden for growing vegetables. This miniaturization of the traditional rural cottage and its way of life was, it must be said, generally well adapted to the situation of lately transplanted migrants. It met with an excellent welcome besides among the working class, whether in the form of strips of building plots offered to workers (West Hill Park, at Halifax, 1862), or the semi-detached houses of French industrialists at Mulhouse, Anzin, Le Creusot or Noisiel-sur-Marne (the first two ensembles were presented as models at the Exposition Universelle of 1867 in Paris, which saw for the first time the question of housing put forward as an essential problem; the other two were built just after the Franco-Prussian war of 1870).

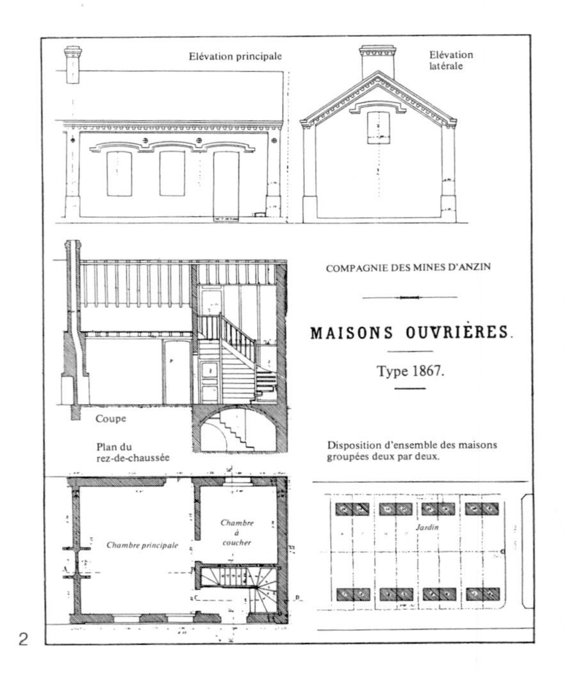

2

ELEVATION OF A 3000-FRANC HOUSE.

3

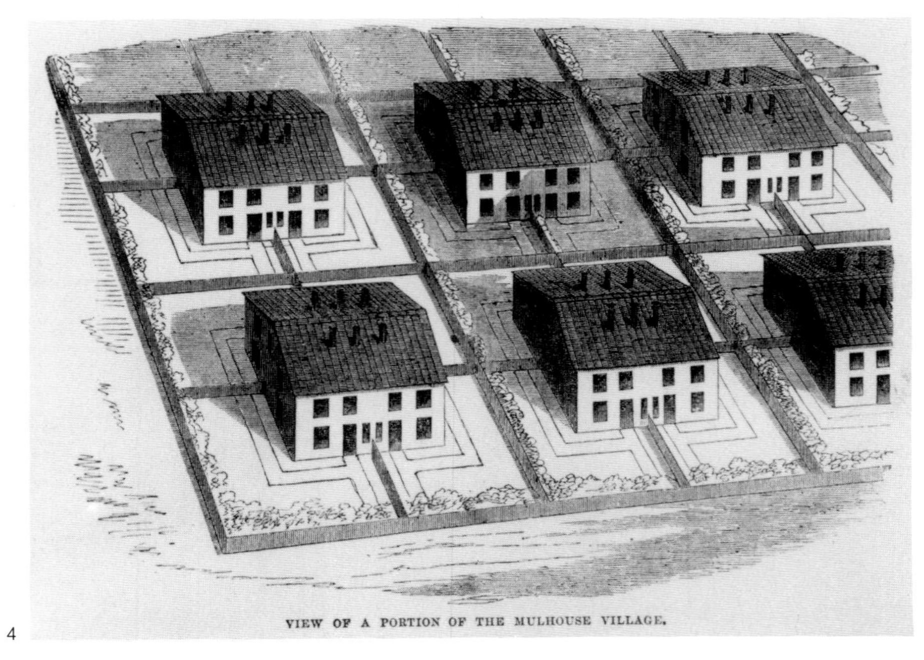

VIEW OF A PORTION OF THE MULHOUSE VILLAGE.

4

1. Le Creusot (Saône-et-Loire): Workers' houses of the Cité Saint-Eugène, 1870-1875.
2. Anzin (Nord): Plan of miners' houses at the Anzin Collieries, 1867.
3.4. Mulhouse (Alsace): Elevation of a worker's house. Partial view of a workers' village. Project presented at the Exposition Universelle, Paris, 1867. *The Illustrated London News*, 1867.
5. Halifax (Yorkshire): West Hill Park, begun 1862. Working-class housing erected with the help of Edward Akroyd, Sir Francis Crossley and other local businessmen.

5

The intense production that marked the mid-nineteenth century corresponded to a profound ideological crisis among architects. To be sure, scholastic quarrels had been rife throughout history. Yet never had architecture been the object of such a debate. It involved both the problem of form and that of the role of architecture. Graver still, questions were being asked about the role of the architect himself and his status in industrial society.
It might be imagined that the expansion of the building sector, while giving architects markets, at the same time gave them a certain form of social importance tied to wealth. That was exactly the case, for the number of architects grew each day, while their social standing rose. Abandoning the building trade, the artist-architect entered, on an equal footing with doctors, the ranks of the professional classes, joining notaries and lawyers in the envied body of notable persons. This remarkable social promotion did not prevent the architect from feeling threatened, as he was, objectively, by competition from businessmen and, more subjectively, by the idea he formed of rivalry with engineers.
In fact, this entire period was one of consolidation of the craft. A network of societies sprang up in France (the Société Centrale, founded in 1840, and the many provincial societies that formed its extension), supported by a specialized press whose birth was one of the great innovations of the nineteenth century. The transmission of formal models was thereafter effected by way of "review architecture," whose role was fundamental in understanding international cultural exchanges as well as in the rapid evolution of stylistics. While assembling a renewed corpus of images, the architects' press also opened its pages to critical reflection, which in the first instance was of corporate concern.

The debate on architecture

To sell art, and nothing but art, is not an easy business. More and more, architects' discourse became self-justifying. It expressed their difficulty in getting problems of aesthetics or semantics across to a public. Without realizing it, the artist was one of the first victims of the law of profit in industrial society. The immediate financial profitability of artistic activity is negative, and its ultimate profitability more than problematic. It is based on a speculation with highly uncertain and, in any case, fluctuating results. The position of other participants in the act of building is more secure; it is not possible to do without them. The architect, therefore, had henceforth to explain the purpose he served and the nature of the aesthetic debates with which he was preoccupied.
The position of the public architect, trained by the Ecole des Beaux-Arts, was totally ill-adapted to bourgeois demand. The new class was only secondarily interested in the representation of civil power; it did not consider the public monument as the prime area for architectural representation, in the same way as it contested the aristocracy's privileged claim to luxury. The evolution of architectural theory reflected this change in the state of affairs. Rationalism, which is a metaphorical discourse on the economy of forms, assimilated to the economy of means (according to that confusion which Malevich, in his political commitments, later carried to extremes!), found favourable terrain in bourgeois mentality, which condemned the idea of prestige architecture on moral grounds. [1]
Concurrently, this didactic effort, in which rationalist style participated by dismantling architectural structures, tried symbolically to take over the engineers' function. Henceforth it claimed to justify architecture as construction. César Daly realized this, moreover, when he reproached architects with stretching out on their own Procrustean bed. It was true that the condemnation of public art cast doubt on the very role of architecture in society.

The academic tradition

The contesting of academicism is a phenomenon which goes back before 1830. In France it emerged apropos of the works sent back from Rome by Henri Labrouste in 1827: "The architectural sketches Labrouste is sending from Rome astonish everyone: they have an unexpected appearance. Beneath a handling which remains discreet, liberties are taken that run counter to accepted usage. There are things there which have no authorized place in documents drawn according to Academy practice. In his diagrams he neglects nothing, records everything, takes down even the sizes of the building stones and incorporates them in his renderings. The organism of the construction can be read easily there. Something like a secondary rhythm is felt that sustains the principal rhythm of the forms." [2]

This fascination with technique did not begin with Henri Labrouste (and moreover it did not start the "revolution" sometimes attributed to him within the Academy). He had been preceded on this path by Abel Blouet, Félix Duban and Augustin Caristie, [3] whose passion for archaeology was equalled only by the taste for exactness and the precision of the sketch, as well as the interest taken in construction, in reaction against the excesses of pictorial architecture by the emulators of Charles de Wailly.

The French architect of the nineteenth century was an archaeologist-architect. The Prix de Rome competition and the obligatory exercises accompanying it during the stay at the Villa Medici had developed, since the eighteenth century, a veritable passion for archaeological studies, the architectural sketch and above all, restoration–which, starting from often uncertain ruins, proposed an ideal re-creation of the original state. The generation of 1830, basing itself on a scrupulous material observation of ruins, paved the way for the scientific practice of modern archaeological restoration.

At the same time, the investigation into construction and its methods led to a kind of paradox. It was within the Academy itself, among the laureates of the Prix de Rome, that rationalist preoccupations were born of which Henri Labrouste would later become the flag-bearer. The technical drawings he furnished of Roman construction, the analyses of the bonding of masonry stones and the structural cross-sections, revealed the student trained by Jean-Baptiste Rondelet. From the observation of technique to its architectural paraphrase, strongly bringing out the effects of structure and the details of construction, there was but an easy step. The consequences are to be seen in the whole of mid-nineteenth-century production, from Louis Duc to Victor Baltard and Léon Vaudoyer.

1. Rome: Villa Medici, north front, 1851-1852. Calotype by Alfred Normand.
2. Selinunte (Sicily): "Temple of Jupiter," 1822-1824. (Now known as Temple G or Apollonion.) Watercolour by Jacques-Ignace Hittorff.

A final aspect of the archaeological interests of the young Prix de Rome architects was that the reaching out towards Greek civilization, and, more generally, towards the East,[4] broke up the unity of classical culture by introducing relativeness into the message of the Roman tradition. To go to Paestum, or like Hittorff to Selinunte, in order to study archaic Greek edifices opened the way to the discovery of the antique architecture of Greece. The development in that direction, however, was long and difficult. It

3

3. Athens: View of the Acropolis from the south-west, 1851. Calotype by Alfred Normand.
4. Paestum (Campania): Section of the "Temple of Neptune" (Temple of Hera II), 1828. Drawing by Henri Labrouste.

4

was only in 1846 that France authorized its *pensionnaires* (architects in training) to cross the Mediterranean to Athens as part of the French School of Archaeology to take sketches of ancient monuments. Alfred Normand was one of the first beneficiaries, bringing back from his trip a precious collection of calotypes;[5] and shortly after him, Charles Garnier, who executed the well-known drawing of the temple of Aegina, correcting the one made by Abel Blouet twenty years earlier.

The journey to Greece, made by way of Sicily, was the occasion of another discovery: that of Byzantine civilization. Going from Venice down to Ravenna, then from Ravenna to the Early Christian basilicas of Rome, the architectural tour of the *pensionnaires* brought them at last to Palermo or to Monreale, and sometimes even to St Sophia in Constantinople. All of classical culture was shaken by that fascinating discovery of colour, that epic sense of monumental composition in painting, in the sumptuous form of mosaics with a gold ground and frescos covering the walls of "Romanesque-Byzantine" basilicas.

Paris: Ecole des Beaux-Arts.
Architects: Félix Duban
Ernest Coquart.

1. Cross-section of the glass-roofed courtyard (Musée des Etudes). *Encyclopédie d'Architecture*, 1876.
2. Interior view of the glass-roofed courtyard (Musée des Etudes), 1871.

3

3. Design for a rich banker's town house. Longitudinal section of the right side with staircase. Watercolour drawing by Jean-Louis Pascal (Prix de Rome, 1866).
4. Design for a traveller's hotel. Cross-section. Watercolour drawing by Louis Noguet (Prix de Rome, 1865).

A last discovery: the canonical rules of architectural order were upset by the practice of redeployment, of associating forms whose syntactical position and dimensional scale were completely disturbed. There resulted unusual effects, curious or harsh, whose bittersweet savour enticed the eye wearied by so many agreed harmonic assemblages. Leon Battista Alberti's rules of unity and arrangement were insidiously perverted by this practice of dissonance, the intention of which was openly anticlassical.
Into the inner sanctum of the Ecole des Beaux-Arts, the keeper of the laws, the heresy penetrated, both in the form of tectonic discourse, paving the way to rationalism, and in the more secret forms of syntactic perturbation, authorizing the most eclectic combinations. Teaching was not entirely untainted by it. In the courtyard of the Musée des Etudes, covered in 1871 with a great metal and glass roof by Ernest Coquart, there was installed a most odd museum of plaster casts, whose accumulation of fragments of architecture or sculpture was almost an inducement to canonical derangement. The three columns of the Parthenon which rose there to touch the glass roof had an almost surrealistic appearance, breaking completely in scale with the arcades of the palace designed by Duban.

4

1. Regensburg: Design for the Walhalla, the "Temple of German Worthies," 1830-1842. Architect: Leo von Klenze. Watercolour drawing by Klenze.
2. Berlin: Neues Museum, 1843-1855. Architect: Friedrich August Stüler. Design for the wall decorations of the south dome. Watercolour by Stüler.

1

The breath of disproportion traversed the production of the School: nothing remained of the spirit of harmony and grandeur dear to the neoclassical in that elaborate reconstruction by Duban of a *Roman Palace Under the Empire* (in a watercolour which has remained famous) nor in the temple at once immense and constricted, designed by Louis Duc for the Vestibule de Harlay in the Palais de Justice of Paris,[6] or in the great prize competitions–the outsize projects for which, made up of dislocated elements, attracted only praises from the juries.
The era of the neo-antique, which was the classically inspired art of the mid-nineteenth century, no longer had anything to do with the neoclassical and its inspiration. Philosophical grandeur was no

2

3

4

3. Paris: Palais de Justice (Law Courts), 1857-1868. Vestibule de Harlay (Waiting-Hall). Architect: Louis Duc.
4. Athens: The Zappeion Exhibition Hall, begun 1874. Ionic portico. Architects: Florimond Boulanger Theophil von Hansen.
5. Berlin: Nationalgalerie, 1866-1876. Architects: Friedrich August Stüler Johann Heinrich Strack. Design for the cross-passage on the first floor. Watercolour drawing by Strack, c. 1870.

5

longer the accepted thing: that stale concept made way for more plastic feelings, the sense of rhythm, the composition round a centre of interest, the search for contrasts and the outspoken taste for vanquished contradictions. There was something Piranesian in the neo-antique vision of the nineteenth century: a dream-dimension deriving from the contextual placing, the permanent frictions of scale and the position of the elements brought into play. How otherwise shall we explain the strangeness of the Walhalla by Klenze, one of the prototypes of the new spirit breaking away from neoclassical equilibrium, or the incongruous platitude of that Greek temple planted in a meanly proportioned public garden, as conceived by F.A. Stüler for the National Gallery of Berlin? How, finally, shall we explain the spellbinding effect produced in the centre of the Zappeion exhibition hall in Athens, by the great circular court designed by the Frenchman Florimond Boulanger [7] as a kind of empty monument, suggesting some return to Marienbad?

The rationalist alternative

1

While neo-antique art, unable to latch on to a theory, enclosed itself in the cult of pure beauty through the elegant and gracile forms of Greek style–somewhere between Ingres, ancient Etruria and the ruins of Athens [8]–the most critical-minded architects were trying to rise above any cramping commitment to a definite style, even if it seemed the most cultivated style in the world, in order to rediscover fundamental laws for architecture that would set it firmly in the reality of the times. In England, in France, in Germany, men like Pugin, Semper, Viollet-le-Duc and Labrouste are found, in the 1840s, to be taking surprisingly parallel roads, despite the diversity of their stylistic repertories.
The question of style, even if it was the object of a public debate bringing face to face those two rival faiths of academicism and archaeological Gothic, enters in here only in a circumstantial way. It is true that Viollet-le-Duc belonged in his tastes to the Gothic school, but it should come as no surprise that ties of friendship united him with Jean Dominique Ingres. As for Labrouste, that founder of rationalism was nothing less than the most brilliant of the holders of the Prix de Rome, a perfect representative of the academic tendency, as we have seen.
For his first public commission, the Bibliothèque Sainte-Geneviève in Paris (1843-1850), Labrouste gave a reading of classicism completely stripped of the artifices of academic composition. The harshness of the parallelepipedal design of the form was a protest against the prevailing abuse of a projecting front and pediments, against a monotonous rhythm of arcades and a pure expression of the internal metallic structure. The decoration of the library, in a word, makes sense only with reference to the structure and arrangement at the same time as to the emblematic vocabulary of the programme (the laurels of science, the cressets of thought, the tablets of authors).
The whole architectural formal arrangement is summed up in the demonstration of a deliberate choice: that of a vast double hall, with slender columns and cast-iron arches filled by a false vault of plaster (fireproof), the hall being enclosed in a stone shell to give it support. Nor were references in any way prevented: there is something Florentine about this palatial library, the simulated pedestal of which houses the stack-rooms; the reading room itself, as has often been observed, is indebted to the admirable medieval refectory of Saint-Martin-des-Champs (used as the library of the Ecole des Arts et Métiers).
Yet none of the references traceable here exists for its own sake. Nostalgia is absent, and indeed it is the affirmation of modernity which prevails, with the use of cast iron in forms that are perhaps not technically daring (cast-iron bridges had been built for the past forty years) but which are daring plastically; for the qualities of

Paris: Library of Sainte-Geneviève, 1843-1850.
Architect: Henri Labrouste.
1. Door of the library.
Drawing by Labrouste.
Revue Générale de l'Architecture et des Travaux Publics, 1852.
2. Perspective view of the main front.
Drawing by Labrouste.
Revue Générale de l'Architecture et des Travaux Publics, 1853.

2

3

finesse and transparency, the matter and colour properly belonging to cast iron, are given a higher value, up to and including the classical capital, calculated in proportion to the shaft of the column and not according to the canonical proportion of the order (which would have made it much thicker).
The technical rationality echoed by the Bibliothèque Sainte-Geneviève and, to a greater degree, by the Bibliothèque Nationale, was not the only message delivered by Labrouste. [9] For the former Seminary of Rennes (1845-1872), the articulation of the central parts of the building, the rhythm of doors and windows, and, distinctively, of the chimney-stacks, functioned as a demonstration of the design, a conception dear to neo-Gothic aesthetics. Classical formalism was wholly attached to the plastic effect, independent of its role. By establishing a codified relationship between the size of the bays and the function of the volume they illuminated, Labrouste introduced a new priority, the expression of function by form (based on a reading of the theoretical works of Pugin, later condensed by Sullivan in a celebrated formula).

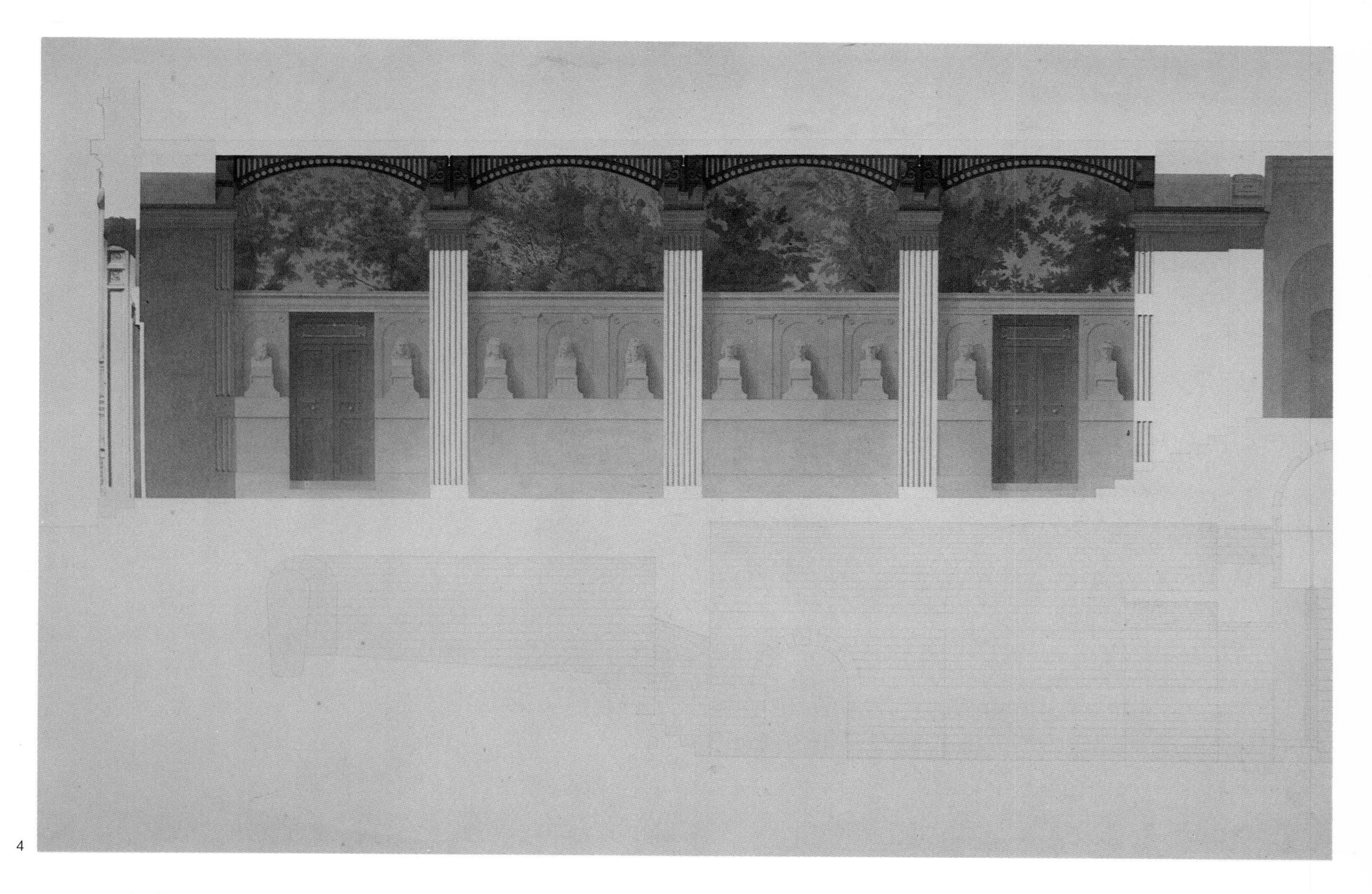

4

3. Rennes (Brittany): Seminary, 1845-1872.
Architect: Henri Labrouste.
Front elevation and cross-section.
Drawing by Labrouste, 1853.
4. Paris: Library of Sainte-Geneviève, 1843-1850.
Elevation and section of vestibule wall.
Drawing by Labrouste, 1850.

It may be asked, besides, whether that entire generation was not steeped in A. Welby Pugin's book *The True Principles of Pointed or Christian Architecture* (1841), which formed an unexpected digest of the whole rationalist ideology. [10] The architectural discourse of Labrouste, in classical language, alludes to it, as does that curious rewriting of the Gothic attempted by Louis-Auguste Boileau or the analysis of structural detail that distinguishes Viollet-le-Duc's view of architectural history.
By redesigning the Gothic so as to free it from the formalism of the stylized profiles of mouldings and cornices, and by daring to transpose certain elements into iron and cast iron, Viollet-le-Duc [11] effectively aimed at reinterpreting the medieval lesson in a rationalist sense–to the extent of trying out new combinations, such as the association of the timber truss with the brick vault or that of the cast iron angle-brace with the vault of stone. Practical-minded,

1 2

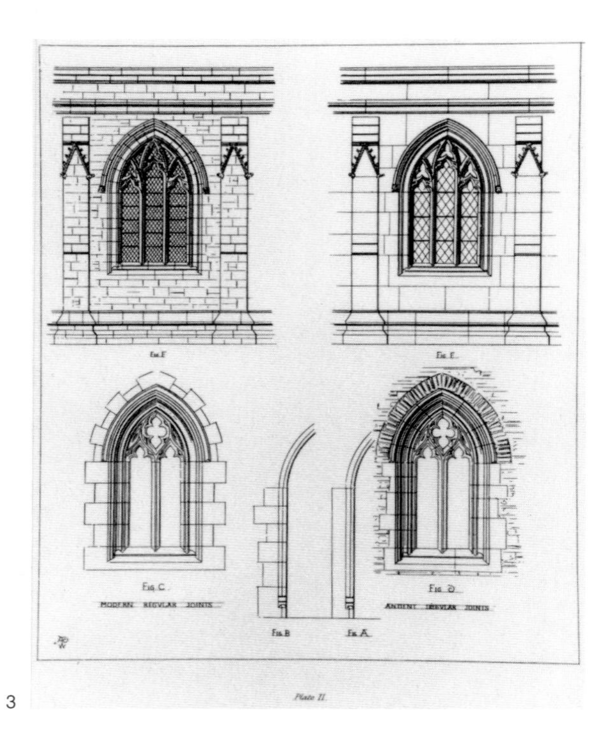

3

all his experience being based on the empiricism of the building site in especially difficult restorations (such as the underpinnings of Vézelay), Viollet-le-Duc never designed a utopian project. The metallic truss he drew in his *Entretiens sur l'Architecture* (1863-1872) reflected the exact state of technology in the Second Empire, with its arches of riveted sheet iron, king-post and tie-beam of steel rods and struts of cast iron (each material chosen for the stresses it would have to bear and with strict account kept of manufacturing costs). To the second volume of his *Entretiens* (written in 1867-1870, published in 1872), he added a design for a house with a steel-work ossature, proving his awareness of the "skeleton construction" in riveted steel devised by Jules Saulnier (for the Menier factory at Noisiel-sur-Marne, then under construction).
The opposite line was taken by Louis-Auguste Boileau, [12] although he too was a builder (starting in 1872 he and his son Louis-Charles collaborated in erecting the Bon Marché department store in Paris). Throwing off the constraints of actual construction, he put forward a vast theoretical scheme, that of the "synthetic cathedral" (an idea which later inspired Gaudí). [13] Redrafted many times in

1. Metal vaulting.
   E. Viollet-le-Duc, *Entretiens sur l'Architecture*, 1863-1872.
2. Paris: Library of the Law School, 1876-1878.
   Architect: Louis-Ernest Lheureux.
   Corner vaulting in the Salle Carrée.
   Encyclopédie d'Architecture, 1876.
3. Ancient and modern masonry joints.
   Drawing by Pugin.
   A. Welby Pugin, *The True Principles of Pointed or Christian Architecture*, 1841.

different forms, this scheme, which set up as being the synthesis of Catholic tradition (combining the plan of St Peter's in Rome with the structure of Chartres!), was composed of a structure of pillars, made of masonry or cast iron, supporting vault quadrants, whose cantilevered revetment wall formed a pyramidal composition, culminating in a sort of giant stepped dome. The interest of this conception, apart from the fact that it allowed the creation of an immense nave, lay in the proposed principle of lighting: the vault segments, receiving the side lighting of huge bays, sent back a reflected, indirect light that lit the building from within. Gaudí got his inspiration from it for the double-vaulting system he used in the Sagrada Familia in Barcelona.

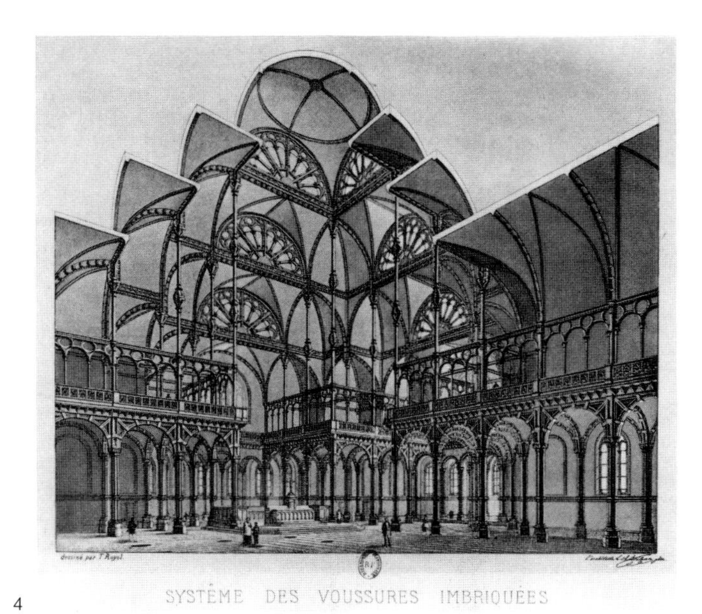

4

4. System of interlocking arch mouldings as applied to the interior of a church, c. 1865. Drawing by Boileau. L.A. Boileau, *Histoire critique de l'invention en architecture*, 1886.

5. Synthetic cathedral, cross-section, 1850. Drawing by Boileau. L.A. Boileau, *Nouvelle forme architecturale composée*, 1853.

5

1

Aillant-sur-Tholon (Yonne):
Village Church, 1863.
Architect: Eugène Viollet-le-Duc.
1. Cross-section.
2. Front elevation.
Watercolour drawings by Viollet-le-Duc, 1862.

Boileau and Viollet-le-Duc maintained difficult relations, from which professional rivalry was perhaps not absent. It is true that the creation of the church of Saint-Eugène in 1854-1855 had placed Boileau in the forefront as demonstrating the possibilities of metallic construction in religious architecture, while Viollet-le-Duc remained wedded to masonry construction. On that point the comparison between Saint-Paul de Montluçon and Aillant-sur-Tholon, two churches of 1863, the first by Boileau, the second by Viollet-le-Duc, is illuminating: they are two opposed examples of practice resting on the same corpus of ideas and references. Montluçon, like Saint-Eugène, was a meditation on the space of the Sainte-Chapelle and its transparency, combined with the ossature of slender round pillars of which the thirteenth-century refectories (by way of Labrouste) were the original model: the architecture of iron and cast iron gave the art of the century of St Louis its ideal expression–an idea which appeared again three-quarters of a

2

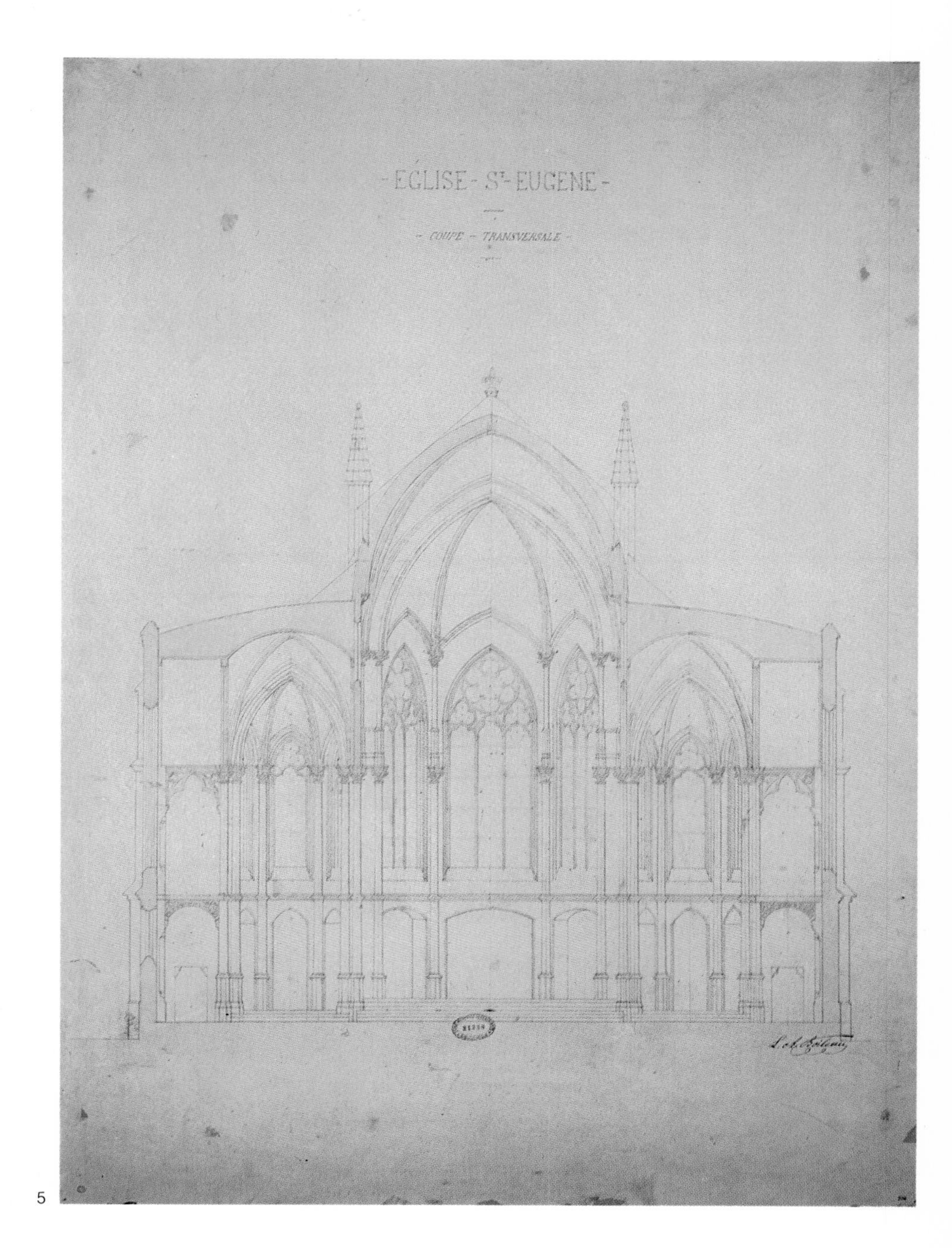

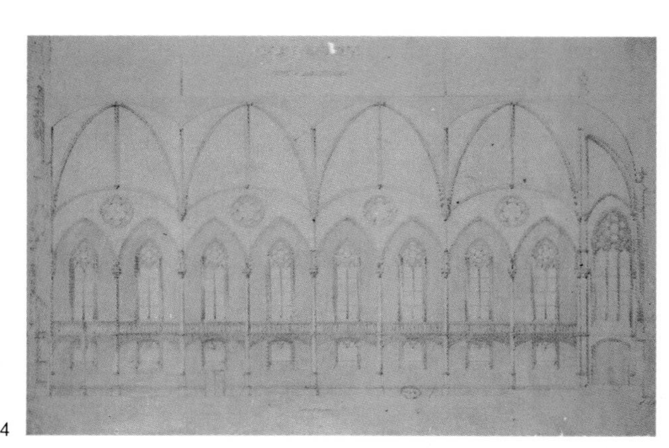

Paris: Church of Saint-Eugène, 1854-1855.
Architect: Louis-Auguste Boileau.
3. Details of the gallery arches.
4. Longitudinal section.
5. Cross-section.
Watercolour drawings by Boileau.

century later with Perret at Le Raincy. Conversely, the building by Viollet-le-Duc was a methodical reflection on a model of neo-Gothic: the church of Cusset, by Jean-Baptiste Lassus, from which Viollet-le-Duc borrowed the gable-façade, the displaced steeple, the lighting by round windows and the wide vaulted nave, while taking care to simplify and rationalize its language and so give it the form best suited to a country church. It has been said of Aillant, moreover, that it is "logical to the point of rigour, ingenious to the point of subtlety." [14]
The demonstrative logic of rationalism would strongly inspire the French generation of the Second Empire (but also the English

1

2

3

architects of the ecclesiological movement). That logic underlies the formal analytics which characterize the work of the greatest architects of the time. Coming from the neo-Gothic, this spelling out of detail made its way through the work of Lassus–accounting for its importance, although its archaeological orientation would limit its scope–to end in edifices as different as Garnier's Paris Opera or the cathedral of Marseilles (the latter by Léon Vaudoyer, 1852-1893). Everything down to decorative designs bore its mark. The studies by Alexandre Denuelle for decorations to accompany the frescos of the Flandrin brothers on a project by Victor Baltard at Saint-Germain-des-Prés, used the arrangement of line and colour as a kind of commentary on the structural organism; they took no liberty, made no step outside the frame, showed no independence of rhythm–ornament was totally subordinated to the tectonic effect.

4

Marseilles Cathedral, 1852-1893.
Architect: Léon Vaudoyer.
1. Side elevation.
Drawing by Vaudoyer.
2. View from the new port.
4. Detail of a dome.
3. Paris: Sketch for the interior decoration of the church of Saint-Germain-des-Prés. Watercolour by Alexandre Denuelle, before 1879.

The practice of eclecticism

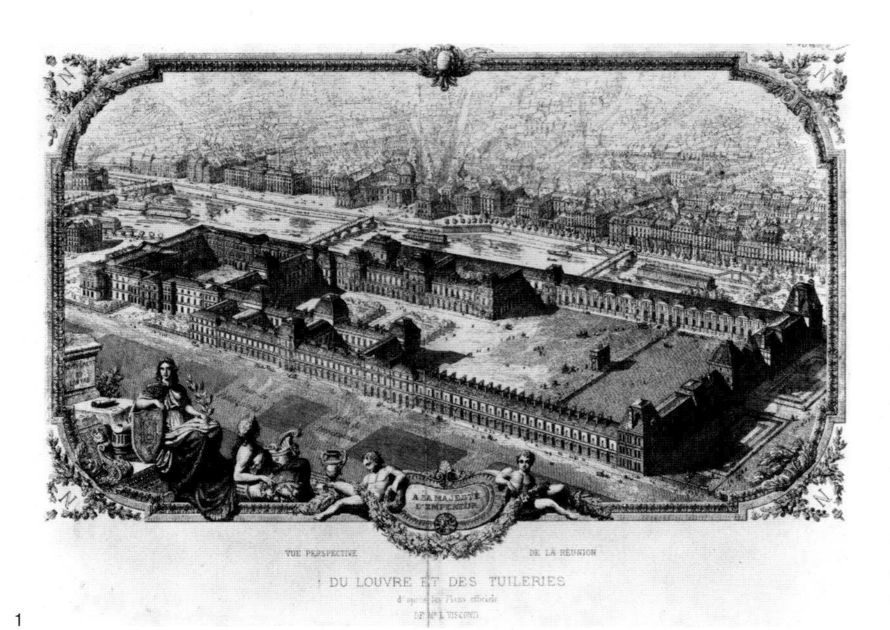

1

It is not by deliberate intent that we have slipped works generally reputed to be eclectic into the domain of rationalism. The theoretical positions expressed by the articles of the specialized press were far from confirming architectural practice. And if, in certain works, the content was more drastic than in others, it was perhaps a question of ideology, but above all, of temperament and circumstances. Eclecticism is not a theory; it is rather a behaviour, an attitude in the face of a project. In the same way, rationalism quite often boils down to a system of design. In "style" architecture, where the repertory of forms is borrowed from history, it is striking that the mode of treatment conforms so little to the initial spirit of the style; something like a whiff of the nineteenth century hangs about, deriving from the excessively articulated spelling out of detail.

Duban and Visconti, in the first works carried out on the Louvre, created a type of composition using "clip-on ornament," [15] in which the décor seems applied to the building structure and composed of autonomous elements, whose own realism clashes with the general unity: each motif is an addition of objects, in a synthesis which is artificial because it is rendered only in broad outline. This formal arrangement of ancient art was a purely analytical rereading which completely violated the spirit of the style, to the point where it has been supposed that the nineteenth century might have lacked talent for the art of pastiche. It was not talent that it lacked, but interest: when it reproduced the art of the past it reinterpreted that art in its own way. Contrary to what has often been maintained, eclectic art seldom mixed styles (it mixed models, but rarely the detail-work of style). What gave historicism its "lack of conviction" was its divergence from the art of the past, by which it claimed to be inspired; in fact, it completely restyled that art.

There is great interest to be found in this exercise, in which the past, in the reading given it, is placed totally at the service of the modern vision of form; and, from that standpoint, it is indubitable that the nineteenth century, which did not possess its own decorative repertory, did indeed have its own style–a certain way of approaching and composing the motif, of placing it or commenting on it. The nineteenth century was indeed the last of the great classical centuries. For what else had the practice since the Renaissance been if not to continuously paraphrase a style–classical ordonnance–by giving it each time a different reading? Historians, besides, had to invent distinctive names to designate the successive phases of classical art–Mannerist, Baroque, Rococo. Pejorative as it may be now, let us accept the term eclectic (which one is nevertheless tempted to describe as analytic instead), and thereby have done with this question. [16]

2

1. Paris: Perspective view of the Palais du Louvre and the Palais des Tuileries as linked together, before 1871. After the official plans by L.T.J. Visconti. Print.
2. Paris: The Nouveau Louvre, Pavillon Richelieu. *Album du Magasin Pittoresque*, 1862. From a drawing by E. Thérond.
3. Paris: The Palais du Louvre, the Arc de Triomphe du Carrousel and the Palais des Tuileries. Photograph by Friedrich von Martens, c. 1865.
4. Vienna: Project for connecting the Hofburg with the museums, bird's-eye view. Pen-and-ink drawing by Gottfried Semper and Carl von Hasenauer, 1869.

3

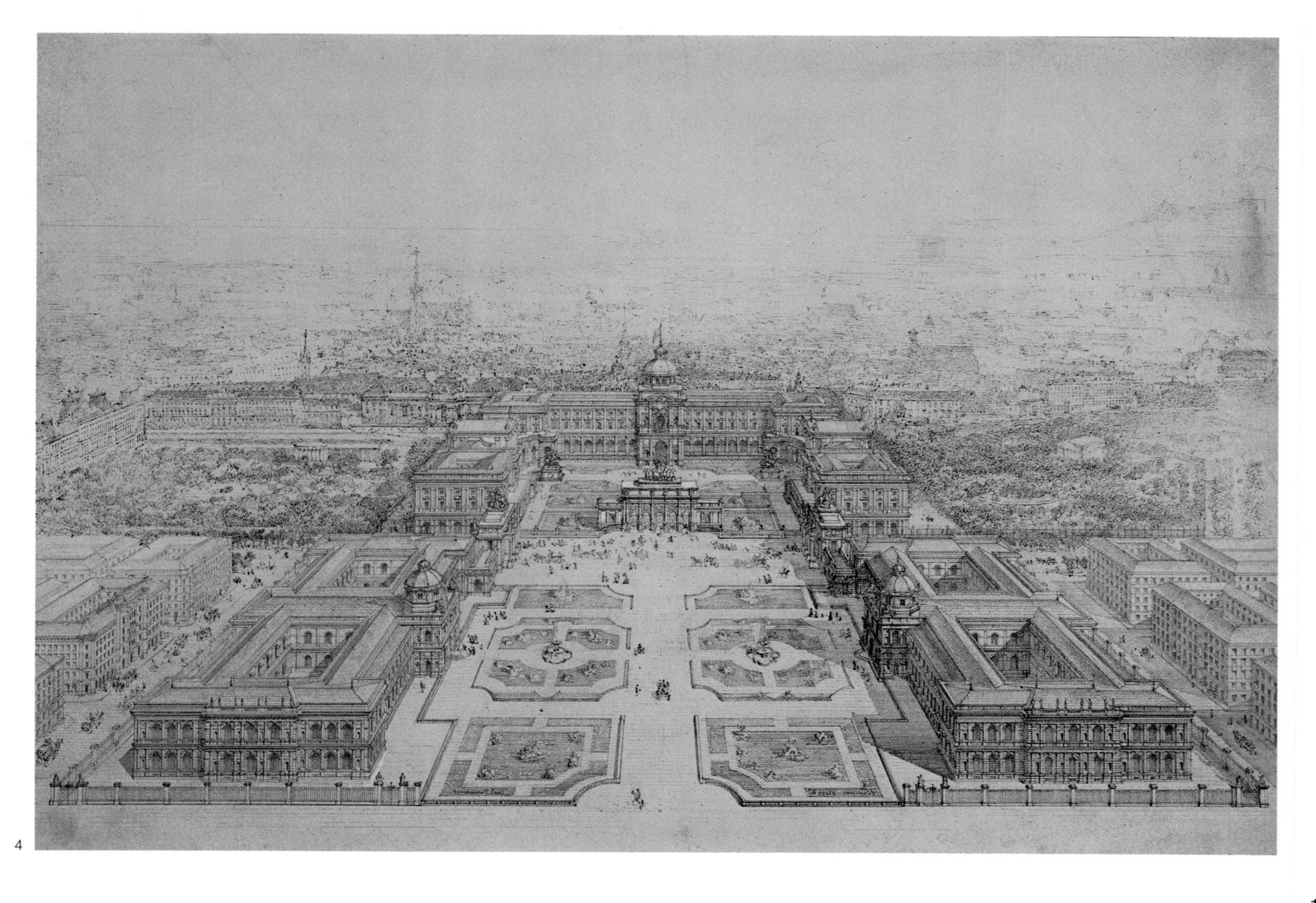

4

The practice of eclecticism opposed the ideology of rationalism to the extent that it rejected architecture as object and gave priority to the problem of fitness. Here, architectural expression did not make construction the object of its discourse; it offered other kinds of artistic commentaries, in which situation and environment became fundamental.
The example of imperial palaces–Semper in Vienna, Lefuel in Paris–is revelatory here. The problem was to associate disparate elements produced by successive intentions and to give the new ensemble the character best suited to it. In the completion of the Grand Louvre, what was aimed at was a historical synthesis. The project designed by Visconti, then given precise form by Lefuel over nearly a quarter of a century, started with a conglomeration of architectures ranging from Henri II to Napoleon I, not without disorder–the Cour Carrée, the Grande Galerie, the Petite Galerie,

1

Lyons: Palais du Commerce, 1855-1860.
Architect: René Dardel.
1. North front.
2. Ornamental clock in the Salle de la Bourse.
R. Dardel, *Monographie du Palais du Commerce élevé à Lyon*, 1868.
3. View of the Salle de la Bourse (Stock Exchange)

2

3

4. Paris: Palais du Louvre, detail of the arcades on the Carrousel side, completed 1878. Architect: Hector Lefuel. *Navigation*, sculpture by François Jouffroy.

the Colonnade, the Rue de Rivoli wing, the Tuileries pavilions. On this amalgam was superimposed a series of designs of which the most important, the one that would serve as the connecting thread to the conception of the New Louvre, was the work of Percier and Fontaine. Visconti took over the façade galleries and associated them with a vertical section derived from Perrault's façade overlooking the Seine, adding to it an ensemble of domed pavilions, the idea for which derived from the Pavillon de l'Horloge by Lemercier. The mixture of all these great architectural concepts, spread over three centuries, produced the powerful neo-Baroque ensemble we know today, superior in its synthesizing spirit to the sum of its components.

The fitness of the programme consisted in the acceptance of the stylistic data of the context, the reference imposed on history, of which the project set up to be the extension (and the amplification!). But the problem of character is no less important, and Baroque solemnity suits an imperial palace; it magnifies the grandeur of the

1

1. Munich: Maximilianeum, 1857-1874. Architect: Friedrich Bürklein. *Ansichten von München*, late 19th century.
2. Paris: Palais du Trocadéro, 1878. Architect: Gabriel Davioud. Drawing by Davioud in *Monographie des palais et constructions diverses de l'exposition universelle de 1878*, 1882.

Marseilles: Palais de Longchamp, 1862. Architect: Henri-Jacques Espérandieu.

3. View from the Zoological Garden.
4. View from the Boulevard Longchamp.

State in another and better way than do the graces of Rococo or the preciosities of the Renaissance–there was not a palace that was not, to one degree or another, Michelangelesque! Semper himself did not escape. The reference to style became, in the event, one more fact to be reckoned with in the elaboration of the programme. The architect submitted to it as he did to the other conditions of the project–aim, site, financial resources, etc.

César Daly,[17] the apostle of eclecticism, preached in the *Revue Générale de l'Architecture et des Travaux Publics* (which he had founded and directed since 1840), this submission of the architect to the economic and social realities of his time, against the theoretical vision of the rationalists. The monumentality of large public programmes did not perhaps find its final explanation in itself, but it did justify itself within an overall conception of urban ordonnance, of which it constituted the hierarchically superior degree, a practice illustrated every day by Parisian Haussmannism.

Architects remained divided before this dual logic: that of the self-evident architectural object, as propounded by the rationalist approach of an Henri Labrouste; and that, no less evident, of setting the building in the right place with reference to a hierarchy, clearly defining a social and political status, of which architecture would be the material representation. In many cases the production oscillated between these two poles, and it was not entirely by accident that these attitudinal changes were tied to variations in the symbolic duties to which a building was assigned. No theoretical solution was possible to such a debate.

2

3

4

The Pompeian House of Prince Napoleon

1

Prince Napoleon, the cousin of Napoleon III and himself republican and liberal, had a private museum built in the Avenue Montaigne on the Champs-Elysées, for which he asked the architect Alfred Normand [18] to draw the plans, after Hittorff had made the preliminary sketches. Residing at the Palais-Royal, the Prince had this building put up to house his collections and to receive there the group of writers which formed his entourage: Renan, Gautier, Sainte-Beuve, Mérimée, Arsène Houssaye, as well as numerous painters and players from the Théâtre Français.
Constructed between 1856 and 1858, the house was abandoned and sold eight years later, as a result of the Prince's political difficulties, and it was demolished in 1891; there remain only the fine drawings which Normand made of the completed work, fearing its demolition. The homage of an hour, the house had been built especially in honour of the actress Rachel, with whom the Prince was very much taken at the time.
Lately returned from Italy and Greece, Alfred Normand had become enthusiastic over the project, which, behind the exterior of a sumptuous villa, aimed at reconstructing a Roman interior based on the evidence of Pompeii. From numerous drawings he had made on the spot, in particular at the House of the Faun, Normand conceived a group of rooms laid out around a glass-roofed atrium (the setting for a famous painting by Gustave Boulanger, *The Flute-Player's Rehearsal*, shown at the Salon of 1861).
The magnificent polychrome décor, Pompeian-inspired, was accompanied by furniture fashioned after antique pieces conserved in the museum of Naples. A slightly mad archaeological scheme, this creation had all the qualities of the total spectacle, in which the visitor is soon tempted to become an "extra". In that respect it was close to the great medieval restoration of Pierrefonds (if only in the daring chords of a colourful harmony which, in both cases, revealed the profound influence of Félix Duban on his contemporaries). The principle of visual saturation of space by colour and design was common to both programmes; whether their archaeology was medieval or antique in this case made little difference.

1. Pompeii: House of the Faun.
   Calotype by Paul Jeuffrain, 1852.

   Paris: Pompeian House, 1856-1858. Demolished 1891.
   Architect: Alfred Normand.
2. Final design of the front.
3. Entrance hall, section.
   Watercolour, c. 1862.

2

3

4

4. Cold room. Watercolour, c. 1856.
5. Atrium. Watercolour, c. 1860.
   Watercolours and drawing by Normand.

5

Reinventing Gothic

1

English neo-Gothic was much less marked than French art by theoretical reflection on structure, as analysed by Viollet-le-Duc and, before him, Lassus. The original inspiration had come from the convergence of nationalism and religion: Gothic art then appeared as national at the same time as pre-eminently Christian art. This orientation, which determined the beginnings of neo-Gothic at the end of the eighteenth century, found favourable ground in the critique of the internationalism of neoclassical style at the same time as its "pagan" character.
Budding archaeology rapidly assembled the catalogue of models that would constitute the neo-Gothic repertory, starting from the selection of a few national models in each European country. In England the ecclesiological movement saw in fourteenth-century art the summit of Gothic style (which the French situated in the thirteenth century under St Louis, a nuance not without importance, for it establishes a close correlation between far-reaching political influence and architectural grandeur).
English neo-Gothic production, however, took an original direction: the High Victorian style, of which William Butterfield was one of the main exponents. [19] It added new perspectives to this catalogue of archaeological references. To be sure, the reading of Pugin was not unrelated to that insistence on limpidity which firmly guides Butterfield's hand, but it is tempered by the decisive orientation which John Ruskin [20] gave by bringing Gothic Italy to the attention of his contemporaries: *The Seven Lamps of Architecture* appeared in 1849, *The Stones of Venice* in 1851, shortly to be followed by G.E. Street's fantastic repertory, *Brick and Marble in the Middle Ages* (1855).
Butterfield's architecture, from All Saints, Margaret Street, London (1849-1859), to such accomplished examples as Keble College, Oxford (begun in 1867), was one of continuous decorative invention. Starting from Gothic examples, he reinterpreted them with a kind of "brutalism" of forms and colouring which totally avoided the mawkishness of Saint-Sulpice. The vitality of this anti-conventional touch [21] nourished all *fin-de-siècle* art: it formed a deep line of cleavage with academic tradition.

2

3

London: All Saints' Church, Margaret Street, Cavendish Square, 1849-1859.
Architect: William Butterfield.
1. View of the interior.
2. Upper level of the nave.
3. The pulpit.

Oxford: Keble College, 1867-1883.
Architect: William Butterfield.
4. View of the College and Chapel.
5.6. Details.

4

5

6

Charles Garnier, last son of the Renaissance

1

The personality of Charles Garnier dominated the eclectic period by a major monument: the Paris Opera, the only edifice of which the architect, by tradition, has had his name attached to it. In itself it epitomized the philosophy of the Ecole des Beaux-Arts, of which Garnier had been the moving spirit for the previous quarter of a century; but it also brought with it a sort of teeming invention which might be seen as not quite reflecting the academic mind. In its very overflow of ideas (quite often called "bad taste" because it ignored every canonical rule), it reflected what was deeply alive in eclecticism: Garnier was to architecture what Offenbach had been to music–a rejuvenating spring!

Garnier's private work is of less importance, for the Paris Opera occupied the best part of his time. Nevertheless, his apartment buildings of the 1880s were distinguished by their monumentality. It was above all in his provincial works, at Vittel, La Capelle-en-Thiérache, Nice, Monte Carlo or even Bordighera, that he expressed the fabulous freedom of imagination which, by the flood of ornamental detail and colour, enabled him to energize the most austere creations. Garnier's works owe their quality to the fact that, beneath simple conceptions outwardly of great formality, the vivacity of decorative animation given by colour suddenly awakens the impression of movement, gaiety and life that buildings so often lack.

Garnier had the soul of a painter; he saw architecture with a painter's as much as builder's eye. If, on the same basis as his contemporaries, he applied a formal analytic borrowed from the rationalists, he did not let himself be imprisoned in the intellectual strait-jacket of reasoning, nor in the plodding submission to "style architecture." It may be fairly said of him that he had no complexes, he neither sought to justify himself nor relied on references, and it was this healthiness which pointed to a way out of the impossible debate between architects.

2

3

1. Paris: Monument to Charles Garnier in front of the Opera House. Architect: Jean-Louis Pascal.
2. Paris: Cercle de la Librairie, 1878-1879. Architect: Charles Garnier.
3. Monte Carlo: Casino, 1878-1879. Architect: Charles Garnier.
4. Nice: Observatory. Bischoffsheim Dome with equatorial telescope, 1885-1887. Architect: Charles Garnier. Engineer: Gustave Eiffel.

4

1

As the laureate of the competition of 1861, Charles Garnier proposed, on the site selected by Haussmann and Rohault de Fleury, an enormous building formed by the addition of independent volumes– foyer, auditorium, arches, rotundas–the dislocation of which was strongly reminiscent of that employed by Vaudoyer in the cathedral of Marseilles. From certain angles this pile of volumes took on a new coherence which made one forget its incongruity. [22]
Garnier handled the gradation of masses, the changes in perception at different distances, the approaches to the building and the entry into it with a consummate knowledge of scales and a sharp sense of detail. Thus, in particular, he managed the transition from the vast open spaces outside to the narrow entry for ticket inspection by an abundant urban furniture of statues, columns and candelabras. The overall unity did not matter in this case because the composition, departing from the principle of static observation from a privileged viewpoint, instead proposed a continuous displacement, a spatial narrative pausing at a certain number of points; hence, composition by "centres of interest," expressing successive stages in the narrative.
In elaborating this kind of language, Garnier had many precedents to fall back on, notably the Baroque style of François Mansart and of Borromini, or the fundamental example of Michelangelo's staircase for the Biblioteca Laurenziana (an example he undoubtedly considered in planning the grand staircase of the Opera). Garnier, however, was a past master in the art of maintaining an absolute separation between form as constructed and form as experienced. That was what fascinated his contemporaries of the 1880s and made them somewhat forget the contradictory positions adopted in the debate of the generation of the Second Empire.
Garnier was indeed the last son of the Renaissance, [23] because he adapted to his own use a whole tradition which came from sixteenth-century Rome, and because he integrated into that tradition, in a lively manner, the formal analytics of the current of rationalist thought. By giving the architecture of his day the sense of scenography, Garnier, after his fashion, blazed the trails of Art Nouveau. In point of fact, he completed the liquidation of an academicism that had long been moribund.
Have we not said the same thing about the Pompeian House, Pierrefonds or All Saints' Church? In differing languages there surfaced in all three a common idea: that of architecture as spectacle, integrating all the forms of plastic expression into the lyricism of illusion.

2

Paris: Opera House, 1862-1875.
Architect: Charles Garnier.
1. Garnier's office.
2. Grand staircase.
Le Nouvel Opéra de Paris, 1880.
3. Candelabrum.
4. View upwards from the grand staircase.

3

4

Art and industry: the relationship between the two formed the object of contradictory speculation for a century and a half, without its being possible, until recently, to identify the bonds which grew up between them in the nineteenth century.[1] Moreover, iron architecture alone, most unfairly, has had attributed to it an industrial character which has gone unrecognized in other materials, such as wood and clay. Everything remains to be said about the development of a material such as brick, from individual casting and baking in a wood-burning kiln to the mechanized production of our day (with baking in a coke-fired kiln and the addition of cement); it has taken such diversified forms as the hollow brick, the gypsum brick, the glazed brick, brick-nogging in floors or the brickwork of chimney-flues. The same is true as regards glass (with the development of laminating), wood or even plaster (moulded staff ornaments).

In a general way, all construction materials have changed in the course of their use, whether as a result of the change in tools (for mechanization is a total phenomenon) or by the improvement in their performance, better understood and better exploited by modern science. Take the example of concrete: used on a large scale by the Romans, it was perfected thanks to the introduction of metal reinforcements in the late nineteenth century, without there being any "invention" of a new material. The technical combination of the mixed ossature–iron rods and concrete sheath–was original, but the components were not.

Industrial architecture

The industrialization of terracotta or glass, the mechanization of woodwork, did more for nineteenth-century architecture than the production of iron, except in its humblest and commonest form: the nail (since instead of being forged it was henceforth extruded at low cost!). One has only to look at nineteenth-century apartment houses, with their parquets of machine-sawn strips of oak, their standardized door-frames and chimney-pieces, their plaster covings and rosettes, which, like the balcony ironwork, were picked out of a catalogue, their false wainscotting made of pine strips contoured and nailed directly onto the wall, their printed wallpaper, to see that even before the birth of a complex technology, all architectural production had been transformed by the development of industrial techniques. The appearance of modern comfort and sanitation only confirmed a trend under way since 1830.[2]

As it happens, most of these technological transformations found formal expression only in a superficial way, although it would be simple to demonstrate how much the interest now taken in contoured decoration reflected the mechanization of the methods of ornamentation. And, equally, how much the taste for repetitive rhythmic cadences expressed the assembly-line character of production (the beauty of the candelabras which surround the Paris Opera depends on the absolute identity of the female figures, modelled by Carrier-Belleuse and reproduced with that slightly distressing uniformity and perfection which belong exclusively to industrial art).

Let us accept, however, that this was only a side-line. The decorative art of the nineteenth century took over for mechanical production the forms handed down from the handicraft tradition, without dreaming for a moment of criticizing them; only in a roundabout way, by accentuating their perfection, did it reveal the change of tools. For that reason the technology of iron, until then in little use, was able to assume symbolic value. It was at once a material whose performance has steadily gained–passing in less than half a century from spans of a few metres to several hundred–and one which had adapted itself to series production in the form of casting of foundry-iron. It is no exaggeration to say that industrial art revealed itself through the technology of iron casting.

Perfecting a technology

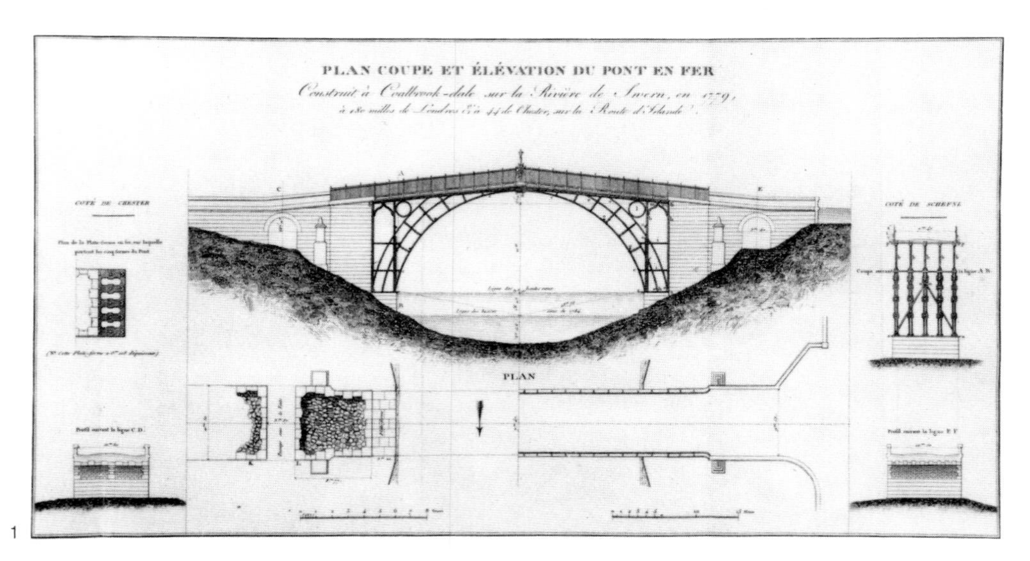

For it was not enough for Abraham Darby to have achieved the impossible by extracting a usable material from the flow of molten iron obtained by smelting with mineral coal (before him, it was common knowledge that only charcoal yielded a pig-iron that was not too brittle; it was through feeling his way many times that he succeeded, on a purely experimental basis, in perfecting techniques to reduce the carbon content of coke pig-iron, anticipating the invention of puddling in 1784). The new material, rough-cast, was as yet only a pig of iron on the foundry floor, with its special properties unknown. It was of course possible, by prolonged working at the forge, to give it the traditional qualities of iron used in metalwork. The industrialists of the late nineteenth century exercised their ingenuity to make a profit out of this "melted iron" by giving it an original character using the technique of casting, whose chief interest lay in the substantial savings (in both heating fuel and labour costs) which the process made possible: cast iron as we know it was born.[3]

Between wrought and cast iron the difference was complete, for whereas forging improved its elasticity, the distinguishing feature of cast iron, by contrast, was its rigidity, increasing its resistance to compression (cast iron is sixty times harder than limestone): this was to make it an outstanding construction material, replacing stone in everything to do with columns or posts. But, at the same time, the malleability of grey pig-iron and its capacity to be cast in perforated plates, making possible the manifold decorative effects of filigree, were to give it a great future as ornamental motif. Much less costly than bronze, pig-iron had multiple uses, the most appropriate being the imitation of wrought ironwork. In this case the economy was double, since to the saving on material was added that, much more substantial, of fashioning it into finished shape by simple casting, replacing the long and difficult work of forging.

The whole history of iron was dependent on the transformation brought about by industry in the economics of its production. The attempt to construct an iron bridge at Lyons in 1775 had failed because of cost. A few years later, Abraham Darby the third was able to bridge the Severn at Coalbrookdale with an span of one hundred feet. The sections, cast in pig-iron, formed a framework of rigid arches (whose semicircular design was akin to that of a stone bridge).

The efforts of the first builders were aimed at improving the assembly of the structural units, because they had observed that bolting, which made it necessary to perforate the units, weakened them, making them more liable to split: for the Pont des Arts[4], L. A. de Cessart and J. Dillon used a system of jointing (inspired by

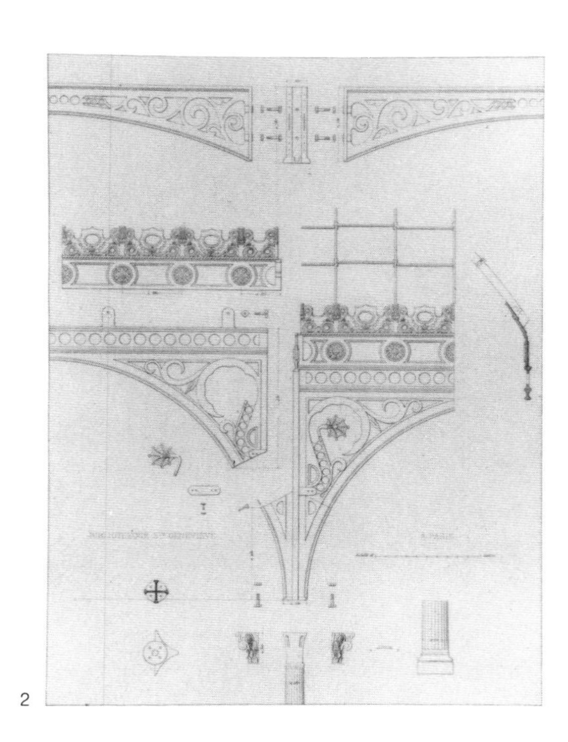

1. Coalbrookdale (Shropshire), England: Plan, section and elevation of the iron bridge built over the Severn by Abraham Darby III in 1779. *Recueil de divers mémoires, extraits de la Bibliothèque Impériale des Ponts et Chaussées*, 1810.
2. Paris: Library of Sainte-Geneviève, 1843-1850. Architect: Henri Labrouste. Details of the art metal-work. *Encyclopédie d'Architecture*, 1853.

timberwork tying) which answered the case. The system was, besides, only a transposing of the principle of the "Delorme-style" timber framework invented by the Renaissance architect. One building made a remarkable synthesis of this experience: the dome of the old Corn Exchange (today the Bourse du Commerce) in Paris. Under Louis XVI, Legrand and Molinos had covered its courtyard with a timbered Delorme-style dome, taking up again this disused procedure. Destroyed by fire, the dome was rebuilt in 1811 by Bélanger, but this time in cast iron.
Nevertheless, the complexity of the assembly system and the slightness of these structures made of metal stalks would have limited their use if parallel experiments with decorative iron

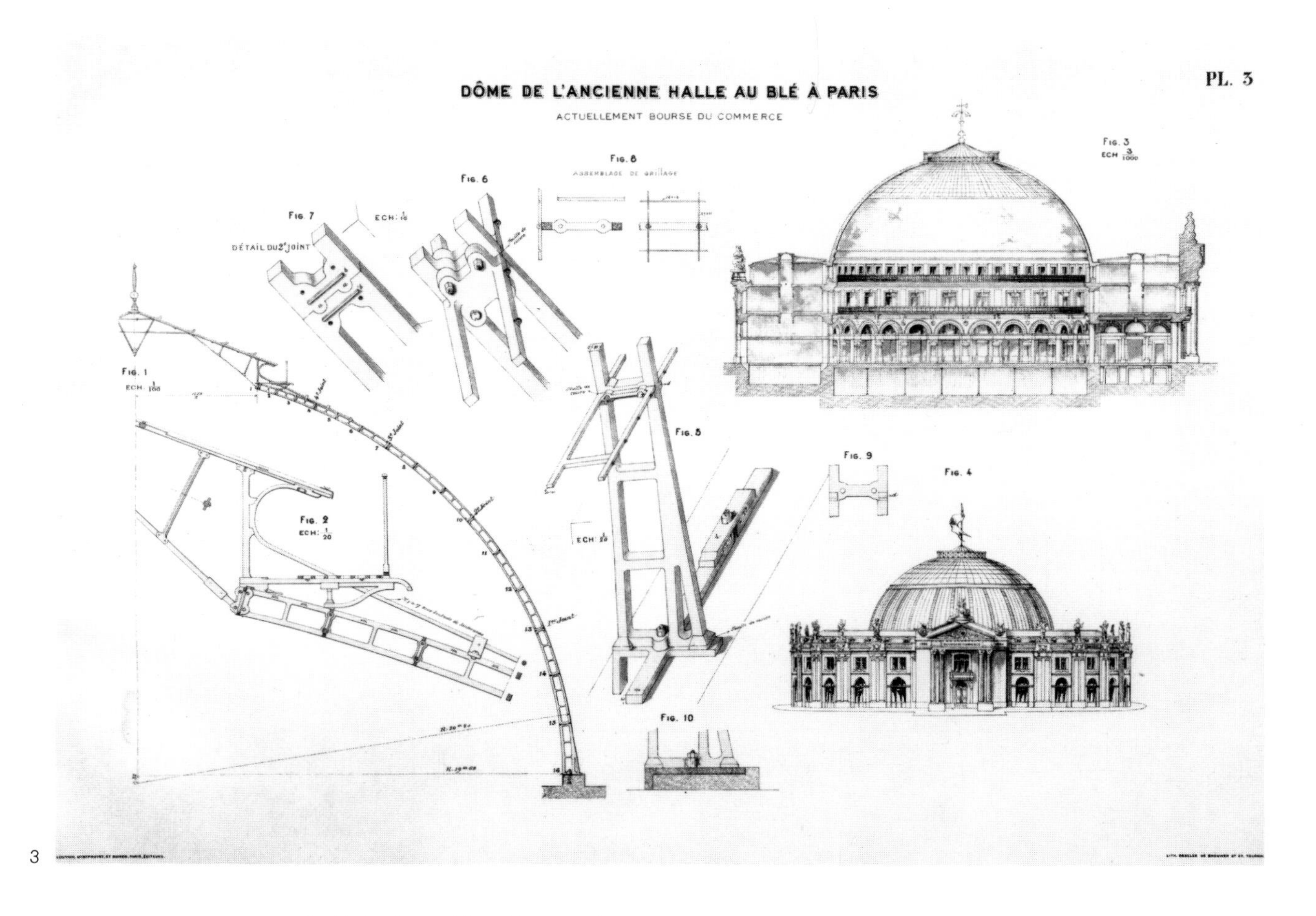

3

3. Paris: Dome of the old Corn Exchange (Halle au Blé, now Bourse du Commerce), 1806-1811. Architect: François-Joseph Bélanger. A. Vierendeel, *La construction architecturale en fonte, fer et acier*, 1893.

castings had not been tried, both in France and England, by the neo-Gothic architects. The churches of St George in Liverpool (1812-1814) or of St Philip in Birmingham (1820-1822) by Thomas Rickman present, inside a masonry shell, a structure of arches, piers and window traceries directly transposing the Gothic skeleton into cast iron. Jean-Antoine Alavoine used cast-iron colonettes (replacing cross-bedded stone in the buttresses) for the restoration of the cathedral of Séez; and starting in 1823 he carried out the fantastic art-work of the spire of Rouen, entirely in openwork

1

2

1. Paris: Library of Sainte-Geneviève, 1843-1850. Ceiling of the Reading Room. Architect: Henri Labrouste.
2. Antwerp: Old Stock Exchange. A. Vierendeel, *La construction architecturale en fonte, fer et acier*, 1893.

cast iron. The technical direction of these works had been given at the end of the eighteenth century by the construction of bridges with cast-iron voussoirs, in which the perforated blocks of cast iron, bolted together, replaced a stone arch, permitting much larger spans (1793, Sunderland Bridge over the Wear, 72 metres).
The prototypes of cast-iron architecture represented by Rickman's churches or Alavoine's spire, around 1820, would perhaps not have produced so great a line of descent if metallic construction had not been made necessary, for the erection of certain public buildings, as a means of fireproofing. It was not yet known that iron, even if it does not burn, warps when exposed to heat, and that in fact it is a material as dangerous as wood (except insofar as it does not catch fire directly from a flame–a constant problem for men who used gas or candlelight).

The iron skeleton was thus an element of the building programme drawn up by the Comte de Laborde for the construction of the Sainte-Geneviève Library. Labrouste tried to go beyond the meagre know-how of his contemporaries (who utilized cast iron only as ornamental motif or, at a pinch, in columns, but never in spanning) by relying on the experience gained in the craft by the Parisian metal-caster Christophe Calla, who executed the project; the series of drawings Labrouste made, beginning in 1842, shows his efforts to go from a metalwork frame in iron rods and bars to the form filled out with moulded ornaments. A parallel approach in England led to the construction of an imposing rotunda all in cast-iron skeleton: the London Coal Exchange (1846-1849), by J. B. Bunning. During the 1840s there were numerous European examples: the elegant Dianabad of Vienna (1841-1843), the dome of St Isaac in St Petersburg (1842) and that of Sainte-Marie in Brussels by Overstraeten (1846).

3. London: Coal Exchange, 1846-1849.
Architect: James Bunstone Bunning.
Print.

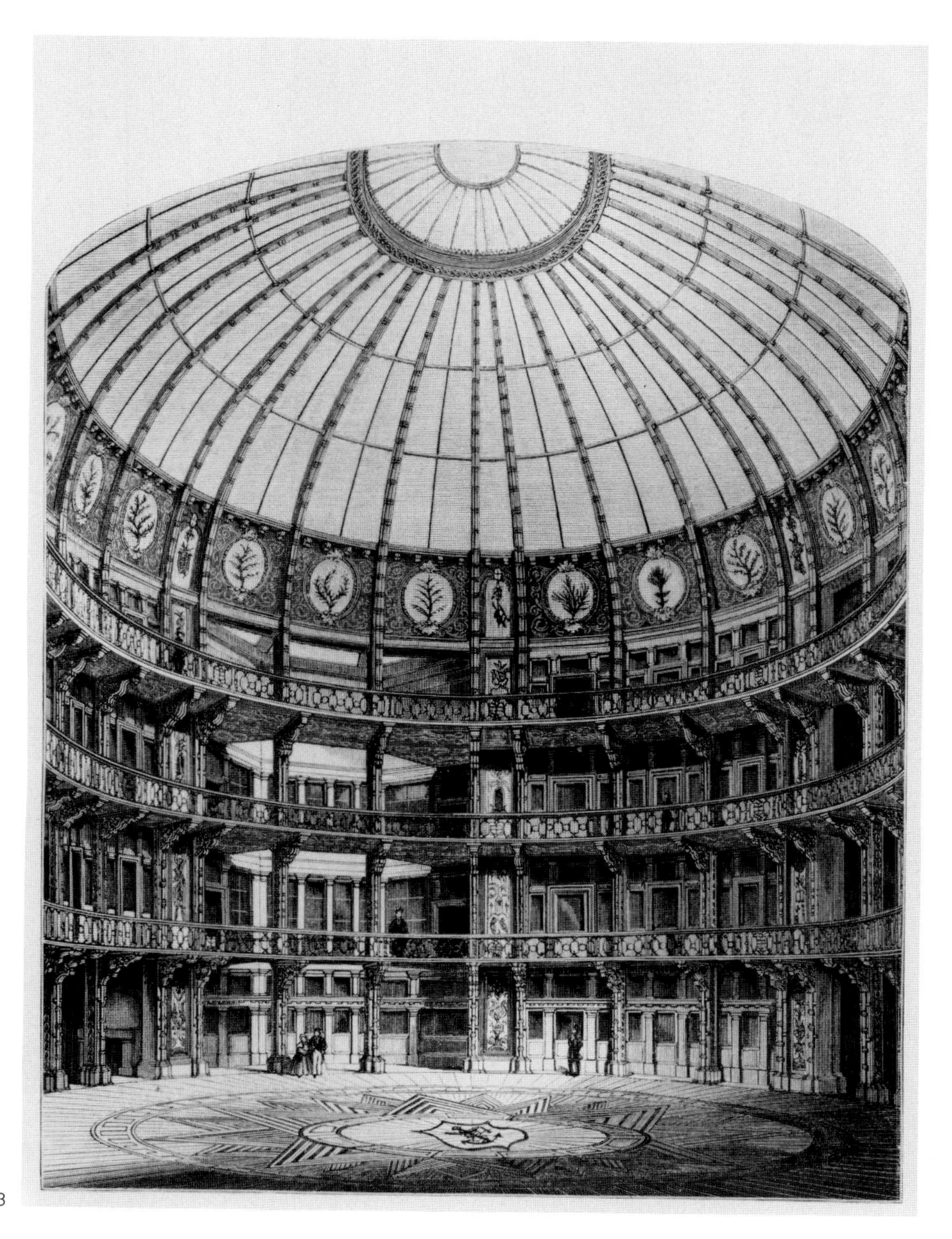

3

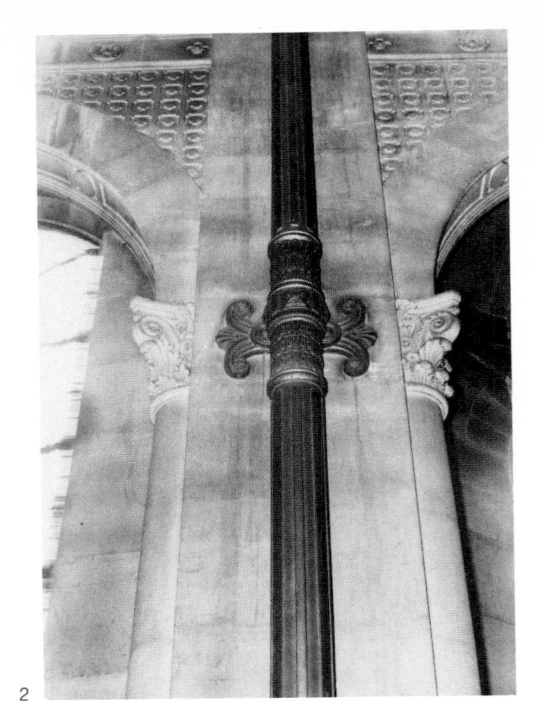
2

1

1. Paris: Bibliothèque Nationale. Reading Room, 1855-1868. Architect: Henri Labrouste.

Paris: Church of Saint-Augustin, 1860-1871. Architect: Victor Baltard.
2. Detail of an imbedded iron column.
3. Cross-section of the nave. *Nouvelles Annales de la Construction*, 1872.

There was little further development in the 1850s, whereas the technical data were being completely transformed. The production of puddled iron increased, making available, at low cost, iron sections or sheets with elasticity far superior to that of cast-iron arches. The perfecting of riveting made possible easy assemblages. The reconstructed beam, formed by latticed ribs, replaced the cast members, more fragile and cumbersome. In 1853, for the Central Markets in Paris, Baltard was already associating a cast-iron skeleton with stiffeners, formed by steel rods fastened with stretching screws. Two years later, Deane and Woodward, for the Oxford University Museum, and Labrouste in 1853, designing the Bibliothèque Impériale (now Bibliothèque Nationale), used the combination of cast-iron columns and reconstructed arches in riveted sheet-iron. It was at last possible, as Baltard did for Saint-Augustin (1860-1871), to use cast-iron columns, brackets and small decorative arcades in association with the riveted iron frame, the main advantage being aesthetic, since the cast members went better with the stone skin than the too-lean forms of riveted sheet-iron. Conversely, Deane and Woodward found how to turn its lightness to account by using it in conjunction with a glass roof; Labrouste, with the white ceiling, luminous and reflecting, of his plaster calottes.

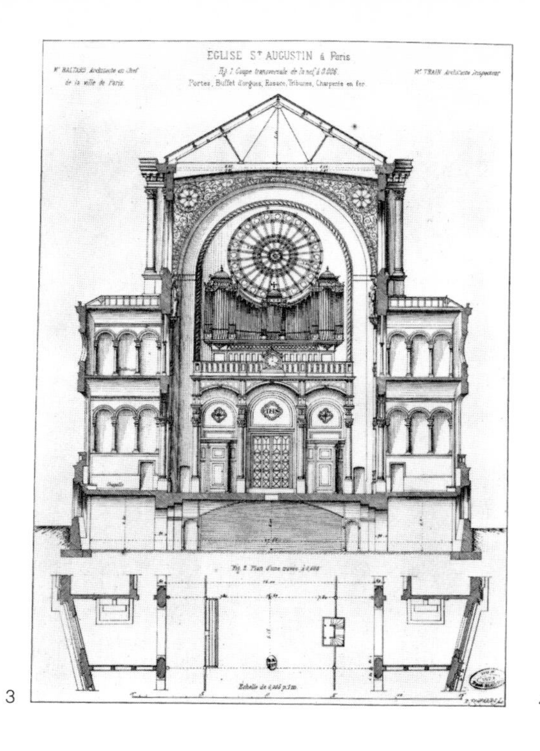

3

4

Oxford University Museum, 1855-1859.
Architects: Sir Thomas Deane
Benjamin Woodward.

4. View in the court.
The Builder, 1860.
5. View of the interior.

5

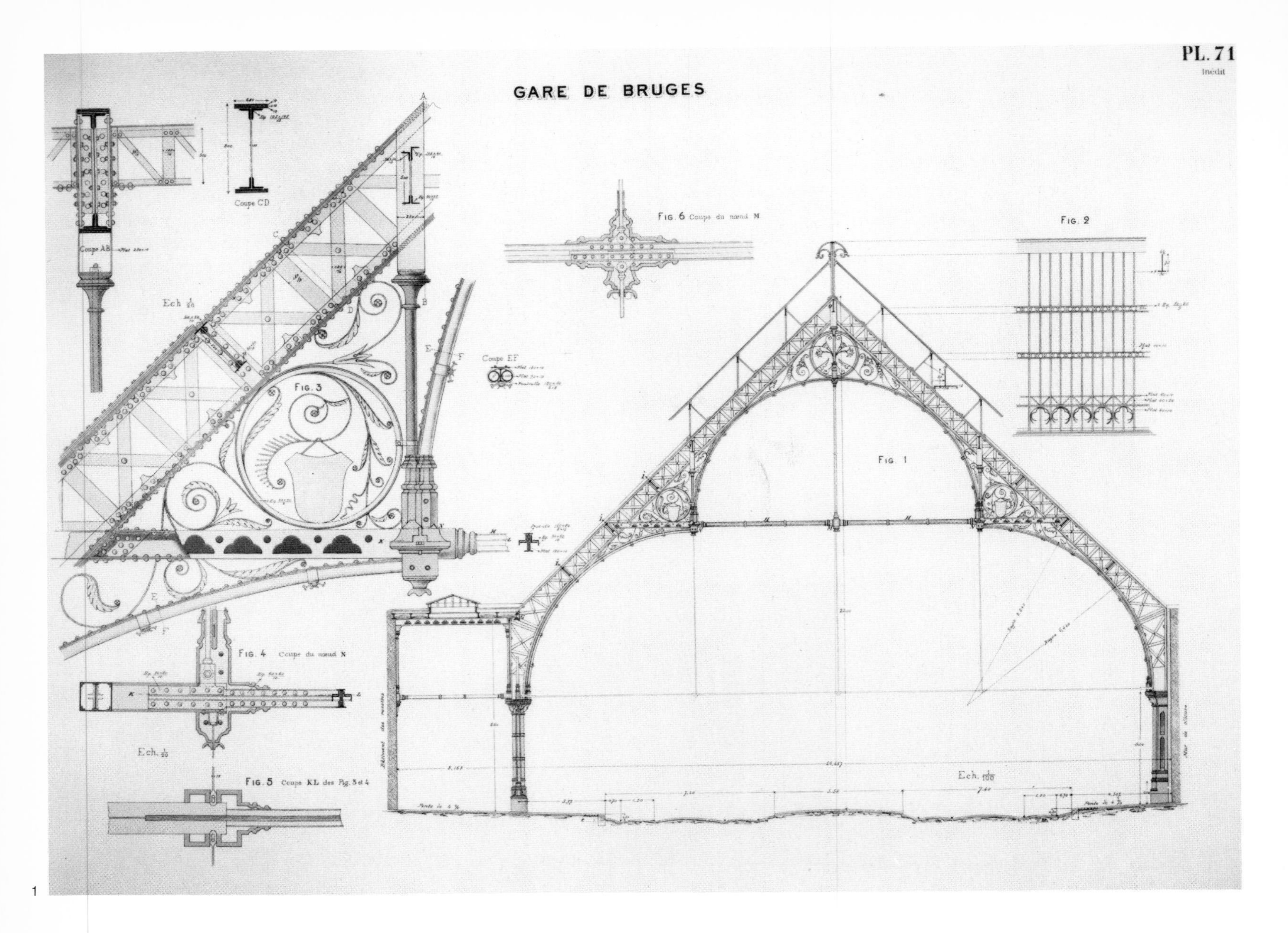

1

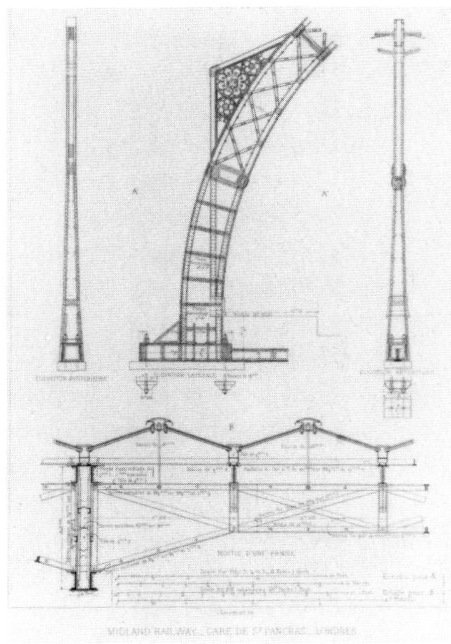
2

This technical advance paralleled that of the frames used for large covered spaces, like train sheds or exhibition halls. The last timber frame, Delorme-style, had been the one for King's Cross Station, in 1851; it soon deteriorated from the smoke of locomotives. In 1854 the glass roof of Paddington Station was still supported by arches in openwork cast iron, while ten years later, from 1861-1864, the great trusses of the Gare du Nord combined riveted iron with cast-iron pillars and brackets, the filigree decoration of which made a great effect (it might even be noted, in the latter case, that tie-beams and king posts subject to stress from traction, were fashioned from steel rods). By the end of the Second Empire, cast-iron members had disappeared. The roof of the Orléans-Austerlitz Station (1869) was formed of a lattice skeleton stiffened with steel rods. From then on, cast iron was not used in any but a supporting role, the only one for which it was truly suited.

It was thus a long way, in less than twenty years, from the first experiments, in which cast iron was queen, to the great roofs of iron, steel and glass such as were the current practice around 1870. In the meantime, some of the qualities attributed to iron (incombustibility, demountability) had failed to meet the test, while others proved their value (transparency, lightness, mass production).

1. Bruges: Railway Station, 1889. Demolished. A. Vierendeel, *La construction architecturale en fonte, fer et acier*, 1893.
2. London: St. Pancras Station, 1868-1869. Engineers: W.H. Barlow, R.M. Ordish. Details of the iron train-shed. *Encyclopédie d'Architecture*, 1873.

3

4

5

3. Paris: Gare du Nord, 1861-1864.
   Architect: Jacques-Ignace Hittorff.
   Detail of the train-shed.
4. Paris: Gare d'Orléans (Austerlitz), 1869.
   Iron train-shed. Polonceau system.
5. London: London Bridge Station, 1844. Demolished.
   Architects: Henry Roberts
   George Smith.

1

2

Iron architecture marked the third quarter of the century by two symbol-monuments: the Crystal Palace and the Paris Central Markets. Both were in glass and cast iron, in accordance with an already superseded technology; but their outstanding architectural qualities left a deep imprint on the history of the art. The Crystal Palace had set out to be not only a unique spatial experience, an immense glasshouse which could enclose even the tops of trees, but also a double technical feat of prefabrication and mobility. Joseph Paxton had no difficulty in carrying the first point: the Crystal Palace was built of standardized elements–columns, arches and skylights–whose exact assembly was organized on a grid allowing all changes. When the building was reconstructed it was possible to augment its size without modifying its structure, by simply shifting the arrangement of the components on the grid. All prefabricated architecture derived from it.
On the other hand, mobility, in theory, championed by metal construction, had no corresponding practical reality. To be sure, the Crystal Palace, built in Hyde Park in 1851 for the Universal Exhibition, would be rebuilt two years later at Sydenham, in Kent, with the same materials. But this purely prestige reconstruction was not at all economic: if the same elements were used, it was necessary to move them onsite and pay for the cost of dismounting and reassembling. The prohibitive cost of this latter operation exceeded the market value of the materials! The idea of mobility corresponded to a quality more intellectual than real, applicable with just as much efficiency to other types of constructions (for example, the first North departure platform in Paris, by Léonce Reynaud: its façades were used again for the new railway station of Lille).

London: The Crystal Palace being re-erected at Sydenham. Destroyed by fire in 1936. Architect: Sir Joseph Paxton.
1.2. Two stages in the reconstruction, 1852.
3. Gangway in the transept. *Photographic Views of the Progress of the Crystal Palace, Sydenham*, 1855.
4. View of the main entrance.
5. View of the roof, looking towards the entrance hall.

3

4

5

1

1. La Roche-sur-Yon (Vendée): Covered market.
2. Dun-sur-Auron (Cher): Covered market.

The impact of the Central Markets of Paris[5] was of a different kind. It was as an architectural model that they played a decisive role in nineteenth-century architecture. Although the model was a very old idea in architecture, it had never before been given this key importance. Most of the architectural publications of the first half of the century appeared as a list of models, drawn from recent construction (like the *Etudes relatives à l'art des constructions* by Louis Bruyère, Paris 1823-1828, or the famous collection by Gourlier, Biet, Grillon and Tardieu, *Choix d'édifices publics projetés ou construits en France depuis le commencement du XIXe siècle*, Paris, 1825-1836).

2

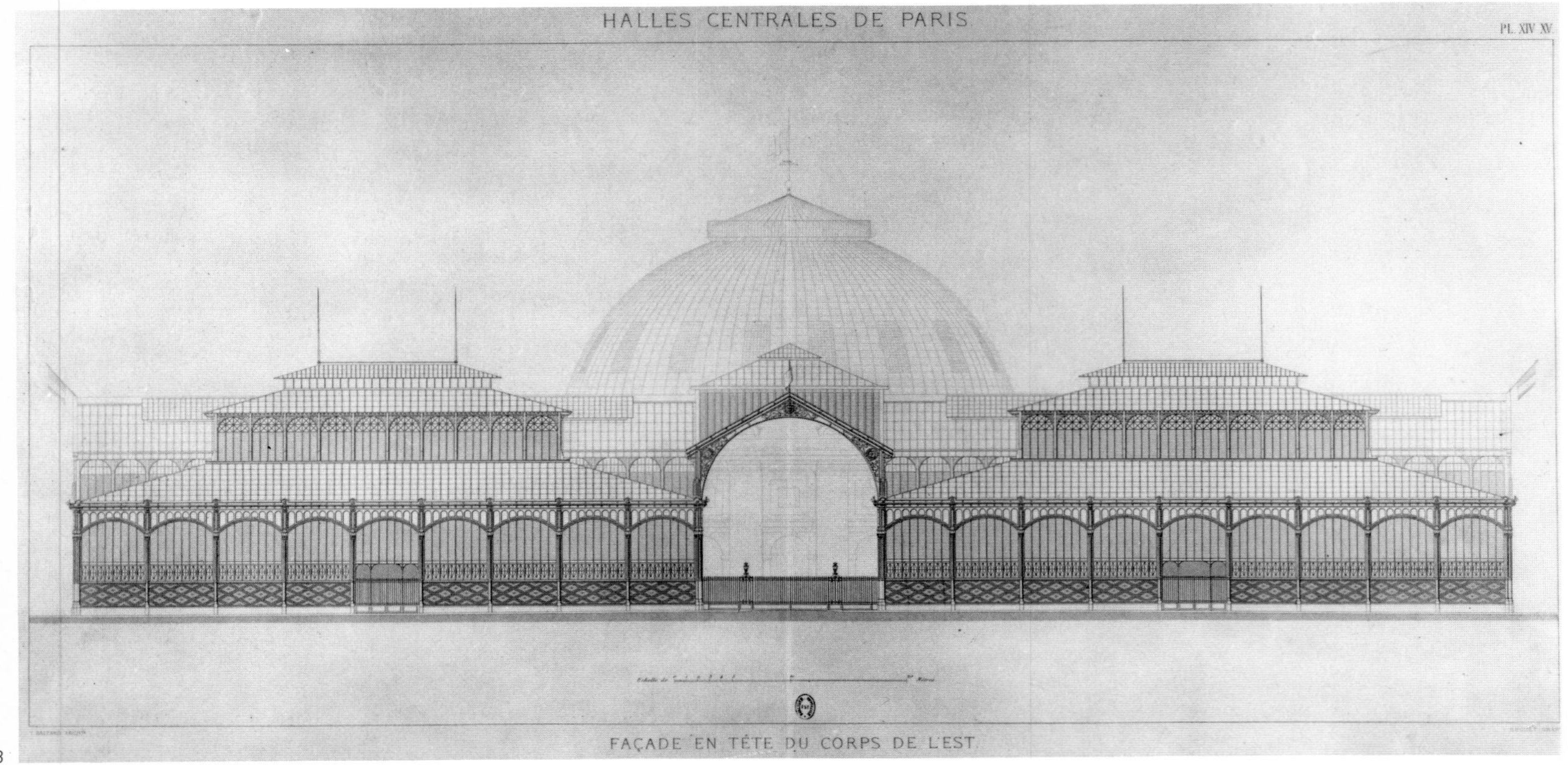

3

4

Paris: Halles Centrales (Central Markets), 1845-1870.
Demolished in 1973.
Architect: Victor Baltard.
3. Front of the east building.
V. Baltard and F. Callet, *Monographie des Halles Centrales de Paris*, 1863.
4. View from the galleries of the church of Saint-Eustache.
Paris dans sa splendeur, 1861.

Baltard's Central Markets formed the crest of this normative wave, in which the imitation of a pre-established model was almost a given condition of the programme. In all French towns were to be found those cast-iron structures, those pavilions with glazed lanterns, those walls of criss-crossed bricks which were the essential features of the course taken by Baltard. The curious thing was that this imitative production did not resemble series construction. Each project was designed by an architect who personally decided on the plan, the forms, the sections, and had them executed by local foundries. Only the basic intention was repeated in broad outline, each architect striving to furnish a personal vision of it adapted to the special conditions of the project–position, function, context, technical possibilities for execution of the structural parts, improvement in the frame, increased richness of decoration. This hymn to series architecture ended in a paradox: if the conception was narrowly normative, that intellectual concern was not expressed in the production, from which all normalization was absent! The case was not unique in the nineteenth century, when the artisan still had great importance.

Furniture and objects in cast iron

1

Starting in the 1830s cast iron showed itself to be an exceptional ornamental material, on a level with terracotta or staff, but in a form adapted to exterior use. If regularly repainted, cast iron is resistant to weather, for it is neither liable to crack from frost nor permeable to water. By its excessive weight and weak resistance to shocks it was ill-adapted for furniture, even though it was widely utilized (mainly in the form of fixed benches); on the other hand it replaced stone, wrought iron or wood in the fabrication of urban furniture, particularly fountains and candelabrum lamp-posts.

With the perfecting of gaslight, under the Empire, public lighting spread. The first gas-jets burned in Paris on 31 December 1829 in the Rue de la Paix (they had existed in London since 1810 and in Paris, in the Passage des Panoramas, since 1817, but the Paris streets continued to be lit by oil-burning lamps). Under the July Monarchy and the Second Empire the whole city became covered with gas-jets, in the form of cast-iron candelabra not more than three metres in height.

Urban furniture was a nineteenth-century invention. Apart from fountains, the Old Regime had had very little public lighting–a few lanterns hanging by chains in the busiest streets. With the development of public transport and the growth of cities, the traditional scale of public highways was shattered in response to the traffic needs.

The outsize scale of the new avenues and boulevards opened up by the Second Empire had been so much resented that there was an effort to correct it by filling those great empty urban spaces with planted areas and furniture to organize them: ornamental candelabra, of course, screens, statues, but also benches, newsstands, urinals, drinking fountains (since with the development of a system of piped potable water the water-supply fountain gradually lost its purpose).

This extension reflected the obsessive concern of urban civilization with hygiene and comfort, just as it was losing the reserves of space which up to then had assured the maintenance of its biological (and sanitary) equilibrium. Latrines and public conveniences were in effect more than indispensable, like the bench or the drinking fountain (before the bistrot took over all these primary functions, combining them with its essential role as a place of exchange and social life). The newsstand, mainstay of publicity, joined them later, followed by the pneumatic clock (used as a trademark by the company which distributed compressed air, the urban chain of which put the first hydropneumatic lifts into operation). Of all this production, that which most impressed the public was due to a generous English patron, Sir Richard Wallace, who, taking his cue from the drinking fountains of London, in 1872 offered the City of Paris a hundred fountains which bear his name, charming miniature cast-iron temples with a central plan and a

2

3

1. Cast-iron urinals for the streets of Paris. A. Alphand, *Les Promenades de Paris*, 1867-1873.
2. French cast-iron lamp-posts. Catalogue of the "Société Anonyme des Hauts-Fourneaux et Fonderies du Val d'Osne," 1870.
3. Geneva: English Garden (Jardin Anglais). Cast-iron fountain with water spouts, 1862.

1

2

1. Cast-iron fountain.
3. Cast-iron drinking fountains (Wallace fountains).
4. Cast-iron kiosk and bridge.
Catalogue of the "Société Anonyme des Hauts-Fourneaux et Fonderies du Val d'Osne," 1870.
2. Troyes (Champagne): Argence Fountain in front of the Lycée.
From a late 19th-century postcard.
5. Marseilles: Zoological Garden.
Wallace fountain.

scalloped dome borne by four female caryatids. The sculptor Charles Lebourg, a pupil of Rude, had looked to Renaissance art for his inspiration, both for the completely detached model, which is best known, and for the backed model to be used for wall fountains.[6]

The influence of Wallace fountains extended far beyond Paris; they are to be found in many provincial towns and even outside France. Like all cast-iron furnishings, they were circulated by mail-order catalogue, with variations depending on the foundry: in particular there existed a variant of the Wallace fountain in which colonettes replaced the caryatids. In the field of multibranched lamp-posts, hundreds of types were circulated, based on the initial model of the "Official List of Candelabra of the City of Paris." Each manufacturer, for business reasons, insisted on publishing his own design, more or less openly derived from the popular models in the great capitals.

Certain foundries[7] occupied a dominant position in world production of cast iron. The largest among them was French: the Société Anonyme des Hauts-Fourneaux & Fonderies du Val d'Osne (founded by J. P.V. André in 1833, subsequently Barbezat & Co.), whose copious catalogue had an exceptional circulation. The kiosk and fountain in the Jardin Anglais in Geneva come apparently from the Val d'Osne. The same fountain had been bought by the city of Tours, which, in order to adapt it to the chosen site, had obtained from the manufacturer a combination of elements belonging to different models. This form of "kit-in-parts" architecture was highly attractive to the nineteenth century!

3

4

5

Each country[8] carved out its own speciality in the domain of cast-iron ornament. If France was famous for urban furniture or balcony ironwork, England and its colonies concentrated on filigreed décor, for covered balconies or two-storied porches of really fabulous inventiveness. In the United States, cast-iron house-fronts were a national feature.

This differentiation reflected the local market, and they adapted to it with remarkable efficiency. In Great Britain, Archibald Kendrick, the Coalbrookdale Company and Walter Macfarlane & Co. of Glasgow executed a great number of plates, the combination of which could produce screen decorations (for railings and the protection of basement areas in front of house façades, giving onto the street) as well as loggias, not to mention whole interiors: covered passageways, covered markets with upper floors, and so on. The English speciality depended above all on adaptable and transportable patterns, which were affixed to all sorts of constructions, sheathing them in a decorative latticework of cast iron of striking uniformity throughout the Empire: from Brighton to Dublin or Edinburgh, from Adelaide or Capetown to Bombay and New Orleans, Anglo-Saxon culture showed its unity and persistence.

Some builders exported entire edifices by boat. Macfarlane put up in India many large buildings, monumental covered markets or kiosks, which he published with a certain pride (*Illustrated Examples of Macfarlane's Architectural Ironwork*, 1912). It was also the case of Belgian or French foundries specializing in colonial bungalows for Africa, an architecture of hutments whose lifespan

1. Carriage entrance with decorative ironwork. Catalogue of the "Société Anonyme des Hauts-Fourneaux et Fonderies du Val d'Osne," 1870.
2. Madras (India): Interior of a bank. *Illustrated Examples of Macfarlane's Architectural Ironwork*, Glasgow, 1912.

3

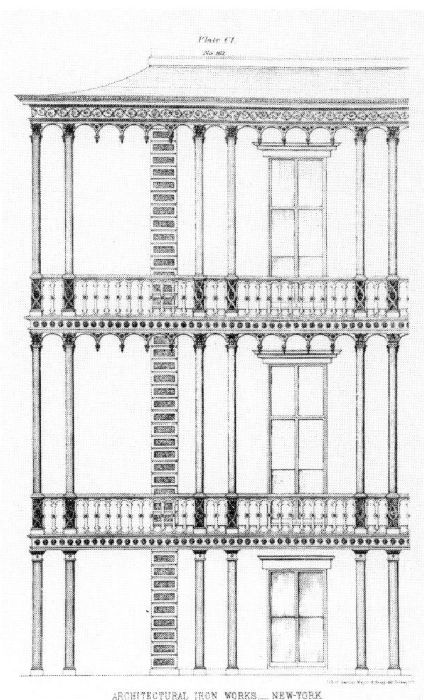

4

3. Johannesburg (South Africa): Macfarlane's, Aegis Building, c. 1894. *Album of Johannesburg*, Grocott and Sherry.
4. Verandah and verandah railings. Catalogue of D.D. Badger's "Architectural Iron Works of the City of New York," 1865.

and ornamental richness were limited, for they were designed to meet immediate needs. In certain countries, economic development had progressed far enough by the third quarter of the century for local foundries to be created: in New York and New Orleans for the United States, in Adelaide and Sydney for Australia.
The originality of French production (apart from urban furnishings which it exported widely) lay in the development of a special ornamental register: that of balcony and supporting ironwork, with the catalogues of Barbezat or Durenne are filled. Derived from bronze ornaments, the first designs published by French illustrators were door ornaments in openwork cast iron (a principle which made it possible to give the appearance of a solid door, by backlighting the vaulted archway leading to the inner courtyard). But, very quickly, ornamental cast iron overran windowsills. It settled on that chief ornament of the Parisian building: the unbroken balcony running along the second and fifth floors.
The history of Parisian ornamental cast iron hinged on the passage from the primitive technique of the openwork plate to that, much more complex, of elements in combination, joined by screws or even by riveting (in short, the assemblage techniques of classical metalwork, but applied to elements formed of cast iron). Up to the end to the Second Empire, the plate dominated, either as a self-supporting panel or in parts mounted on a frame of square pieces of iron. Progress, in this décor, was reduced to the extreme skill-

1

fulness with which these plates took on the appearence of the traditional ironwork motifs which inspired them.
Castings in relief, made from the 1830s on, enriched this work by making possible the joining of motifs onto the original grille. Little by little, these panels became surrounded by castings of frames which increased the variety of possible effects. In this way the plates tended to diminish in surface area as the secondary castings multiplied. At the end of the nineteenth century the changeover from cast iron to steel permitted a mixed operation, starting from castings reworked on demand and giving the illusion of wrought-ironwork. This overlapping of the industrial technique of cast iron and the technique of the artisan at the forge once again illustrates the relationship of complementarity which the period sought to maintain–not without success. One last example will enable us to furnish proof as far as architecture was concerned. If the dream of "portable, incombustible, durable, comfortable, enlargeable houses" conceived by Hector Horeau in 1857 produced no result, metal construction nonetheless allowed North America to create imposing urban décors very rapidly and at low cost. The catalogue of D. D. Badger in New York (*Architectural Iron Works of the City of New York*, 1865) presents a collection of models suited to the rush construction of the new towns of the West. Starting in 1854 James Bogardus had put up buildings with cast-iron fronts in New York, such as the Harper Brothers Building; in 1856 he proposed buildings with a cast-iron skeleton. This latter solution was perhaps not as widely used in American construction as is imagined, but

that was because it was combined in a mixed procedure, in which the front alone was constructed of metal, the rest being carried out in brick masonry, at low cost.
At St Louis, as in New York (in the "Cast-Iron Districts"), there are still to be found numerous examples of these cast-iron fronts, with neoclassical decoration, taken from manufacturers' catalogues. This prefabricated decoration suited a country in which the profession of architect was as yet uncommon, while demand, stimulated by commercial competition, grew incessantly. Ornamentation, which no local workman could have made and which no architect was on hand to design, arrived on the scene by railway. It was thus that the Savings & Loan Society had been built in San Francisco in 1870, according to the plans of J. P. Gaymor, the regular architect of the Badger firm of New York.[9] Examples could be multiplied. The important fact is that this "mail-order architecture" existed, in far more systematic forms than in Europe (one only has to see the difference between it and "model architecture" exemplified by covered markets), but in an adaptation flexibly responsive to building-site conditions, there being a continuous two-way traffic between the artisan and industry.

3

2

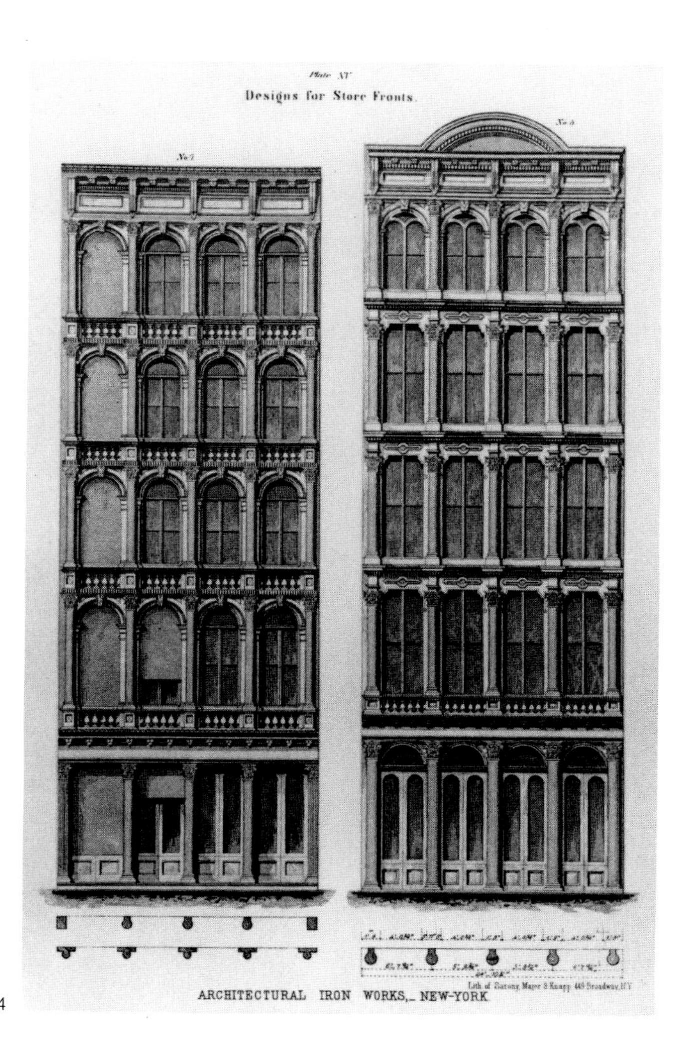

4

1. New York, 93 Reade Street: Cast-iron front of five stories with cornice, 1857. Architect: John Jones.
2. Cover of D.D. Badger's "Architectural Iron Works," New York, 1865.
3. Three designs for capitals from Badger's catalogue.
4. Two designs for store fronts from Badger's catalogue.

The steel revolution

1

This form of reciprocity, which had lasted a half-century, came to an end when the equilibrium was upset by the technical breakthroughs of skeleton construction in steel. Steel construction made necessary the working out of a new decorative language, in appropriate materials, just as it called for a radical change in assembling procedures.

Till then, the product had been industrial, consisting of factory-made, mass-produced components, but it was made functional by the artisan; a few men and a scaffold had sufficed for the handling and fitting of these light elements, which could be adapted or wrought into shape. Henceforth things would be different. The great steel constructions demanded the industrialization of the building site. No metalworker could put up a skyscraper on his own; he had no machines to hoist and assemble the units and his financial resources could not meet the necessary investment. The changing economics and technics of construction entailed the industrial concentration of building firms, with repercussions on all those involved in building work. In the long run it put an end to that liberal independence which had distinguished the architectural profession throughout the nineteenth century.

The steel revolution corresponded to, and reflected, the second Industrial Revolution. The technical epic which distinguished it, and which made the late nineteenth century a great period, had as its corollary the increasing alienation of individuals. Art, both in its means of expression and final aims, found itself at the crossroads of this conflict between man and society, a conflict which the artist, individualist by training, keenly experienced. He found himself forced into a difficult choice between praise and blame: between the panegyric upon industry embodied in its great creations–the Eiffel Tower, the Galerie des Machines, bridges or skyscrapers (for which he devised a kind of Babylonian or Roman monumentalism of flagrant inhumanity)–or that condemnation implied in the return to artisan labour, the interest taken in the family house, the search for the sources of European culture and its deliberate actualization in the forms of domestic architecture.

2

1. Chicago: Fire of 1871, view northwards from the Court House. Stereopticon slide.
2. Chicago: Fair Store, 1890-1891. Architect: William Le Baron Jenney. The steel frame during construction. *Industrial Chicago*, Goodspeed Publishing Co., Chicago, 1891.
3. Chicago: Home Insurance Building, 1883-1885. Architect: William Le Baron Jenney.

The new technical adventure began with the Exposition Universelle of 1867 in Paris, when the steel manufacturers presented structural sections and laminated iron sheets of resistance far superior to that of cast iron, at competitive prices. The factory of Noisiel (Seine-et-Marne) by Jules Saulnier (1871-1872) and the beautiful design for a house with a metallic frame proposed by Viollet-le-Duc in the second volume of his *Entretiens sur l'Architecture* (1872) are the direct consequence of this development: "It will have been observed that cast iron used for supports," wrote Viollet-le-Duc, "presents disadvantages and difficulties when it is to be combined with laminated iron; that iron sheets used intelligently offer more

3

1

1. Chicago: Monadnock Building, 1889-1891.
Architects: Daniel H. Burnham
John Wellborn Root.
Detail of the front.

security and allow assemblages of quite incomparable solidity." [10] The whole idea of skeleton construction is contained in that sentence. The old dialectical principle of structure, based on the post-and-lintel combination, had no justification after the post itself was made of laminated iron, like the lintel; the assemblage of the two parts was no longer effected by simple superposition, which had made all metal architecture a house of cards, whose solidity could only be ensured by strong enveloping walls. Henceforth the whole frame formed a kind of cage, all the parts of which were joined; the wall no longer played any other role but that of a filler within this frame. The system was well known in the timber-frame architecture of the Middle Ages. Not surprisingly, Viollet-le-Duc was one of the first to grasp its implications, even if engineers were already applying it in bridges or the hulls of ships.

More than twenty years were needed before the system was perfected, by passing from iron to steel (which made the structure still more resistant, and therefore suitable for high-rise building). The motivation came from the needs of business. The reconstruction of Chicago, [11] after the fire of 1871, spurred the construction of tall buildings, rising to ten storeys, which the recent development of lifts made it possible to use for habitation. Traditional construction in stone or brick was not without risk above a height of six or seven floors; the building foundations might be crushed by the building's own weight. Attempts were therefore made to reinforce the basements with steel rails embedded in the masonry. The upper levels were also reinforced by tying and bracing with metal, since they risked splitting open if the perpendicularity of the façades was not perfectly maintained. Finally, the piers were reinforced by including in them a steel column which increased their resistance, as in the Home Insurance Building of William Le Baron Jenney (1883-1885). All of this construction nevertheless remained traditional until around 1890. The Masonic Temple by Daniel Burnham and John Root (1891-1892), the world's tallest building of its day, was a structure with bearing masonry walls, as was the fine Monadnock Building, all in brick, by the same architects (1889-1891).

It was in a seven-storey building, the second Leiter Building (1889), that William Le Baron Jenney tried the first experiment in steel-frame construction–so successful that it was called "Chicago construction." It was given a façade decoration of masonry plaques, as was the Fair Store two years later. But this sheath was no longer necessary: the Chicago architects invented the great

2

3

4

2. Chicago: Tacoma Building, 1887-1888.
Architects: William Holabird
Martin Roche.

3. Chicago: Reliance Building, 1890-1895.
Architects: Daniel H. Burnham
John Wellborn Root.

4. Buffalo, New York: Guaranty (Prudential) Building, 1893-1895.
Architects: Louis Sullivan
Dankmar Adler.

1

New York: Bayard Building, 1897-1898.
Architects: Louis Sullivan
Lyndon P. Smith.
1. Detail of the front.
3. Entrance.

three-panelled bays–the "Chicago window" (one fixed pane with two flanking sashes)–and they also devised a completely ceramic sheath, in the form of profiled window-jambs and breast-panels moulded in relief (Reliance Building, Burnham and Root, 1895) or simple frame lines (Cable Building, Holabird and Roche, 1898).
The architect who did most to create a new language adapted to the character of frame construction was Louis Henry Sullivan.[12] To the assemblage of cold industrial materials, of the glass and ceramic that made the Reliance a very modern building, he preferred the richer materials of brick and terracotta, definitively ruling out the cast-iron sheath widely used by others. The reason was not technical but aesthetic. The lacy décor of cast iron added to the gauntness of the steel skeleton; it aggravated its effect of

2

2. St. Louis: Wainwright or Getty Tomb, drawing by Louis Sullivan for a limestone frieze, 1892.

slightness. Terracotta, on the other hand, created by its colour and substance a warm envelope which maintained a harmonious dialogue with the glass pane. It gave the skyscraper its monumental, its "Babylonian" character, so typical of late nineteenth-century architecture.

There remains the question of ornamentation. Contrary to work in cast iron, relief was not employed. The flattened décor gave to the surface a discreet graphic quality, a simple vibration of cast shadows; it had a kind of matness to it that contrasted with the glossy surface of the great expanses of glass. The whole was only a skin: it did not try to give the impression of a bearing structure of masonry, but insisted rather on its character of a sheath stretched over a structure. The experiment of Sullivan, coming between his first efforts as yet not completely free of the Florentine allusion (Wainwright Building, St Louis, 1891) and a major work (Guaranty Building, Buffalo, 1895), was as impressive as it was decisive for the elaboration of a new language, on the fundamental principle it had enunciated: "form follows function." In reality, form followed structure instead, but it did so with rare intelligence.

3

The spire of Rouen Cathedral

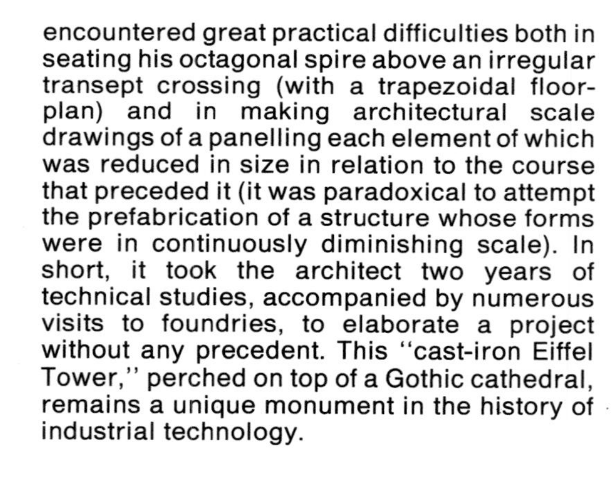

1

The new spire reconstructed by Jean-Antoine Alavoine over the transept crossing of Rouen Cathedral[13] is probably the earliest nineteenth-century edifice entirely in cast iron, not counting bridges. The old spire had been destroyed by fire in 1822; the reconstruction plans are dated 31 May 1823. The first castings arrived on the site in 1827, after several years of technical studies, and the work continued until 1838. It was then interrupted, to be completed only much later, between 1876 and 1884, the year in which the small lantern and the pinnacles were built.
It may seem curious that the most modernist project of the period, calling for a new material (which had never been used in that form), had to do with a historical monument, and it may be even more astonishing that Alavoine's proposal met with unanimous approval, from the prefect (who declared: "This monument, both by its height and the nature of the materials used [cast iron]... will always be one of the most remarkable that has been raised in the past century... its execution seems to me epoch-making in the history of the arts.") to the Inspector General of the Council of Civic Buildings, Gourlier: "Everything leads me to think," he wrote, "that this work is worthy of the Council's approval and high praise."
The blend of modernity and archaeology that characterized Alavoine's spire is typical of the period, in which the discovery of Gothic art became confused in people's minds with the spirit of the avant-garde. By raising the summit of the spire 148 metres above the ground, the architect gave it the character of a master-stroke leaving far behind the archaeological justification it presented (the spire claimed its inspiration from Salisbury!). Its chief interest lay in the fact that the structure, wholly self-supporting, was composed of openwork cast-iron plates. Alavoine encountered great practical difficulties both in seating his octagonal spire above an irregular transept crossing (with a trapezoidal floor-plan) and in making architectural scale drawings of a panelling each element of which was reduced in size in relation to the course that preceded it (it was paradoxical to attempt the prefabrication of a structure whose forms were in continuously diminishing scale). In short, it took the architect two years of technical studies, accompanied by numerous visits to foundries, to elaborate a project without any precedent. This "cast-iron Eiffel Tower," perched on top of a Gothic cathedral, remains a unique monument in the history of industrial technology.

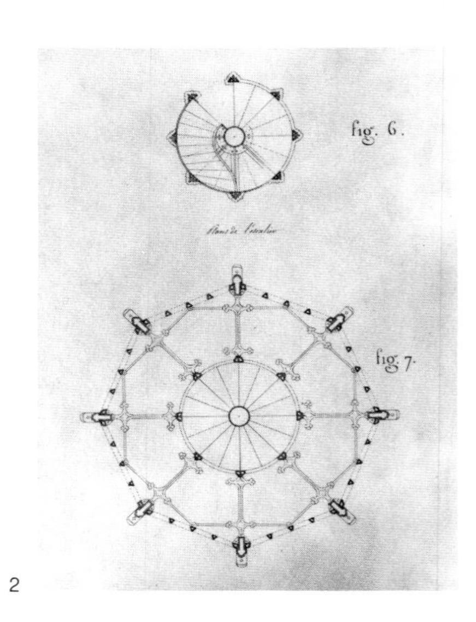

2

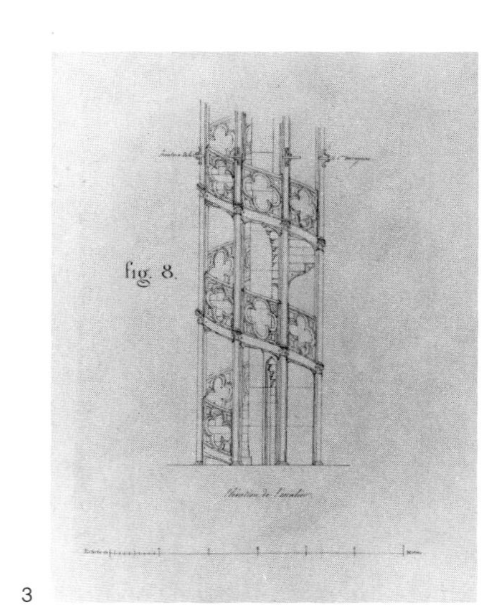

3

4

Rouen: Spire of the Cathedral, 1827-1838, completed 1876-1884.
Architect: Jean-Antoine Alavoine.
1. Internal stairway.
2.3. Plan and elevation of the stairway. *Premier supplément au Mémoire du 31 mai 1823, de J.-A. Alavoine*, 1823.
4. Initial design for the spire. *Mémoire, de J.-A. Alavoine*, 1823.
5. West front and spire of the cathedral.

5

Musical kiosks

1

In kiosk architecture cast-iron furniture found one of its most popular and international expressions, based on elaborate examples dating from the Second Empire–models often constructed in wood, but whose appeal was increased precisely by translation into industrial materials.
A form of holiday architecture, the kiosk derived initially from garden pavilions, Ottoman or Oriental. Nineteenth-century culture turned it into a small pavilion with a central, generally octagonal floorplan. Used as a bandstand, it always had a masonry base enclosing a wooden floor which acted as a resonance chamber. The construction was as light as possible, so as not to shut off the sounds; the canopy covering enhanced their transmission.
Because it was the architectural expression of the popular feast, the kiosk always preserved the character (accentuated by the polychrome and ornate carving of the roof) of flagpoles, theatrical backdrops and lampions. In all that dwelt something of the fanciful spirit of Hector Horeau!
Like the covered markets, kiosks revealed treasures of decorative invention by their immeasurable diversity, while the defined intention remained unchanged. More than any other construction, it was an exercise in style: with eight cast-iron supports, eight filigreed arcades, an iron screen, a brick base, a zinc roof and wooden frieze, decidedly one could do anything. From a school exercise destined for architectural reviews to the actual kiosk, in Cherbourg, Reims, Bastia or Mexico, there were endless variations to bring ornamental cast iron and chased zinc onto the stage.

2

3

4

1. Kiosk of metal and porcelain tiles, designed by Eugène-Adrien Forget. V. Champier, *Documents d'Ateliers. Art Décoratif Moderne*, 1898.
2. Cherbourg (Brittany): Kiosk in the Place de la République.
3. Bastia (Corsica): Kiosk in the Place Saint-Nicolas.
4. Reims. Kiosk (Kiosque des Marronniers) with the band playing.
5. Oaxaca (Mexico): Kiosk.

5

The Menier factory at Noisiel

USINE DE NOISIEL
POUR LA FABRICATION SPÉCIALE DU CHOCOLAT MENIER

1

The first building erected on the principle of skeleton construction, later to be used in the Chicago skyscraper, was the Menier Chocolate Factory at Noisiel (Seine-et-Marne), put up in 1871-1872 by the architect Jules Saulnier.[14] Noisiel was also the site of a housing estate which the chocolate manufacturer Menier had built for his workers.
The daring of the scheme owed much to the ideas on metal construction advanced by Viollet-le-Duc. It was also indebted to the specific nature of the programme–a mill driven by the waters of the Marne. Like most water mills, that of Noisiel was a bridge structure, carried out in partitions of iron and brick headers, a simple transposition of the traditional system of half-timbering. It was, for that matter, a mill of this type, built in 1840 and enlarged in 1855, which the new factory replaced.
But the conversion was of great boldness and logic. On piers sunk in the river-bed (separating the turbine housings) rested four riveted iron beams, 72 metres in length. Above, the storeys of the factory were formed by a sheath of walls "arranged like bridges, in iron latticework, and forming beams themselves." This load-bearing cage enclosed metal floors, strengthened by iron posts which ensured their resistance to the weight of the machines. The most striking innovation was aesthetic: it was the first building since medieval times to use the diagonal bracing structure as the frame for its décor. The polychrome partitioning (accompanied by glazed-tile roofing) followed the webbing of this structure, the brick ornament being inspired alternately by the Menier monogram and the stylized flower of the chocolate-tree (the glazed bricks came from Ivry, from the firm of Muller–one of the leading figures of Parisian Art Nouveau at the turn of the century).
All the elements of this language were already latent in the gaze which the rationalists turned towards the Middle Ages (in particular certain elements can be recognized as taking inspiration from the synodal hall of Sens, restored by Viollet-le-Duc). But their union, as well as the artistic treatment they received, resulted in a key work for the understanding of late nineteenth-century art.

Noisiel (Seine-et-Marne):
Menier Chocolate Factory,
1871-1872.
Architect: Jules Saulnier.

1. Overall view.
   Print.
2. Iron construction of the façades.
   Encyclopédie d'Architecture, 1877.
3. View from downstream of the building on the river.
   Encyclopédie d'Architecture, 1874.
4. Lucarne with clock.
   Encyclopédie d'Architecture, 1877.
5. Details and side view of the lucarne.
   Encyclopédie d'Architecture, 1878.
6. Details of the façade.
   Encyclopédie d'Architecture, 1877.

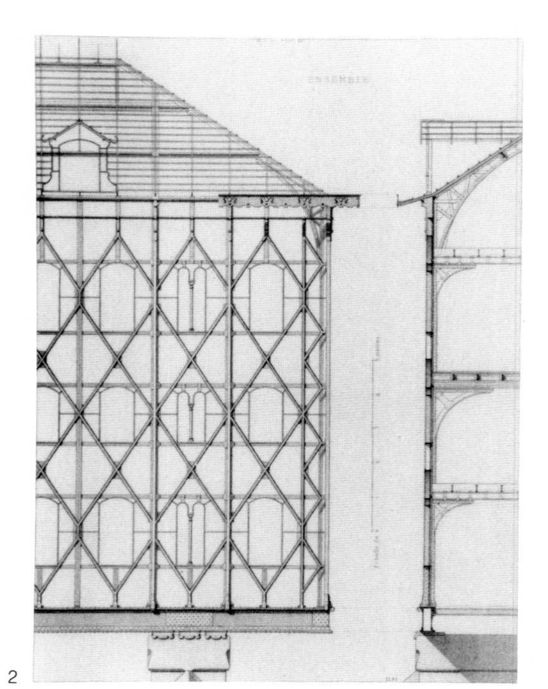
2

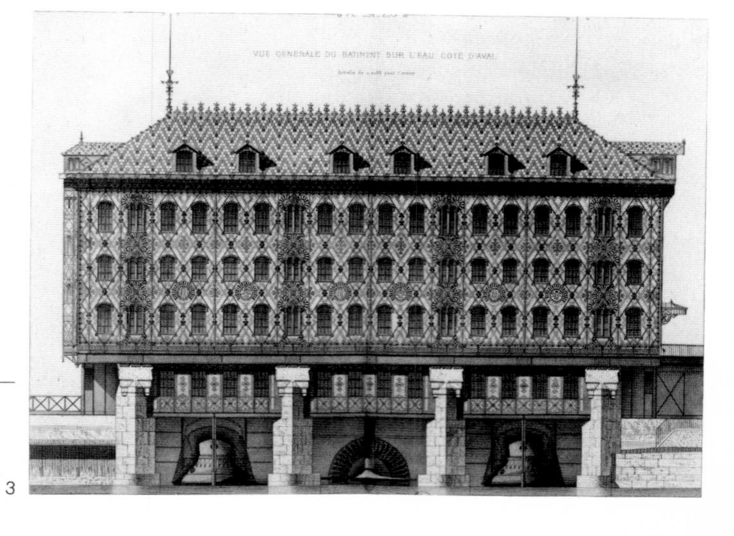
3

4

5

6

IIII

ART NOUVEAU

The War of Secession in America (1861-1865) and Prussia's wars against Austria (1866) and then France (1870) in Europe overthrew the old political and economic structures just as the second Industrial Revolution was getting under way. Economic concentrations, urban sprawl (starting a new wave of rural exodus), technical changes and political upheavals all combined to transform contemporary civilization in depth.
Both the War of Secession and the War of 1870 were civil wars. The Franco-Prussian struggle would not have assumed such significance if it had not ended in the collapse of the French Empire and the bloody episode of the Commune. A whole society was in transformation, rejecting the old hierarchies, the old authorities, and demanding by war or revolution a new distribution of whatever was to be had. A distribution that went as far as the conquest of colonial empires, securing the control of the sources of raw materials as well as consumer markets.

Past and present 1870-1890

The heyday of the two great empires, France and England, and of the two great cultures associated with them was passing. Industrial Europe would soon be Germanic, if not Russian; at the same time American power was on the rise. In Europe itself the shift in economic centres was revealing. Towards the end of the century Brussels, Amsterdam and Barcelona were to play a major cultural role, which they disputed with the great established capitals. In this new landscape the noiseless confrontation over Fashoda took on a different meaning: it was the admission of change, the symbol of a lost hegemony.
The third generation of the last third of the nineteenth century was not that of laws and institutions, nor of steam and the railway, but that of the great technical discoveries: the telephone, electricity, the phonograph, the automobile, would change ordinary behaviour patterns by breaking down the physical limitations of distance, of daily rhythm, of memory. At first sight, their consequences were perhaps smaller than those of the great industrial concentrations; but they extended so deeply into life-styles and human exchanges that they threw culture into a turmoil.
With the spread of photography, born half a century earlier, and that of artificial comfort (central heating, sanitation), which touched architecture most particularly, this whole group of inventions affected at once the use, transmission and conservation of cultural facts, whose survival was now guaranteed by the image and the phonograph record, while at the same time they went more rapidly out of fashion under the double effect of technical changes and commercial consumption.
Finally, and perhaps most important, the transmission of news speeded up until it became instantaneous and universal, breaking through the barriers of time and space, the frontiers of the old cultural order, even giving immediacy to the stalest of news, that of history as revealed by archaeology. One of the strongest features of the late nineteenth century was the simultaneity of cultures, through the immense harvest of texts and images placed before the eyes at every instant. It was only natural that architecture should have been shaken to its foundations.

History, the object of conflict

It is seldom helpful to speak of "periods of transition"; every period is a transition between what has been and what will be. And yet the 1870s were indeed characterized by a continuous shift in the system of references from what had been the ideal of the generation of 1830–Victoria or Louis-Philippe–and what would be, properly speaking, Art Nouveau. The "fin-de-siècle" spirit went into a kind of skid compared with the combativeness shown by the preceding generation. The first signs of it were evident at the fall of the Second Empire, around the time of the Paris Universal Exhibition (1867), which gave concrete form to a turning point in mentalities and, subsequently, to the change in dominant architectural models. Garnier, Abadie or Viollet-le-Duc[1] from then on had more importance than Scott, Barry, Lefuel or Baltard–an insensible shift in generations, but a fundamental shift in ideologies, for it was the theory of rationality which triumphed, curiously by joining forces with the lyrical monumentalism of the great artists of late romanticism. We have already pointed out that bivalence of the architectural project, which involved chasing after two contradictory or rival notions: the evocative power of the language, the enrichment of its semantic content, and, simultaneously, the purely autarchical discourse of a formal demonstration expressing technical rationality.

However much we may feel it today, this contradiction was only apparent. Indifferent to scholastic conflicts, an exacerbated sense of the architectonic united these two ambitions within a common language. The critic Lafitte sensed this fusion between rival theories when he wrote (in *L'Architecture contemporaine*, 1866): "Our epoch is no longer an epoch of principles, but an epoch of dealings between contrary principles."[2]

For what mattered was to get out of the dead end of ideological debate. Each edifice was a stock-taking, and it became as well a prototype containing the seeds of a new art. It was beyond eclecticism (more and more considered as a form of opportunism) that architecture wanted to rediscover its reason for being: in itself. It expressed itself as a monumental art, a rhetoric indifferent, in the real world, to the question of style. That was why it did not neglect monumentality, even making it the rule of its expression, as opposed to the mundane preciosities of the decorative style currently in fashion. Grandeur and sobriety were therefore to be the norm.

But legibility as well: a wind of didacticism was blowing through architecture, making every form demonstrative, from silhouette to structure and from structure to detail. Everything was explained, analysed, underlined,[3] as if the building became the paraphrase of its own intention. The differentiation in scales permitted the most

Rheinfelden (Switzerland): Feldschlösschen Breweries, 1874-1876.
Architect: Zimmermann Atelier.

heterogeneous forms of discourse, without their rivalry being troublesome. What the silhouette expressed, the detail could ignore, and what the scale of each floor had to say, that of the mass could contradict. The divergence of discourse within the same object was one of the striking traits of this period. It alone made possible the escape from the impasse into which criticism had blundered.
The driving force of this transformation, in which pragmatism carried the day over ideology, was once again industry. Its galloping expansion gave it the resources of a Maecenas and the craving for architectural representation. For the first time, the factory would be not only a place of production, but also an image, a monument of architecture, whose silhouette invaded letterheads and publicity posters. The architect got his share: considerable resources were made available to him in this henceforth privileged domain of architectural production. One need only mention the Godin factory at Guise, expanded by its cooperative, the textile plant "Le Fil au Louis d'Or" in Lille, Motte-Bossut in Roubaix, to evoke the image of those "castles of industry"[4] erected at the turn of the twentieth century by the great employers of labour.

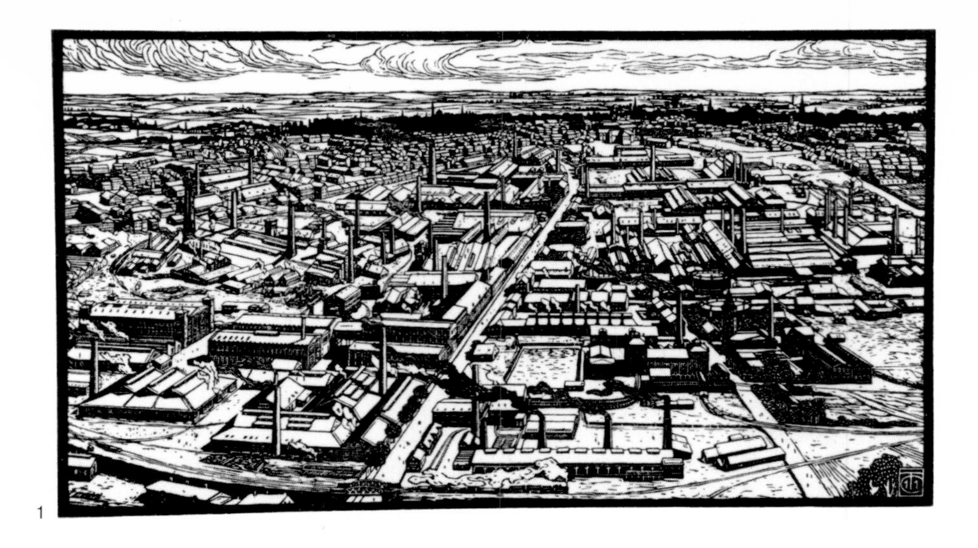

1

One of the finest examples (among so many monuments which contemporary industrial architecture is only just rediscovering) remains the Feldschlösschen brewery at Rheinfelden (1874-1876), on the rail line between Zurich and Basel.[5] Enlarged several times, in the same spirit, the building has the complex silhouette of a fortified castle, with imposing crenellated battlements, a monumental structure of red-brick arches standing out from the filler of yellow brick, like some giant viaduct, some impregnable fortress, enclosing within its sides the meticulous detail of a sumptuous machinery of oiled cast iron and gleaming copper.
The endless extension of the Krupp factories in Essen or the colossal steam-hammer of Creusot (1876), in the iron and steel hall which housed it, were other examples of that industrial power which fascinated the contemporary public and with whose worship art was increasingly associated. Even if immediate economic interests did not spur the systematic architecturalizing of factories, there was a latent preoccupation with it. When the pretext was not solely luxury it was dictated by commercial ambitions. Thus the Benedictine liqueur distillery at Fécamp based its trademark on its factory, one of the most improbable constructions of the end of the century (but not without charm).

2

1. Essen (Ruhr): The Krupp Works in 1887. *Krupp 1812-1912*, 1912.
2. Le Creusot (Saône-et-Loire): The Great Steam-Hammer, 1876. Engineer: Eugène Bourdon.
3. One of the six relief panels of the *Labour Frieze* decorating the monumental gateway of the Exposition Universelle, Paris, 1900. Sculptor: Anatole Guillot.
4. The Director: "Cheer up, my boy. Since your father has been killed in the mine, the Company, shrinking from no sacrifice, reserves his place for you." Lithograph in *Le Chambard Socialiste*, 1895.
5. Poster for the Belgian Workers' Party, 1899. Lithograph by J. van Biesbroeck.

3

Even if factory architecture is not to be reduced to the product of commercial advertising, it gained therefrom, for it was the point of convergence of several distinct aims. The expression of an industrial power measured by the perenniality of its establishment, it also revealed management success through the identification of man with the tool of his trade; finally, by its mere physical presence, it crystallized a working-class soul in quest of its identity. The factory or the mine, the smokestack or the pit-head frame, were to the worker what the field was to the peasant: a part of himself and of others; a place of alienation, but also of existence and recognition.

Artists were fascinated by the world of labour taking shape before their eyes. To the architectural and spatial creations of the great "industrial minarets," immense factories or black-country slag-heaps, answered collections of images which, in photography, poster, or bas-relief, sought to make a synthesis of working-class life, to idealize it by raising it to the level of highbrow culture. Images of a force in full expansion, through strikes and political struggles, by which the working class sought to win social recognition. Images, too, of the world of labour: miners with gnarled torsos, comrades in leather aprons, maul in hand–with which all the friezes of public monuments were suddenly adorned.

10 Centimes

Le Chambard
SOCIALISTE

BUREAUX
19, rue du Croissant
PARIS

Satirique — Illustré — Paraissant tous les Samedis

Rédacteur en Chef : GÉRAULT-RICHARD

ABONNEMENTS

A MONTCEAU-LES-MINES

LE DIRECTEUR. — Console-toi, mon garçon. Puisque ton père a été tué dans la mine, la Compagnie, qui ne recule devant aucun sacrifice, te réserve sa place.

4

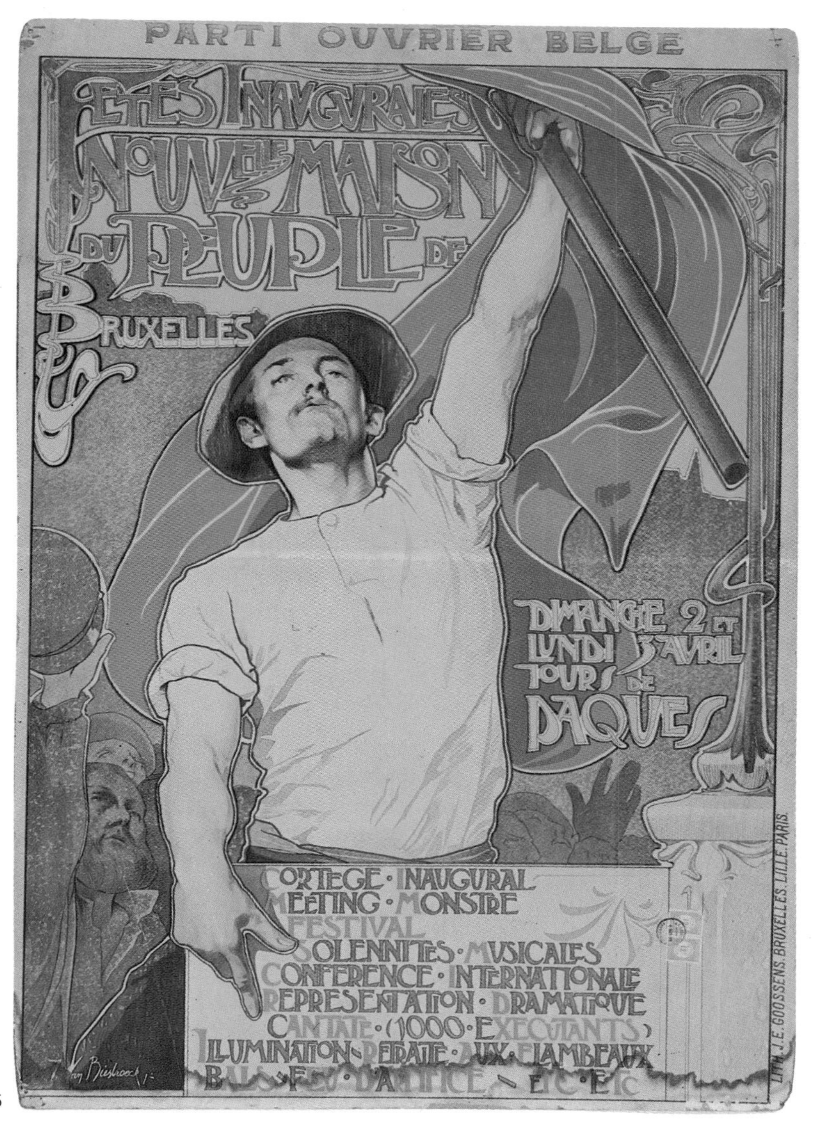

5

The paradox was but all the more striking alongside the sterilities of an official culture locked inside the Byzantine debates of a climate of archaeology-worship. The conflict between past and present was first of all a conflict between culture and barbarism, between the blind force of the proletarian and the refined erudition of the poet or the collector–a confrontation between culture and anti-culture of which the dramatic days of the Commune had made it possible to measure the full extent, in the burnt-out rubble of the Tuileries or the Hôtel de Ville. There were plenty of artists who expressed that twilight anguish of a civilization about to become useless by evoking, not without aiming to please, the bloodthirsty games of the circus or the fall of the Roman Empire.[6]
Positions hardened; they would harden still further, from the anarchist attacks to the October Revolution. The turn of the century was wholly absorbed in this conflict between *past and present* (the title of a basic work of Anatole de Baudot on the architecture of his time).[7] Implicitly, the message of architecture became political: the reference to culture was split; it represented stakes in society, it

1

2

1. Paris: *Science*, sculpture by Blanchard in front of the Hôtel de Ville.
2. New York: John Jacob Astor House, Fifth Avenue and 65th Street, 1897. Demolished. Architect: Richard Morris Hunt.
3. New York: Cornelius Vanderbilt Residence, Fifth Avenue and 57th Street, 1908. Demolished. Architect: George B. Post.
5. Paris: Hôtel de Ville (Town Hall), 1874-1882. Architects: Théodore Ballu
Edouard Deperthes.
Photograph of 1882.

made of the past, still more than an allusion, a message. No longer was it a matter of indifference whether a building was in the style of the sixteenth century or that of the reign of Louis XV.
It was of even less indifference whether it respected the forms of those styles or departed from them by some excessive liberty, by a modernity foreign to literal interpretation. Great care would be taken to justify by circumstantial examples the "liberties" taken with style, the abandoning of a model, the failure to respect the norm. Historicism identified itself with the cult of archaeology. When New York hotels imitated the châteaux of the Loire, or when the Hôtel de Ville of Paris (rebuilt from 1874 to 1882) reproduced the building destroyed by fire, there are good grounds for questioning the creative capacities of the period: there was a philosophy of pastiche which turned the copy into a justification. At the same time, it purged the insidious doubt with which art had become filled, through the precious forms of a mannerism manifestly anti-classical. From that angle, the road that led Théodore Ballu and Edouard Deperthes from La Trinité and Sainte-Anne d'Auray to the Hôtel de Ville[8] in less than ten years, is revealing. Whether out of fear or rejection, historicism found it harder and harder to accept the changes of the present.

3

4

5

4. Paris: Hôtel de Ville (Town Hall). Unexecuted design by Julien Guadet for the reconstruction, south front, 1873. Watercolour drawing by Guadet.

1

2

Lyons: Basilica of Notre-Dame de Fourvière, 1872-1914.
Architects: Pierre Bossan
Sainte-Marie Perrin.

1. Interior view.
2. Design for the north side.
4. North-south cross-section.
Watercolour drawings by Pierre Bossan, 1866.
3. Paris: Sacré-Cœur Basilica, Montmartre, 1874-1919.
Architects: Paul Abadie
Lucien Magne (bell-tower and choir).
Print of 1890.

Only in religious art did public architecture retain its stylistic prolixity, without archaeological justifications or pastiche. It is true that, in the French context, the proclamation of the republic modified the traditional relations between throne and altar. The church took on a symbolic value in the struggle against the economic and social changes now being achieved with such startling rapidity.
A confusion sprang up between industrial revolution and revolution pure and simple. Everyone knew that industrialization had been at the origin of the disturbances of the Commune. From there to seeing the latter as a divine punishment was but a step, soon taken. The great pilgrimage churches were churches of reparation, an offering made to God for the redemption of past faults and the crimes committed against His servants. A vengeful God had brought down upon a perverted France–and on its capital, the modern Babylon–the double punishment of defeat and civil war.

The new temples by which His wrath would be appeased were testimonies of popular fervour, material proof of a state of moral health, expressed by the sacrifice of a gift, in which the whole country participated (the National Assembly itself, by passing a law, made an offering of the basilica of Montmartre to the Sacré-Cœur). At Fourvière, at Lourdes or at Domrémy, in the bastions of militant Catholicism out to reconquer the dechristianized milieux of the large cities, doubt was not accepted currency: it was by simple means, accessible to all, that the religious message was transmitted.

The splendour of the liturgy, the spectacle of its feasts and processions, acquired its full meaning only by culminating in a lavish architecture. Montmartre crushed Haussmannian Paris by its massiveness and sparkling whiteness, overshadowing the domes of the Louvre, the steeple of the town hall, the elegant curve of the Palais du Trocadéro. At Fourvière, that colossal "Sainte-Chapelle" which Pierre Bossan placed above Lyons, the luxury of the interior fittings was Byzantine: the marbles, mosaics and stained-glass windows joined in a riot of ornament that took over for its own advantage, for the spectacle of faith, the riches of Garnier's Paris Opera.

3

4

Because the building had political and social significance, it brought conviction in its train: to this day, the Sacré-Cœur of Montmartre remains one of the best known buildings of the world. At Domrémy–whose basilica is the very symbol of French nationalism, through the heroic figure of Joan of Arc–Paul Sédille (who also designed the Printemps department store) rediscovered the monumental inspiration and stylistic complexities that Léon Vaudoyer put into the Cathedral of La Major in Marseilles. Above and beyond the class struggle, nationalism would be the great cement of French unity. By proclaiming France "the eldest daughter of the Church" the Catholic hierarchy hit upon a formula giving it a pre-eminent position in institutional representation–in absolute contrast with the blows which the lay authority multiplied against it. Indeed, the Church took over public architecture for its own profit: thousands of village churches, rebuilt during the last quarter of the century, are there to bear witness.

1. Domrémy (Vosges): Statue by Mercié in front of Joan of Arc's birthplace, 1902.
2. Domrémy (Vosges): Basilica of La Pucelle (The Maid), 1881. Architect: Paul Sédille.

3. Marseilles: Basilica of Notre-Dame de la Garde, 1853-1864. Architect: Henri-Jacques Espérandieu.
4. Rome: Monument to Victor Emmanuel II (popularly called "The Typewriter"), 1882-1888. Architect: Giuseppe Sacconi.

In other countries this identification between great public architecture and religious architecture does not obtain. The Jubilee Church of Wilhelm II in Berlin is more a dynastic monument than a religious symbol; and the colossal mass of Giuseppe Sacconi's "Typewriter" in Rome (1882-1888), dedicated to the glory of Victor Emmanuel II, stands out in a provocative face-to-face with the Vatican City and St Peter's dome. It is by design that we have brought together this symbol of institutional rivalry, a rivalry expressed in terms of the urban landscape, with those other political monuments, the French basilicas of pilgrimage.

A positivist attitude

Monumentalism or the cult of archaeology: the debate of the 1850s had shifted insidiously onto a new ground, leaving the rationalists in an ambiguous position. Recognized through the institution of external ateliers of the Paris Ecole des Beaux-Arts and that of the diocesan architects, the rationalists now had a key role in the training of young architects, at a time when the Beaux-Arts teaching methods were most influential at international level. They filled most of the high public offices and triumphed in the great competitions. The centenary exhibition of the French Revolution, the Paris World's Fair or Exposition Universelle of 1889, was a hymn to the glory of these French rationalists, dominated by J. C. Formigé's Beaux-Arts pavilion and Ferdinand Dutert's decoration of the Galerie des Machines.

This official recognition was offset by the complete overtaking of their architectural models. Labrouste died in 1875, Viollet-le-Duc in 1879. All the technology behind their work was superseded. Construction was no longer in iron and cast iron, but in steel, with mighty spans unimaginable twenty years earlier. The triumph of the rationalists, in fact, remained a corporate affair: it was the engineers who dominated the profession, fulfilling the prophecy of César Daly. And the engineer, trained by the great schools, believed he could do without the architect. When he did call him in, he confined him to the role of a decorator–that of Stephen Sauvestre for the Eiffel Tower or Dutert for the Galerie des Machines.

The architects' response to the engineers' technical feats was quite inadequate. The counter-project drafted by Anatole de Baudot as an alternative to the Galerie des Machines was a kind of giant glasshouse, covered by umbrella vaults in iron and glass deriving from English Gothic (via the plates in Viollet-le-Duc's *Entretiens*). Set against the power and formal sobriety of the great three-jointed metallic trusses conceived by Victor Contamin, Baudot's vaulted Gothic design had something puerile about it. If architects followed the theoretical rules which they themselves had laid down, they were obliged to disappear as architects. Industrial society may need scientists; it can easily do without artists. A bitter lesson to an avant-garde philosophy that was coming to an untimely end.

The only way out of such an impasse was to give up technical rivalry with the engineer and thoroughly study the plastic working of form, a field in which the nullity of the engineer was obvious. Here the rationalists did admirable work, benefiting from the lessons of their predecessors with a keen sense of efficacity and sobriety. The banded mass of Formigé's columbarium at Père Lachaise, a strange *campo santo* whose volumes were taken from Delorme and the polychromy from Siena, was of startling effect, as was the aquatic atmosphere of Dutert's museum, where the

1. Paris: Central dome of the Beaux-Arts Pavilion at the Exposition Universelle, 1889. Architect: Jean-Camille Formigé. Glucq, *L'Album de l'Exposition 1889.*
2. Paris: Museum of Natural History. Gallery of Comparative Anatomy, 1894-1895. Architect: Ferdinand Dutert.

4

3. Paris: Exposition Universelle, 1889.
Gallery of Machines.
Architect: Ferdinand Dutert.
Engineer: Victor Contamin.
4. Paris: Viaduc d'Austerlitz, 1903-1904.
Architect: Jean-Camille Formigé.
Engineer: Louis Biette.

1

1. Paris: Columbarium of the Père Lachaise Cemetery, 1889-1907.
Architect: Jean-Camille Formigé.
Main front, watercolour by Formigé, 1886.

Paris: Church of Saint-Pierre de Montrouge, 1864-1872.
Architect: Emile Vaudremer.
2. Main front.
3. Side elevation.
Encyclopédie d'Architecture, 1872.
4. Interior view.
5. Paris: Church of Saint-Jean de Montmartre, 1894-1904.
Architect: Anatole de Baudot.
Interior view.

monstrous skeletons of prehistoric animals bathed in the greenish light from immense glass roofs, hemmed by the serried rhythm of cast-iron balustrades ornamented with stylized ferns, whose mechanical repetition was the only guide-mark in the vastness of those great bare halls.

In matters of detail, the beauty of Emile Vaudremer's masonry, his artful use of empty spaces and the subtle dialectic he observed between live parts and fillers were exceptionally fine. He conferred on the architecture of white brick and stone its patent of nobility, through that "Third Republic" style characteristic of French schools and hospitals.

Starting from the same premises, the road taken by Anatole de Baudot,[9] Viollet-le-Duc's favourite pupil, who later became the architect of Historic Monuments (and, in that capacity, restorer of many buildings), led him from 1894 on to conceive structures in reinforced concrete whose boldness and intelligence of design were equalled only a half-century later by the Italian architect-engineer Pier Luigi Nervi.

2

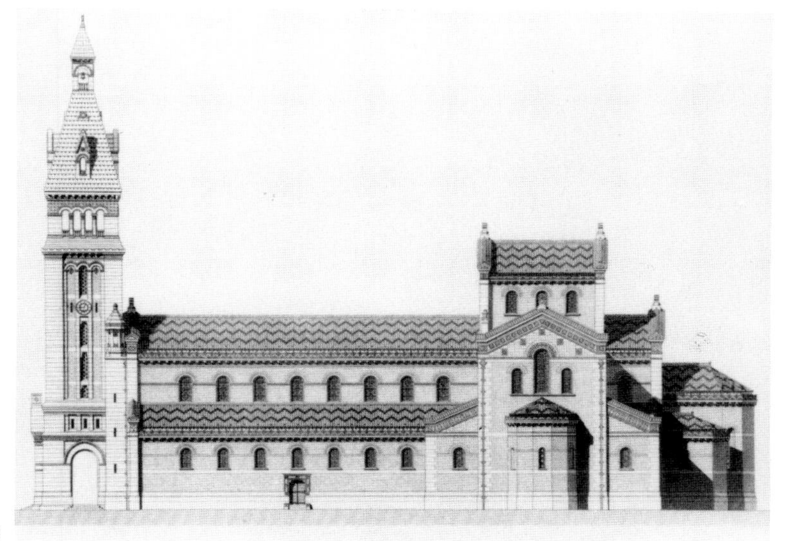
3

4

5

1

2

3

1. Paris: Lycée Molière, 1888.
   Architect: Emile Vaudremer.
   View of the yard.

   Grenoble: Lycée de Garçons (Boys' High School).
   Architect: Emile Vaudremer.
2. Front and back.
3. Arcades in the courtyard of the administration.
   Encyclopédie d'Architecture, 1886-1887.

4

5

6

Sceaux (south suburb of Paris):
Lycée Lakanal, 1882-1886.
Architect: Anatole de Baudot.
4. View from the yard.
6. Front.
La Construction Moderne, 1885-1886.
5. Paris: Lycée Victor-Hugo, 1894-1896.
Architect: Anatole de Baudot.
Covered yard.
La Construction Moderne, 1893-1894.

The right to culture

1. Karlsruhe: Homburger Bank, 1898-1901.
Architects: Robert Curjel
Karl Moser.
Die Architektur des XX. Jahrhunderts, 1902.
2. Basel: St. Paul's Church, 1898-1901.
Architects: Robert Curjel
Karl Moser.
Die Architektur des XX. Jahrhunderts, 1902.
3. Boston: Trinity Church, 1873-1877.
Architect: Henry Hobson Richardson.
Elevation with no porch,
design of 1874.
4. Boston: Ames Building, 1881-1883.
Architect: Henry Hobson Richardson.
5. Cambridge (Massachusetts): Austin Hall (Harvard Law School), 1881-1883.
Architect: Henry Hobson Richardson.
View of 1901.

It might be imagined that the aesthetic impasse of eclecticism, imprisoned in the cult of archaeology, and the theoretical impasse of rationalism, overwhelmed by the technical innovation of engineers, enclosed the years 1870-1880 in a double record of failure. That would be to ignore the sensitive refinements brought to form by pushing the virtuosity of design and execution to their uttermost limits, and to overlook the lessons of grandeur and economy of means promoted by way of new reflection on the meaning of form.

It is therefore not surprising that, from the conjunction of the two abortive approaches, there was born an Art Nouveau, prefigured during the 1880s, but, as if by chance, outside the traditional centres of culture.

In the forefront stands the figure of Henry Hobson Richardson, [10] an American architect from Boston trained in Paris in the atelier of Labrouste's brother and a great admirer of both Butterfield and Vaudremer.

Richardson's innovative work is usually reduced to the Marshall Field department stores in Chicago, which ushered in the experiments of the nineties by their influence on Adler and Sullivan. But that is leaving out Trinity Church in Boston, which, in the year of the Montmartre competition, 1874, gave a less emphatic and more effective version of neo-Romanesque, by the sobriety of its design and the beauty of the natural polychromy of pink sandstone–with a powerful, monumental, harmonic detail, and a perfect balance between the sense of mass and the integration of the detail.

But it mattered little whether all this was Romanesque or not, whether the Irish interlace ran through it, associated with Anglo-Norman elements, peppered with quotations from French Gothic. The essential thing was that the regional building material suddenly showed itself in its plastic originality, as though its proper use had never been known until then; that the mass was made manifest; that the relation of solids and voids demonstrated a clear law (the rhythmic narrowing of the Ames Building in Boston to bring out its structure, or the hierarchical assertion of the size of the bays, revealing the major spaces, in the Allegheny County Courthouse in Pittsburgh); that, finally, the detail served as a commentary whose graphic animation placed an accent on a few chosen centres of interest–well provided breathing pores, sharp punctuations, sudden accumulations that roused the attention. It was a whole new language coming into place, indifferent to historicism, in which it still superficially participated.

Richardson's influence (and that of Frank Furness [11] in Philadelphia) was decisive in Northern Europe at the end of the century, in

3

4

5

1

Amsterdam: Stock Exchange, 1898-1903.
Architect: Hendrik Petrus Berlage.
1.3. Views of the interior.
2. Initial design for the south front.
Watercolour by Berlage, 1896.

2

Germany (Curjel and Moser), Switzerland and Holland. It explains why H.P. Berlage[12] turned away from a Flemish neo-Gothic inspired by his mentor Cuijpers (whose best known works of that period are the Rijksmuseum and the main station in Amsterdam) to the powerful, bare forms of the Amsterdam Stock Exchange (1898-1903), in a searching meditation on the works and thought of Viollet-le-Duc. Cuijpers, like Beyaert in Belgium, admired Viollet-le-Duc: the simplicity and logic of his architecture vouch for that. But admiration was not enough: he also had to give to his own style of design the force too often lacking in the elegant detail of Second Empire work.

The redundant style of Louis Cordonnier,[13] together with his flair for combining historical forms, had made him the uncontested laureate of the Amsterdam Stock Exchange competition in 1884. Fifteen years later, Berlage, his unlucky rival, had gone far beyond the forms of historicism by learning the joint lessons of French rationalism and Richardson's monumental style. Berlage combined economy of means with a keen sense of materials and colour, so much so that Mies van der Rohe was to see in him the founder of modernism.

3

4

5

4. Rotterdam: Warehouse of the firm of W.V.D. Lugt en Zoon.
Architect: J.P. Stok.
Neubauten in Holland, 1900.

5. The Hague: De Nederlanden Fire Insurance Building.
Architect: Hendrik Petrus Berlage.
Neubauten in Holland, 1900.

Catalan architecture of the 1880s moved towards exuberance, with Doménech i Montaner, Puig i Cadafalch and Antoni Gaudí.[14] The fascination with terracotta dominated this production of brick and glazed tiling, whose bright polychromy was associated with an orientalizing style inspired by Mudéjar art, in forms which told at every moment of the careful reading of Viollet-le-Duc's *Entretiens* and *Dictionnaire*.

The inventiveness of this vocabulary proved that the theoretical lesson of Viollet-le-Duc had borne fruit. Transcending the copy or quotation, it dynamized a type of creation that depended on an original exchange between modernity and archaeology. To modernity belong the desire of renewal, the systematic use of new materials, the rationality of structure and the avowed functionalism of the design; to archaeology, the constant reference to local examples, by architects who were often also great archaeologists (to Puig i Cadafalch we owe the standard work[15] on Visigoth architecture in Spain). It was from Catalan Gothic[16] that Gaudí drew his references, but it would be absurd to call his work purely neo-Gothic: the quotation was a source, not a model.

1. Barcelona: Group of three terraced houses. Architect: J. Puig i Cadafalch. Elevation. *L'œuvre de Puig i Cadafalch*, 1904.
2. Barcelona: Casa Vicens, 1878-1880. Architect: Antoni Gaudí. Original aspect before the remodelling of 1925.

4

By the end of the nineteenth century the stagnation of the 1870s had been overcome. Art Nouveau was born of a fusion between the monumental lyricism of a public art, the theorists' demand for rigour and the respect for a permanent reference to history. But the prevailing mentality had changed. History was no longer historicism. When an earlier building was taken as a model, it was recast in relation to the technical and economic particulars of the time. Imitation and pastiche were refrained from. And from this fusion of an affirmed scientism of approach and a cultural sensibility steeped in history, forming a continuity with its examples, a living art was born. A difficult gauging of two ingredients: from the preponderance of one or the other would quickly result a cleavage between culturalism and modernism (following the expression of Françoise Choay)[17], depending on the emphasis given to the continuity of the cultural link with history or to the expression of the new data of civilization. In the art of the nineteenth and twentieth centuries the relationship to history remained difficult, even when the past was thought to be stale and done with.

5

3. Astorga (León): Episcopal Palace, 1887-1893. Architect: Antoni Gaudí. Interior.

Barcelona: Palau de la Musica Catalana (Palace of Catalan Music), 1905-1908. Architect: Lluís Doménech i Montaner.

4. The great entrance hall.
5. The concert hall in 1912.

Metal constructions

1

The economic and technical concentrations achieved during the second phase of the Industrial Revolution, during the last quarter of the century, were characterized by industrial megastructures. Most conspicuous was the change of scale made possible by the technique of the steel frame.
Two kinds of new bridges revealed it as early as the mid-century: the Britannia tubular bridge over the Menai Straits, by Robert Stephenson, in riveted sheet steel forming a sort of gigantic hollow beam, within which passed railway trains (which, paradoxically, turned this bridge into a tunnel!); and the Brooklyn Bridge in New York, by John and Washington Roebling, a suspension bridge of spun steel cables, capable of spanning the breadth of the East River, at the southern tip of Manhattan, in an unbroken flight.
Neither of these structures had much of a future. Their progress was certainly spectacular in relation to arched spans formed by cast-iron voussoirs. But technology was to make another leap forward, by perfecting the trelliswork beam, made of riveted industrial sections. Reviving the idea of tubular structure developed by Stephenson, the bridges of the last quarter of the century were all three-dimensional structures (even if the methods of calculation remained two-dimensional, necessitating the decomposition of volumes by orthogonal planes), following the principle of skeleton construction, which should rather be called "cage-construction," for that is what it amounts to.
Technique made further progress with the so-called bowstring bridges. The Garabit Viaduct (1880-1884) by Gustave Eiffel is a fine example, paving the way for odd conceptions like the Forth Bridge near Edinburgh (1882-1890) by Benjamin Baker and John Fowler–the arches left the piers in symmetry like the arms of a crane, to be joined at their key by a slender footbridge–or the Hamburg bridge over the Elbe, formed by two sinusoids crossing on the tops of the piers like some monstrous braid dropped there by chance. Independently of the engineer's not always very happy feats of prowess, certain structures, exploiting the technical data of steel construction, were indisputable artistic successes: for example, the viaducts of the elevated railway of Berlin, more elegant in design and more modern in structure than those of the Paris Métro (where the arched member remained coupled with cast-iron pillars, raising it above the public way, an effective, but often unaesthetic procedure, and in any case possessing very little unity).

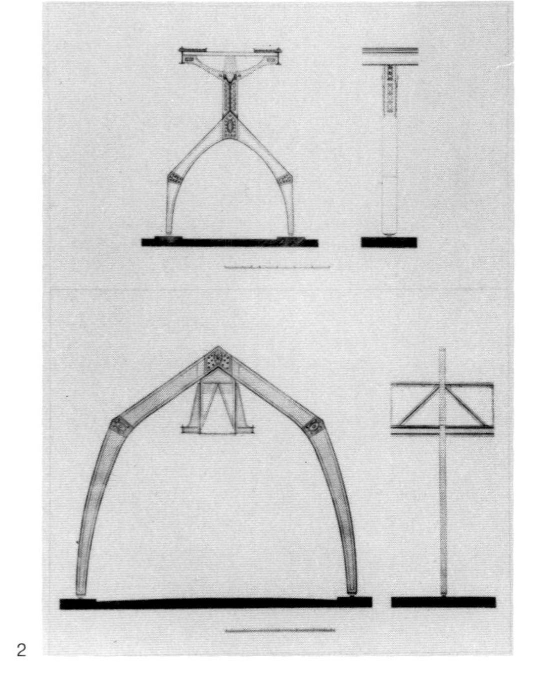

2

1. New system of support for metal bridge. *Encyclopédie d'Architecture*, 1874.
2. Berlin: Forked and arched iron supports for overhead metropolitan railway. B. Möhring, *Stein und Eisen*, 1903.
3. Hamburg: Iron railway bridge over the Elbe, 1868-1872. Engineer: Lohse.
4. New York: Brooklyn Bridge over the East River, 1869-1883. Engineers: John and Washington Roebling.
5. Garabit (Cantal): Viaduct over the Truyère, 1880-1884. Engineer: Gustave Eiffel.

3

4

5

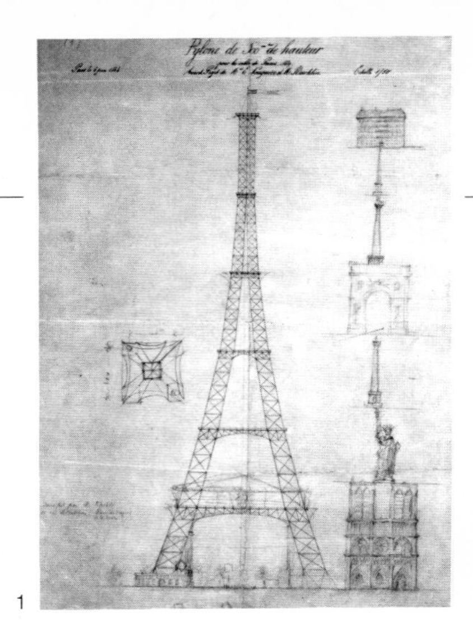

1

2

3

The industrial megastructures were not limited to bridges and viaducts: the barge hoist at Fontinettes, built in 1888, or the pit-head frames of mines, foundry halls, drying or cooling towers, water towers or silos springing up in a thousand places where their unaccustomed presence, the product of a technical necessity and not a political or social will, disturbed the traditional order.
A major symbol of industrial art, the thousand-foot tower, an old architectural dream, was erected for the Paris World's Fair of 1889: the Eiffel Tower, dominating the Parisian cityscape. A prodigious technical success, but a wild intrusion into the world of culture: "It cannot be conceived," wrote J.K. Huysmans,[18] "that this funnel-shaped grating is completed; that this lone suppository riddled with holes will remain that way. This look of a scaffolding, this arrested attitude, in a now completed edifice, makes absolute nonsense of art. What, besides, is one to think of the ironworker who has his work daubed with Barbedienne bronze, making it seem as if soaked in cold meat gravy? ... On going inside the tower you are confronted by a chaos of intersecting beams, riveted with bolts, hammered together with nails. You can think only of props holding up an invisible building on the point of collapse. You can only shrug your shoulders at this glory of wire and plate, at this apotheosis of the viaduct pier, the bridge apron! ... One might guess it to be the steeple of a new church inside which is being held the holy service of the High Bank ... In that case, its safe-deposit-box material, its beef-stew colour, its factory-pipe structure, its oil-well shape, its skeleton of a giant dredge for extracting the gold-bearing mud of the Stock Exchange would be accounted for. It would then be the spire of Notre Dame of Bric-a-brac, a spire deprived of bells but armed with a cannon announcing the opening and closing of services, inviting the financial markets to agio vespers, a cannon sounding, with its salvos of gunpowder, the liturgical feasts of Capital!"
Industrial architecture could not be written off with greater humour.

4

Paris: Eiffel Tower, 1887-1889.
Engineers: Gustave Eiffel
Maurice Koechlin
Emile Nouguier.
Architect: Stephen Sauvestre.

1. The 1000-foot Tower, with comparative heights of Notre-Dame, the Statue of Liberty and other monuments. Preliminary design by E. Nouguier and M. Koechlin, 1884.
2. Under the Eiffel Tower. Glucq, *L'Album de l'Exposition 1889.*
5. Detail of the girders.
3. Henrichenburg (Ruhr): Disused barge hoist on the Dortmund-Ems canal.
4. Blanzy (Saône-et-Loire): Pit-head frame at the Pré-Long mine.

5

The handling of detail

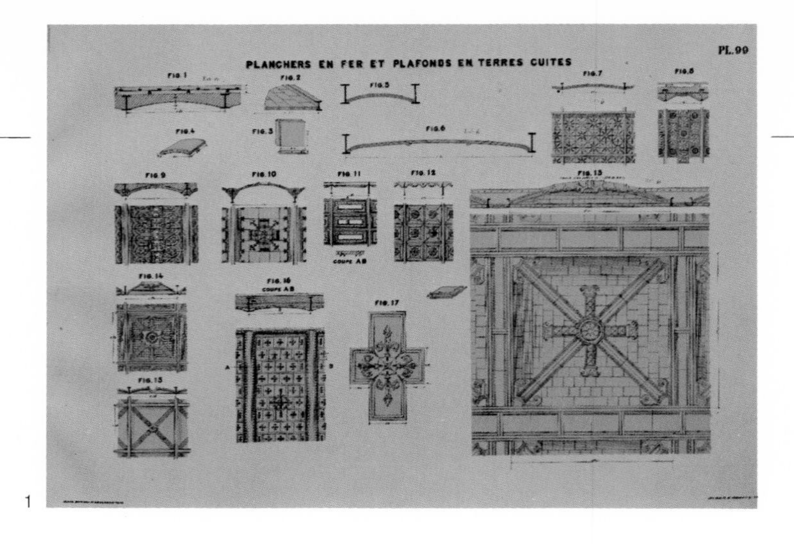

1

The systematic ordering of detail was one of the main features of the rationalist heritage in the last quarter of the nineteenth century. If the analyses of broad options were often subjected to the great compositional laws of the Beaux-Arts, if the treatment of space and light fitted into a pictorial tradition stemming from Boullée (faithful to a formula going back to the late eighteenth century), it was in the domain of detail that modernity triumphed, opening a breach in the academic tradition of the hierarchy of architectural orders and their settled detail, just as it rejected the sort of borrowing constituted by historical revetment, accepted by conventional architects.

The question of style, from this standpoint, has so little importance that it is not impossible to find in rationalist detail diverse historical allusions: colonettes whose foliate capitals owe something to the twelfth or thirteenth century, wide pilasters that are Renaissance-like, classical modillions and even the traditional proportions of the architectural order or of the hierarchy of levels–arcaded substructures, principal upper storey with entablature and pilasters, Attic-style gables–in keeping with the formulas cherished by classical tradition.

The essential did not lie there, but in the thought given to the post-and-lintel relationship, in the analysis of the components of an arcade or in the expression of a dialectic between skeleton and filling-in, between live and inert structural components. The effect of polychromy, gained by using stones of different origin or different tints of brick, was a main element of clarification in the analytic study of detail. In the same way, solid and voids constituted graphic networks whose varying mesh marked out the role of each structural plane. Finally, the placing of ornament plotted out the sensitive points of the constructed organism: the spring of the arch on the springer and the hooking-on of the floor timbers behind the plane of the façade (hooking that exposed numerous decorated cramp-irons, following the method of Labrouste for the Rennes Seminary); the passage of the beam or metal breastsummer that cut a groove across the façade, bringing forward large flat surfaces of glass; the springing on a colonette which reinforced the span in mid-career.

One of the finest examples of this mode of stylistic detail was the group of offices built for the French Railways by Adrien Gouny (Rue du Faubourg-Saint-Denis, Paris, 1887). But the appeal of this kind of plastic commentary on structure was so great that it may still be seen in the monumental façade of the annexes of the Crédit Lyonnais, by André Narjoux, at the start of the twentieth century.[19]

2

1. Iron floors and terracotta ceilings.
   A. Vierendeel, *La construction architecturale en fonte, fer et acier*, 1893.
2. Paris: Office building of the French National Railways (originally Chemins de Fer de l'Est, now SNCF), 1887.
   Architect: Adrien Gouny.

   Paris: Annex of the Crédit Lyonnais bank, 1908.
   Architect: André Narjoux.
3. Front in its present state.
4. Detail of the front.
   L'Architecte, 1909.

3

4

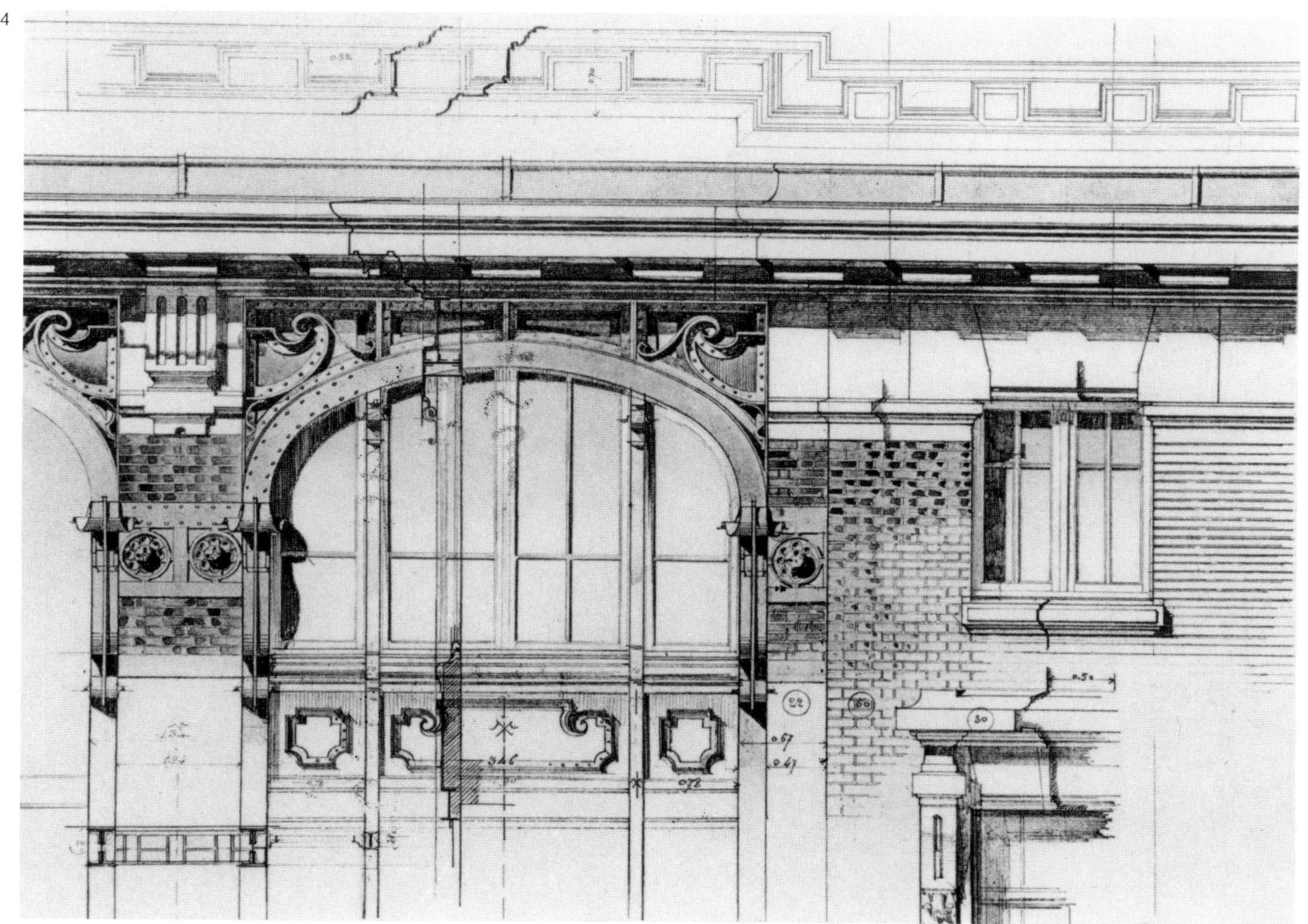

1

2

Everything which this handling of detail owes to the influence of Emile Vaudremer is apparent, from the first experiments of Saint-Pierre de Montrouge, under the Second Empire, to his major work, the Lycée Buffon. At Montrouge, the dialectic of the brickwork was still under the influence of its Romanesque antecedents; only the terracotta roof-gutter, its design a Labroustian quotation, was handled powerfully. The whole, by its flatness, strove to express the inner recourse to a covering structure of timberwork–thus without buttresses or slanting thrusts.
In the Lycée Buffon, the formula of stone and yellow brick façades, reviving the Gothic analytics of live and filled-in parts of the building, was applied to perfection, accompanied by segmented arches or metal beams which ensured the broad spans desired for the hygienic lighting of the classrooms. The rigorous skeleton revealed itself within by the exposing of floors in small brick arches on metal joists, without any disguise. This lesson in construction was in the true French tradition.

3

1.3. Paris: Lycée Buffon, 1887.
Architect: Emile Vaudremer.

2. Sceaux (south suburb of Paris): Lycée Lakanal, 1882-1886.
Architect: Anatole de Baudot.

4. Paris: Church of Saint-Pierre de Montrouge, 1864-1872.
Architect: Emile Vaudremer.

4

Form and meaning

1

The formal analytics of the rationalists often resulted in works whose logic did not escape barrenness, as contemporaries were well aware. With renewed interest in the spectacle of form, in a dramatization emphasizing the effect of mass, the contrast of light and colour as well as the emblematic aspect, the Art Nouveau generation reacted against the excesses (sometimes formalist, which was the last straw!) of rationalist styling. Viollet le-Duc pointed the way, with the universally admired example of Pierrefonds. And J. K. Huysmans placed himself at the head of the movement, in that essential book for the understanding of Art Nouveau, *La Cathédrale*,[20] which transmitted Ruskin's "Bible of Amiens" message with a rigour and archaeological culture which admirably served its effortless style.

By playing on the spectator's sensibility, by elaborating forms which, through the play of masses and volumes, the modulation of light, produced a purely aesthetic emotion, and then adding to that form an iconographic commentary packed with literary allusions, cunning devices and deliberate obscurities, architects strove to enrich the content of architecture, to go beyond the limits of that redundancy of formal discourse on technique (the *tectonic* as the expression by image of technique, on principles stemming from Gothic ornamentation). They wished to join forces with other art forms, those in which the discourse had a meaning: painting, sculpture, literature. It was at times with naivety that they stuck discourse onto architecture, by laborious allegories, puerile symbols or emphatic inscriptions, but the effort was worthy: it sought to exceed the bounds of that abstract science that was architecture, to make it commune with other artistic expressions, within the total art which each of them dreamed of establishing.

It is useful to compare the Diamond Workers' House in Amsterdam (1899-1901), by H. P. Berlage–in the concentrated formula he gave it, around the light well of a patio-courtyard dominated by the revolutionary legend: "Workers of the world, unite!"–with the Metz railway station, a manifesto of the official style of the Imperial German Administering Authority in the occupied territories. Jürgen Kröger, laureate of the 1902 competition, achieved at Metz an edifice in a style akin to the neo-Romanesque for political reasons (the Imperial style could only be Romanesque, or better still Carolingian!), but whose ubiquitous system of emblems was of striking interest.[21]

2

1.2.4. Metz (Lorraine): Railway Station, 1905-1908.
Architect: Jürgen Kröger.
Details of the interior.

3. Amsterdam: The Diamond Workers' House, 1899-1901.
Architect: Hendrik Petrus Berlage.
Cross-section.
Watercolour drawing by Berlage.

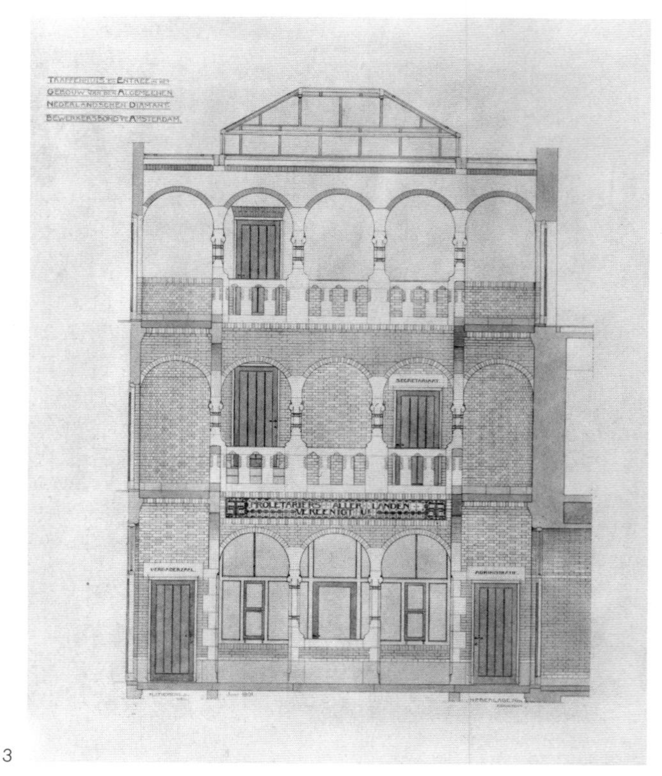

3

4

1

In the choice of style, apart from the political pretext, it was Richardson's influence that dominated. With Berlage, as with Kröger, the care for plastic handling dominated, affirming, in one case, the rigour and power of the Workers' International; in the other, the triumph of Germanization in the annexed provinces. But in the last analysis it mattered little: it was the link between the form and the message, perfectly brought out in both cases, which formed the novelty of the discourse (contrary to that dissociation between structure, space and ornament which had marked all of the nineteenth century and had forced eclecticism upon it).
With Doménech i Montaner, in the auditorium of the Palace of Catalan Music, where figures in relief escape from a background of mosaic and broken tilework, while the winged horses of the capitals take off above the hall, this fusion between architecture and symbol is patently achieved. The décor of the auditorium, conceived on the lines of the Salle Gaveau in Paris, was oriented on Wagnerian themes, in a startling saturation of light and colour.
Antoni Gaudí, attacking the conception of structures by a continuous shuttle between the logic of construction and the evocative power of the image, was to carry the experience still further–to madness, it was said at the time. But this total lyricism was nonetheless to leave a unique patrimony in the history of architecture by the intensity of the aesthetic emotions it aroused and the indissociable bond between the quality of that spectacle of form and the philosophical content it transcribed.[22] There was something in common between the ambition of Pierre Bossan and that of Antoni Gaudí: perhaps that common ground was Art Nouveau?

2

1. Barcelona: Casa Batlló, 1905-1907. Architect: Antoni Gaudí.
2.3. Barcelona: Casa Milá, 1905-1910. Architect: Antoni Gaudí.
4. Barcelona: Palace of Catalan Music, 1905-1908. Architect: Lluís Doménech i Montaner. The winged horse Pegasus.

3

4

CREDIT
LYONNAIS

The second Industrial Revolution may be said to have begun around 1865, corresponding in France to the last years of the Second Empire. The transformation of structures which it brought about resulted, in the closing years of the century, in a state of equilibrium characterized by steady expansion in industry and economic life, thus promoting art and literature at the same time.
A serious economic depression had occurred in England in 1876-1879, then on the continent in 1882-1885. Several spectacular financial crashes (Crédit Immobilier, 1873, and Union Générale, 1882) touched off a train of bankruptcies and led progressively to new economic concentrations; and so the first trusts appeared in Germany and the United States. The tentacular power of some of these industrial groups was such as to put them beyond government control; indeed, pressure from them was strong enough to bend the government to their will, not without creating scandals that burst occasionally into the open (like the Panama scandal in France in 1892).
As these huge industrial complexes grew, spreading out around immense plants with their exchange infrastructures and developing into gigantic workers' cities (the Krupp works at Essen is a characteristic example), the owners had to face social problems of ever growing magnitude. The close of the nineteenth century was the age of the great social laws. Government interference in the social sphere had at first been purely political: such, in France, were the press laws instituting freedom of expression (1881), the compulsory education law (1882) and the trade-union act legalizing unions (1884); such, in England, were the trade-union acts of 1871 and 1876, guaranteeing similar liberties.

The "Belle Epoque"

1890-1914

But the economic slump again brought to the fore the issue of workmen and masters. The growth of anarchism between 1882 and 1894, with the wave of bomb outrages in 1892-1894, showed how serious that issue was, calling for far-sighted legislation, not for stop-gap measures. Growing out of much earlier schemes, the workers' housing policy[1] first laid down in France in 1867 was displayed and demonstrated at the Exposition Universelle of 1889; it was followed up in 1894 by the passing of the first French law on low-cost housing.
For all the difficulties and delays attending workers' housing policy in France, the mere fact that such a policy now existed was decisive. It banished the spectre of revolution; it helped to integrate the working class into society as a whole; it raised the level of the proletariat by encouraging home ownership and participation in cultural benefits, placating the spirit of contestation. The Marxist theory of revolution was thus belied by the facts, while the aspiration towards a middle-class dignity became the driving force of social ascension; and this was a cultural phenomenon of essential importance.
Conflicts of interest between social classes were diminished at home, but were shifted into another sphere, into the policy of hegemony which carried the leading industrial countries into the colonial venture and later into war among themselves. Economic growth and social peace combined to impose a steady extension of markets, and in consequence an ever keener rivalry between producing countries. Protectionism and liberalism ensured the defence of national interests at home. Abroad it was another matter. Here the clash of interests was ruthless and by the 1880s economic warfare was endemic between contending empires. The Belle Epoque saw a permanent escalation of that clash which could only end in war.
Art benefited nevertheless from business prosperity, the extension of markets abroad, the prestige of the great entrepreneurs and the affluence of the upper classes. With it went a carefree holiday spirit that made the awakening all the more brutal, in the mud and blood of the trenches. For the collapse of European culture, after a century of flourishing industry, was caused not by wild hordes of revolting workers but by military arrogance arising from the uncontrolled clash of rival economic interests in a society dominated by the law of profit. Who could have foreseen such a downfall, just when art had achieved so enviable a place in society? For never before had the artist's work been so much admired and encouraged in Europe and America.

The triumph of the West

1

The relation existing between money and display slowly changed with the rise of industrial capitalism. The wealthy businessmen of the early eighteenth century were often satisfied with unpretentious houses, and in the interior decoration went no further than an opulent discretion; one thinks of the Genevese bankers, the shipowners of Saint-Malo, the wine merchants of Bordeaux. By 1900 it was otherwise. Luxury by then, and indeed for decades already, was no longer the apanage of aristocrats, it was flaunted by an international society whose names were widely known and publicized.

The international exhibitions and trade fairs, popular festivals of industry and consumption, had for thirty years been a privileged place of rendezvous. All the crowned heads paraded through them, also the great landowners, fund-holders and businessmen. At inaugurations and first nights, and in the fashionable cabarets, they met and mingled, coming together there as they came together at the other ceremonies of society life–at the roulette table in the continental casinos, in the palace hotels of fashionable watering-places, on the transatlantic liners.

2

The setting was everywhere the same, one of spectacular luxury. As against the great fitting up of city streets and squares typical of the Paris World's Fairs of 1878 and 1889, preference was given now to sumptuous but perishable décors, made up of wooden scaffoldings, painted canvases and staff, so many stage sets which turned the exhibition into a theatrical display, with all the elaborate machinery, light and water effects, and even costumed actors, that properly belong to the theatre.

The World's Columbian Exposition of 1893, in Chicago, was the first of its kind, an elaborate evocation of Venice and Rome, complete with artificial canals and lagoons, Baroque palaces by the lakeside, Berninian fountains, and domes, monumental arches and colonnades surpassing in extravagant grandeur anything seen before. In Paris, for the Exposition Universelle of 1900, the colossal riverside refreshment hall in the Champ-de-Mars and its electrical fairyland fulfilled a similar purpose, so well that one may wonder even now whether the Grand and Petit Palais, erected for the occasion, are real or imaginary buildings. Even the admirable gate by René Binet, at the beginning of the Cours-la-Reine, with its polychrome cabochons decorating the metal frame, has something outlandish, with its feverish rash of ornament.

When one sets out to entertain, one is not always very fussy about the choice of guests. The international society of 1900 was a mixed company of captains of industry, swindlers, parasites, aristocrats and upstart bourgeois, thrown together willy-nilly. Class distinctions no longer held good. The new social order was a plutocracy. Birth, whether high or low, mattered little. What mattered was income. (This is the society satirized in the stories of the woman writer known as Gyp, herself an aristocrat and descendant of

1. Paris: Exposition Universelle, 1900.
   Monumental gateway.
   Architect: René Binet.
2. Paris: Exposition Universelle, 1900.
   Palace of Electricity.
   Architect: Eugène Hénard.
   Fountain.
   Architect: Edmond Paulin.
   Le Panorama, 1900.

Mirabeau, representing the class now being overwhelmed by the men of wealth.) In France, in particular, anti-Semitic and anti-German prejudices were rife among these financiers and businessmen who had seized economic power from the *notables* of the past.

Architecture is indeed a permanent reflection of the class struggle, but not in the caricatural sense too often given to it. In terms of culture, the working class, at least in the nineteenth century, found no outlet of expression, had no right to one. If it had a culture of its own, deriving from its rural origins and such traditions as were maintained among immigrants to the big cities (among the Auvergnats in Paris, among Sicilians in New York), it was a residual culture, the still living trace of their struggle against proletarian alienation. So it is within the middle class, in the rivalry between social groups, that one must look for the significant social cleavages.

3

Chicago: World's Columbian Exposition, 1893.
3. Columbian Fountain.
Architect: Frederick MacMonnies.
4. General view of the fair buildings.

4

1

One of them is to be found in the conflict between the lavish display of palatial homes and the cheap picturesqueness of suburban villas.[2] Not only were there the rich and the others, but there were the rich and the less rich, vying with each other in a struggle for social recognition. This conflict was reflected in politics, as it was in journalism and literature. In France, from the time of the Dreyfus Affair (1894), die-hard intransigence and xenophobia became the detonators of a society threatened with disruption. It was only to be expected that architecture should become a party to these disputes.
Because, unlike literature, architecture is a luxury art, it is here that the differences are most revealing. Little is signified by subtle differences between styles of reference, one catering for the taste for display of the nouveau riche and imitating Art Nouveau, another going back to the more stately and decorous style of the Louis XVI period. The important thing to note, over and above any distinction between cultures of reference, is the unity which asserts itself in the art and architecture of the propertied classes and opposes them as a group to the lower middle class–a unity which imposes on the wealthy the paradoxical necessity of asserting their opulence as a demonstration of force. The art of the Belle Epoque is an art of display only made possible by money and pompously centred on fashionable ceremonies, like the return from the races, the promenade in the Bois de Boulogne, the outing in the country.

Paris: Hôtel Lutétia, 1910.
Architects: Louis-Henri Boileau
Hervé Tauzin.
1. Detail of the front.
5. View of about 1910.

2

It is a conventional art, in a Louis XV or Louis XVI style whose systematic décor of Rococo ornaments or beribboned fillets, whichever the client preferred, adapted itself to any circumstances.[3] The architect, reduced to the status of a decorator, simply organized the life setting of the upper classes: he supplied them with an elegant, superficial product, easily consumable. However luxurious, such work was inescapably stereotyped, imprisoned in a style of sameness common to the palace hotels and the office buildings of big companies. It is the very reverse of the bourgeois individualism with which the nineteenth century is generally credited.

This art, when not identified with the political power, could only refer back to convention. When culture ceases to be an instrument of creation, it becomes a system of exchange, a "password" between the members of one social group, acting as a means of exclusion, determining the contours of the group and isolating it from others. By keeping to an outmoded style, that of the eighteenth century, this art gave the ruling classes a comfortable sense of cultural monopoly. The Louis XV or Louis XVI style was to the fine arts what Latin was to literature: a powerful means of class identification, and also of class exclusion. Hence the eagerness with which the ascending bourgeoisie took over the classical style as soon as it could afford to do so.

3

4

2. Paris: Palace Hôtel des Champs-Elysées. Architect: Georges Chedanne. *La Construction Moderne*, 1899.
3. Madrid: Hotel Ritz, 1908. Architect: Charles Mêwès.
4. London: Piccadilly Hotel, 1905-1908. Architect: Richard Norman Shaw.

5

An architecture and decorative manner of pure convention, of pure ostentation, in which no hint of individualism is allowed to enter, is common to all the grand hotels of this period catering for the international set–so unmistakably common that it has been fittingly called the Grand Hotel style. On the individual level there were few who could vie with it. (One who did was a Monsieur Vaissier,[4] an immensely wealthy textile magnate who built an outlandish Palais du Congo at Tourcoing in Northern France, a monument of megalomania and bad taste.) A few touches of Art Nouveau, plenty of Louis XV, and classical forms taken from Gabriel and rehandled in the spirit of Lefuel: that sums up the formula as we find it in Paris in Georges Chedanne's elegant Palace Hotel on the Champs-Elysées and the powerful Hotel Lutétia of L. H. Boileau and Hervé Tauzin;[5] in London in Richard Norman Shaw's Piccadilly Hotel (the one owing most to Gabriel); in Madrid in the Ritz of Charles Méwès; at Nice in the Negresco of Edouard Niermans, and many, many more.

The recipes of the Beaux-Arts spirit, the French formula-loving spirit par excellence, were so effective and generally acceptable that they could be made to fit many types of buildings. From the grand hotel to the apartment block, the transition was imperceptible. It is true that the clientele was practically the same.

1. Budapest: Apartment house, Waitzen Boulevard. *La Construction Moderne*, 1895-1896.
2. Paris: Private house, No. 3, Square Rapp. Architect: Jules Lavirotte. *Die Architektur des XX. Jahrhunderts*, 1901.

3. Paris: Apartment building, 7, Rue Rembrandt and 51, Rue de Lisbonne. Architect: Gustave Rives. *Salons d'Architecture*, 1897.
4. Paris: Apartment building, Avenue des Champs-Elysées and Rue de Berri. Architect: Paul Friesé. *Moniteur de l'Architecte*, 1900.

The Parisian apartment house[6] of 1900 is one of the most luxurious in the world. Intended for well-to-do tenants, it was designed to attract them by the majesty of the façade, the beauty of the bonded stonework, the quality of the sculptures (including the human figure more and more often), the generous proportions of attic and roofing, the size of the drawing rooms, the scope given for interior decoration. Here, in this favoured field of urban architecture, even by way of a stereotyped idiom, the personality of the individual architect finds full expression. Turning the corner of a street, one readily recognizes the handiwork of Gustave Rives, Paul Friesé or Jules Lavirotte, who number among the most gifted practitioners of this virtuoso style so highly characteristic of the bourgeois Paris of 1900. That Lavirotte also flirted with Art Nouveau is a circumstance of secondary interest. He shared this liking for Art Nouveau with several other French architects, chief among whom is Georges Chedanne: see, for example, his very fine Hôtel Mercédès in the Avenue Kléber.
The French decorative style spread rapidly and gained an international status, thanks to its all-purpose simplicity. As a mere ornamental covering, its repertory of conventional forms could be made to fit any structure and extended to any scale. It could be applied equally well to metal construction or to reinforced concrete, which by now was widely used for flooring.

It was an art of facing, of revetment, and here the Beaux-Arts spirit revealed itself to be highly modern and close to the compositional devices of Art Nouveau, in which decoration was always conceived as an overlay and embellishment of form. The great interest of this French decorative style, thus acting as a revetment, lies in the fact that it answered better than any other to the technical requirements of modern construction. This is particularly true of office buildings, whose modern types were emerging at this very time, working themselves free from the traditional model of the bourgeois apartment building.

The creation of extensive floor spaces with thin partitions, which were often movable, called for ample lighting from the façade. Hence the increasing prominence of broad glass surfaces in office architecture, not only to provide the indispensable lighting but to emphasize the metallic structure of the building. Glass openings meant a loss of heat, but this drawback was compensated by technical advances in central heating with water-heated radiators.

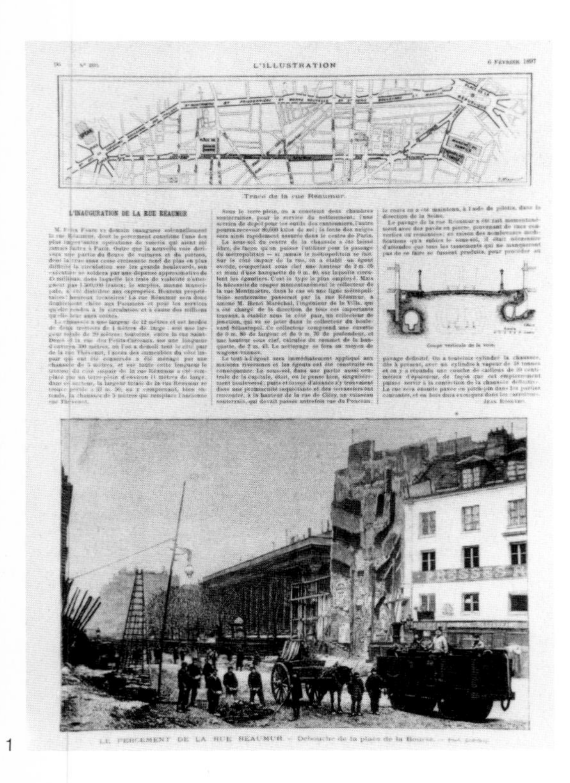
L'ILLUSTRATION

1

2

3

1. Paris: Opening of the Rue Réaumur, 1895-1896. *L'Illustration*, 1897.
2. Paris: Building at 132, Rue Réaumur, 1901. Architect: Jacques Hermant. *La Construction Moderne*, 1900-1901.
3. Madrid: La Equitativa Insurance Company, 1891. Architect: José Grases Riera.
4. Paris: View of the Rue Réaumur.
5. Paris: Winning design for the New York Life Insurance Building. Design by Georges Morin-Goustiaux and Paul-Alexis Lecardonnel.
6. Paris: Rue Caulaincourt and Rue Lamarck, 18th arrondissement. Pre-1914 view.

With the laying out of the Rue Réaumur in Paris in 1897, this street became an open-air laboratory of office architecture,[7] in a developing dialogue between classical pilasters and entablatures on the one hand and glass-faced fronts on the other–both in a characteristic post-Haussmannian style of domes and high barrel-roofing, whose sweeping protuberance emphasized the majestic volumes of these buildings, silhouetted at each intersection. The ones erected by Jacques Hermant (132, Rue Réaumur, 1901) and Charles Guirard de Montarnal (130, Rue Réaumur, 1898), both men award-winners in the first façade competition organized by the city of Paris, have some striking similarities not only with the apartment buildings of the residential quarters then in course of construction (at the corner of Rue Lamarck and Rue Caulaincourt in the 18th arrondissement, for example), but also with the big office buildings in other European capitals (La Equitativa, Madrid, by José Grases Riera, 1891). All these buildings are typical of the urban style of architecture that flowered around the turn of the century.

4

5

6

The more forceful office buildings of New York give that city a less coherent image, one suggestive, in European eyes at least, of that spirit of ruthless competition animating the world of liberal capitalism which they represent. And yet they belong to the same trend of architecture, with a similar emphasis on structure, a similar use of the classical repertory reduced to the revetment of form. Here the French Beaux-Arts spirit reappears as if clarified and amplified by a more direct translation of the needs and purposes of commercial architecture.
Innocent of any innovation in style (as if the still recent experiments of the Chicago School had never been), the New York skyscrapers of the early 1900s treat ornament as a mere covering texture, overlaying the main structural features as marked by the division of the skeleton support. This graphic schematism is common to the Hotel Plaza (Henry J. Hardenbergh, 1905-1907), the mammoth imitation of a Haussmannian building; to the strange "Flatiron" or Fuller Building of Daniel H. Burnham (1902), which is rather Farnesian; to the City Investing Building (Francis H. Kimball, 1908), with its Norman bell-tower roof; also to the Singer Building (Ernest Flagg, 1907-1908, demolished in 1967), the handsomest and most modern of them all in its straightforward use of the glass panel and the soaring lines of its silhouette.

2

1

1. New York: City Investing Building. Architect: Francis H. Kimball. *L'Architecte*, 1908.
2. New York: Hotel Plaza, 1905-1907. Architect: Henry J. Hardenbergh.
3. New York: Singer Building, 1907-1908. Demolished in 1967. Architect: Ernest Flagg.
4. New York: Fuller or Flatiron Building, 1902. Architect: Daniel H. Burnham.

3

4

The charms of leisure

1

Efficiency dictated the design of the New York skyscrapers of 1900, whose show of ornament does not take us much beyond the rudimentary (and is far removed indeed from the Art Deco fireworks of America in the 1920s). For the truth is that, in its sources and forms, Western art remains a purely European phenomenon. It is probably true, too, that the emphasis on artistic features in European architecture of this period was an instinctive reaction to the shift of economic power from Europe to America, a reassertion of cultural originality calculated to attract and hold a cosmopolitan elite of tourists and travellers susceptible to the image of Europe as the cradle of civilization. Emulation played its part in maintaining a high level of creativity and asserting European cultural superiority (so clearly reflected in the Swiss architectural debate over nationalism vs. internationalism).[8]

The distinctive image of the main European countries was crystallized in their railway stations, such as the neo-Baroque Gare d'Orsay (1898-1900) on the Seine embankment in Paris, designed by Victor Laloux (plagiarizing Lefuel) on lines anticipated by the French architects Blanc and Marcel who built the station in Bucharest (1894); or the austere Carolingian Romanesque chosen by Jürgen Kröger for the imperial station at Metz (1905-1908). It is a striking fact that from the refreshment room of Metz station to that of the Gare de Lyon in Paris, the same atmosphere prevails, created by the visual wealth of the mural revetments, the expanse of panoramic wall and ceiling paintings, the systematic dwarfing of the furniture by the size and decoration of the rooms and the powerful lighting. The solemn atmosphere has an almost religious inwardness (following the formula applied by Baltard to the Paris church of Saint-Augustin), tempered here by the palatial superabundance of large ornate frames.

2

3

Into this setting of academic grandiloquence, Art Nouveau made its way as if by accident–because it was the fashion of the day and an architecture of show and pomp could not help identifying itself with fashion. Characteristically, the creator (with Louis Majorelle) of the most admired Art Nouveau decoration in Paris (the interior of Chez Maxim's, Rue Royale, 1899) was Louis Marnez, a Parisian architect whose buildings in a frenzied Louis XVI style owe as much to Piranesi as they do to Neufforge and Delafosse. The Chez Maxim's decorations were more showy, but less fine than those done by Majorelle alone (Restaurant Lucas-Carton, Place de la Madeleine, 1905) or the shop-fronts of Charles Plumet and Tony Selmersheim.[9]

For the image of the Belle Epoque in France is not without ambiguity in its relation to history: if culture was a winning card, so was modernity. The international currents of Art Nouveau were continually overlapping with uninspired expressions of the

4

1. Paris: Gare d'Orsay, 1898-1900.
   Architect: Victor Laloux.
   Interior view.
2. Metz (Lorraine): Railway Station, 1905-1908.
   Architect: Jürgen Kröger.
   First-class waiting room.
3. Bucharest: Winning design for
   the Main Station, 1894.
   Architects: Louis-Pierre Blanc
   Alexandre Marcel.
   Salons d'Architecture, 1897.
4. Paris: Maxim's Restaurant, 1899.
   Architect: Louis Marnez.

1

academic style–as if the open reaction against Art Nouveau at the Exposition Universelle of 1900, where its forms were excluded,[10] had answered no purpose. It is true that the art language of modernity steadily pursued a parallel destiny to that of official art and that it succeeded in gaining the upper hand in the field of commercial architecture, by fulfilling one particular requirement: that of the big department store.[11]

Paris: The Printemps Department Store, 1881-1885.
Architect: Paul Sédille.
1. Dome and belvedere crowning the corner pavilions.
Encyclopédie d'Architecture, 1885.
3. View of the interior.
2. Milan: Galleria Vittorio Emanuele II, 1865-1867.
Architect: Giuseppe Mengoni.
Late 19th-century view.

Originating in the covered gallery housing a row of shops, the department store has an early model in the Galleria Vittorio Emanuele II in Milan (Giuseppe Mengoni, 1865-1867) and other precursors in Paris in Les Magasins Réunis (Gabriel Davioud, 1865-1867) and the Magasin au Bon Marché (L. A. Boileau, 1872-1874). The formula was fully worked out by Paul Sédille in the Magasin Le Printemps (1881-1885). The construction consisted of an undisguised steel skeleton, with no internal partition walls to cut off the view. The superimposed floor areas, patterned by slim iron columns, were well lit by natural light streaming in from the glass-panelled façades, and they were divided into a series of courts of various shapes, each covered by a large glass skylight.

2

3

4

5

4. Saint-Etienne (Loire): Nouvelles Galeries Department Store, 1894-1895. Architect: Léon Lamaizière.
5. Paris: Grand Bazar Department Store, 138, Rue de Rennes, 1906. Architect: Henri Gutton. *L'Architecte*, 1907.

This latter device (today abandoned on grounds of safety since it favoured the spread of fire) largely accounts for the beauty of Sédille's Printemps department store, by harking back to the original model, apparently very different, of the covered gallery. From the skylights came an influx of light, illuminating the colourful ranges of low counters and the lofty iron passerelles or bridges leading from court to court. Outside, the glass and steel envelope was patterned with a sculptured decoration of Florentine inspiration, embellished with mosaic panels and wrought iron, while each corner of the store was built out like a pavilion and domed. The department store with corner turrets became a recognized model in France, reproduced throughout the provinces in "Les Nouvelles Galeries" and "Les Dames de France," with endless variations, from the late nineteenth century (Léon Lamaizière at Saint-Etienne, 1894-1895) till after the First World War (Emmanuel Le Ray at Le Mans, 1923). In Paris a "streamlined" version of Sédille's department store was evolved by a greater insistence on the clarity of the structure and the transparency of the filling-in (Henri Gutton, Grand Bazar, Rue de Rennes, 1906, and Frantz Jourdain, La Samaritaine, 1905-1910).[12]

The thoroughgoing rationalism of Sédille's Printemps store, whose interior only owed its attractiveness to the quality of the light, answered to the aims set forth by Louis-Charles Boileau, when in 1876 he wrote in the *Revue d'Encyclopédie d'Architecture*,[13] with reference to the Bon Marché: "Light, instead of being made to play over plastic forms, should be opposed to itself in the ambient air circulating through the building; and, by allowing it to enter profusely or sparingly, it should go to create shimmerings or half-lights or reflections, making the daylight of the room space sparkle or glow, just as glass chandeliers are made to scintillate by the variety of cut-glass prisms. In this concert of light, the solid architecture will act as the setting does for a fine jewel: it will count in so far as it sets vibrating, with all possible intensity, this interior lighting which the glass surfaces and the half-lit depths beyond them will have made more inviting, more resonant, more rich and varied, than the pure and simple daylight outside."

This idea of 1876 was still strong enough to dominate the rotunda of the Galeries Lafayette (Ferdinand Chanut, 1910-1912). Even without its grand staircase, now demolished, this large glass dome bathing in a harmony of red and gold remains one of the finest, most satisfying interior spaces to be seen in Paris; the quality of the stucco and wrought-iron ornaments designed by Louis Majorelle amplifies its form and gives it that refinement of detail so often lacking in the academic style of the day (in the Gare d'Orsay, for example, where the style of Victor Laloux reveals its poverty of invention).

1

2

Paris: Galeries Lafayette Department Store, 1906-1912.
Architects: Georges Chedanne
Ferdinand Chanut.

1. Grand staircase. Demolished in 1974.
2. Glass dome.

1

2

The vogue of Art Nouveau in commercial architecture, vying with the academic repertory of bourgeois art, contaminated most of the buildings erected outside the great historic capitals, where classicism remained the rule. Combined with eclectic orientalizing formulas, the 1900 style invaded the seaside resorts, taking over from a trivial and hackneyed picturesqueness. The old antinomy between classical and picturesque, between urban and suburban, which had marked the architectural tradition since 1830, shifted now to another plane, one which opposed the frivolities of fashionable art, where any licence or abuse was permissible, to the serious and monumental character of urban art identified with public art.

By maintaining this opposition, the art of the early twentieth century kept closely to the cultural tradition which had arisen since the Romantic period. The deep-seated dualism of Reason and Feeling was maintained in this renewed form–in, it must be said, a very strange relation with the classicism and ideology which it represented (in this century of ours when no architect considers himself academic and every architect is to some extent). Drained by now of any lingering vitality, the classicism of 1900 was a ghost of its former self, looming up in a few columns erected here and there as meaningless quotations from the past.[14] Which is as much as to say–reversing the statement just made–that every architect had become an eclectic (if any meaning could still be attached to that term).

One might add that every architect had become a modern, because the technical and economic facts of the profession had completely

3

4

Nice: Casino. Demolished.
Architect: Henri-Eugène Meyer.
1. View from the Promenade.
4. View from the beach with breakers.

2. Vittel (Vosges): Casino, 1884-1885. Demolished.
Architects: Charles Garnier
Fernand Nachon.
View of 1886.

3. Monte Carlo: Casino, 1878-1879.
Architect: Charles Garnier.

1

changed and because the architecture of the industrial age had found its form, after three-quarters of a century of uneasy experimenting. But that modernity was accepted by architects with more or less of guardedness and applied with more or less success, according to the men and places concerned. The triumph of the Beaux-Arts style about 1900 and its easy conjunction with Art Nouveau is not to be explained in any other way. The formal Beaux-Arts style was, by its very superficiality, readily adaptable to the new requirements of the profession. It was no enemy of Art Nouveau but simply a competitor; it only remained to share out the market between them by prior agreement. The dialectics of urban and seaside architectue amply demonstrated this. In the architecture of recreation, both in the seaside resorts and the spas, the tradition of modernity already went back a long way (being found in full expression at Brighton in the early nineteenth century) and was strengthened now by examples of international renown. The double achievement of Charles Garnier at Vittel (casino and baths, 1884-1885) and at Monte Carlo (casino, 1878-1879) proved decisive, amplifying earlier examples like the casino at Arcachon, a masterpiece in the Moresque style (1862-1865, demolished).
Coming as the end-point of a whole building design developing on the urban scale, the casino became a focus of architectural

2

3

endeavour and effects. The "garden pavilion" of Arcachon became in Garnier's hands a palace adorned with sculptures, mural paintings and mosaics, and built out on the seaward side with a marvellous terrace. The beach which, at Biarritz or Deauville, still formed the focal point of the design (as the pump-room did at watering-places), gave way to the place of public amusement–the casino, containing café-restaurant and gaming saloons, and halls in which concerts, plays and public balls could be given. Where the cure had taken precedence before,[15] recreation took precedence now. The most sumptuous examples of these pleasure houses were the casino at Nice (unfortunately demolished) and the Kursaal at Ostend (Alban Chambon, 1898-1906), thanks to their unusual siting on the water or the dunes.

4

1. Biarritz (Basses-Pyrénées): View of the beach.

Ostend (Belgium): Casino, 1898-1906. Architect: Alban Chambon.

2. Design of the front, 1903.
3. View of the interior.
4. View of the Casino in the early 1900s.
5. Brighton (Sussex): Palace Pier, 1891-1901. Architect: St. John Moore.

5

Ernest Hébrard at Evian (Cachat Pump-Room, 1903) and François Lecoeur at Vichy (where the casino is connected with the covered walks of the wrought-iron designer Emile Robert, made for the 1889 Exposition Universelle in Paris and re-erected here in 1900) succeeded in combining architecture and urbanism in an ensemble of remarkable unity and irresistible charm; both kept to a moderate scale and set off the buildings with lawns and trees, relieving covered with open spaces. The formula worked out at Evian and Vichy culminated in the great covered gallery at Vittel (1897-1905, now no more), a steel and cast-iron construction put up by the Schertzer building company of Nancy, in front of the baths of Charles Garnier: under this light umbrella of iron, the fusion of architecture and landscape, as dreamt of from the time of the first winter gardens of 1830, was fully realized.[16]

The inventiveness poured so abundantly into the architecture of recreation is in marked contrast with the formalism of the Beaux-Arts style which, even though it triumphed in public art and in the city streets, never quite succeeded in carrying conviction. However one looks at it, there is always something stilted and hypocritical about this showy architecture. Too smugly representative of state power, it has the heaviness of a uniform. The architect of today can only shudder at this unrelieved mass of conventions, whereas he imagines with pleasure the grounds and buildings of the spas of 1900.

1. Poster for the mineral waters of Evian on the Lake of Geneva (Haute-Savoie).
2. Evian (Haute-Savoie): Cachat Pump-Room, 1859. Remodelled in 1903. Architect: Ernest Hébrard.

3

4

3. Vittel (Vosges): Covered Gallery, 1897-1905. Demolished. Builder: Schertzer & Co., Nancy.
4. Vichy (Allier): Covered Walks, 1900. Architect: François Lecœur. Wrought-iron by Emile Robert.
5. Poster for the Vittel springs. In the background, Vittel as it was around 1890.

5

Likewise with upper-class housing. There would be little point in surveying the French town houses of this period. Numerous though they are, they have no real interest. They are a compound of recopied forms, lifeless layouts and shabby details. Even the luxurious "Palais Rose" (the Hôtel de Sagan built by P. E. Sanson for Boni de Castellane in the Avenue Foch, Paris, and now demolished) was only an abridged copy of the Grand Trianon, with interiors taken over from Versailles, such as its reconstruction of the Escalier des Ambassadeurs, a finicking copy based on witness accounts of the seventeenth century. It is of interest only in so far as pastiche is interesting.

Where architects did find an outlet for imaginative expression, and also a good source of income, was the large residential villa. Here they worked for a wealthy clientele who gave them all facilities for this villa architecture–a far cry indeed from the meaner housing of the workers' suburbs.

As the heir not only of Viollet-le-Duc's country houses but of a whole scholarly tradition of picturesque architecture going back

1

2

3

1. Lausanne: Villa La Sauvagère, 1905-1906.
   Architect: Alphonse Laverrière.
   Watercolour by Laverrière, 1905.
   Biarritz: Villa Oceana, 1903.
   Architect: Henri Sauvage.
2. Interior view.
3. South front.
   Art et Décoration, 1904.

several centuries, the residential villa in France often attains to a size and complexity that in earlier times would have merited, and received, the name of château. It has all the characteristics of the château: the grounds, the outbuildings, the luxurious interior appointments integrating the conception of the furniture and of the objects of everyday life.

What was expected of the architect was invention, so that the nuances of this or that architectural style have no place here, apart from a distant allusion or an elegant echo in the wholly personal manner of the architect in charge.

A few successful works of this kind and the architect's reputation was made. A commission for a villa thus assumed as much importance in his eyes as one for a public building. The architects chosen, often among the most promising of the younger men,[17] generally made a name for themselves: Alphonse Laverrière in Lausanne (Villa La Sauvagère, 1905-1906), Henri Sauvage in Biarritz (Villa Oceana, 1903, oddly published later on as "Villa in Brittany"), or L. H. Boileau, who had built the Hôtel Lutétia in Paris and whose monumental "Artist's House by the Sea" (1908) was no doubt not merely imaginary. As if by chance, all these men were among the most prominent exponents of Art Nouveau in France.

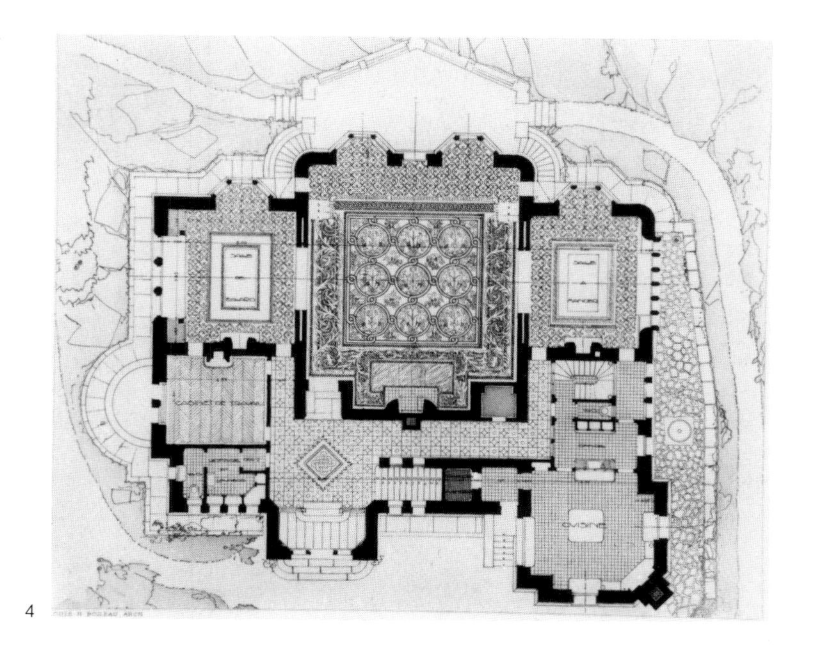

4

"Artist's House by the Sea."
Architect: Louis-Henri Boileau.
4. Ground-floor plan.
5. Front elevation.
L'Architecte, 1908.

5

Country life

The summer stay in the country was an integral part of upper class life in France of the Belle Epoque. For two generations, it had been the custom to alternate between two homes: winter in town, summer on one's estate. The move to the country was no small affair, involving as it did the whole family and domestic staff, and once installed there was a continual coming and going of friends, together with the ritual round of visits to neighbouring châteaux for courtesy calls, a shoot, a betrothal, an entertainment.[18]
Long since converted to business and drawing its wealth from there, aristocratic society maintained its provincial rank for reasons of both prestige and interest. Show was a habit, but also a necessity. In the hierarchy of notables, the great families were the interpreters and representatives on the national level of a whole local network of influences. It was important to keep in touch with local affairs and take part in them personally, attending to requests and complaints, and bringing them to a successful issue through one's own network of contacts. Existing alongside the industrial structure of the modern economy, this personalized system of politics operating through the notables, the men of name and distinction, lingered on for a surprisingly long time in old Europe, where the aristocrat's power of intervention and mediation remained strong (for his class was the focus of high society and therefore the most influential). It often happened, moreover, that the hierarchy of the notables was closely copied by the political structure of local or regional institutions.
The rebuilding of one's château was generally decided on as a means of reasserting one's local power and prestige, now threatened by changing mental habits.[19] The owner was able to do so thanks to the financial affluence he drew from business profits. Rebuilding, embellishing, enlarging, was important because the château was the very symbol of his social status. As such, the château must not look like a villa (even though it might well cost less to build or rebuild than some of the great villas). It had to be historic, since the aristocrat's legitimacy was sanctified by history, and it became archaeological because archaeology was thought to offer the only guarantee of authenticity.
But all too often it was a fanciful archaeology, and this for two reasons. First, because the estate owner set out to transform a comfortless ruin into a fine family residence fitted with all the luxury to which he was accustomed in town. Secondly, because he cared little about the specific architectural forms peculiar to the region; his reference models were those of a popularized culture, taken from dictionaries or encyclopaedias offering a very sketchy picture of architectural history. For the French aristocrat, the style of his château had to be that of the castles on the Loire (for his English counterpart, it had to be Perpendicular or Tudor).

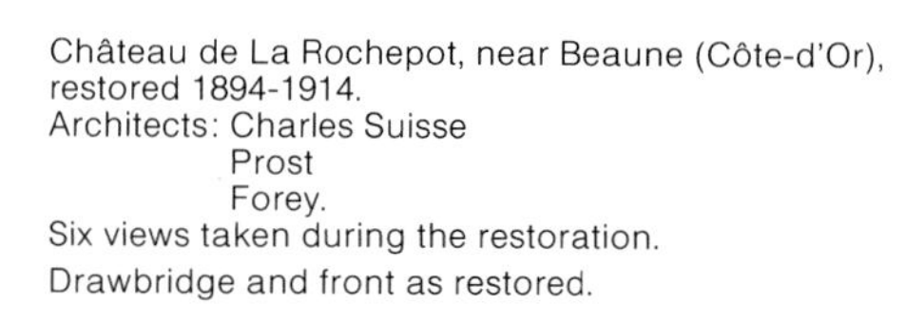

Château de La Rochepot, near Beaune (Côte-d'Or), restored 1894-1914.
Architects: Charles Suisse
Prost
Forey.
Six views taken during the restoration.
Drawbridge and front as restored.

1

2

To this meagre cluster of references was added the impact of an unchallenged model: the château of Pierrefonds as restored by Viollet-le-Duc. The twofold language he employed here (half way between a modern idiom, stemming from a critical rereading of medieval architecture, and an imaginative idiom stemming from an archaeological scholarship) was amplified by each reinterpretation of it, until the French château of the early twentieth century became a pure architectural invention. What the owner would never have tolerated for his town house, he was delighted with in the country. His château was the release of dream and fancy from the constraints imposed elsewhere by social standing, by breeding, by good form.[20]

Two French examples may be taken from the Allier region: Thoury and La Rochepot. An abandoned manor, Thoury was purchased in the later nineteenth century by the Comte de Bourbon-Chalus, a distant descendant of the famous Connétable de Bourbon. His purpose was to make it his summer residence, in a region where he owned extensive tracts of land and forest. The count applied first to a local architect, Alexis Besson of Moulins, who submitted five designs between 1881 and 1885, all calling for a complete reconstruction. Dissatisfied with them, he finally turned in 1889 to the Parisian architect Paul Selmersheim, inspector general of Historic Monuments and "diocesan"[21] of Moulins, and the work was carried out in 1890-1891. Preserving the original structure, Selmersheim remodelled the sixteenth-century square tower in the style of a fourteenth-century keep, remotely derived from regional

examples, and at the back of the original château he added a complex of galleries and a staircase whose design was taken from the Louis XII wing of the château of Blois. The result was a severe, monumental restyling of French Gothic. Nothing picturesque was attempted or lapsed into; each form fits smoothly into the overall pattern, making the whole in effect a pure product of rationalism. The odd thing is that this drastic restoration strikes one now as fundamentally unsound. To the practised eye, the continual allusion to other work is unsettling (the stairway modelled on that of a chapter house in Moulins, for example), while some reconstructed details of the keep are fairly comical.
The wealth of archaeological reference proved in the end self-defeating. A disciple of Viollet-le-Duc and father of one of the finest Art Nouveau artists, Paul Selmersheim was nevertheless a skilled and interesting architect.
The château of La Rochepot was restored by the widow of Sadi Carnot, president of the French Republic, as a tribute to the memory of Carnot (assassinated in 1894 by the anarchist Caserio). The architect in charge was a well-known personality of that day, Charles Suisse, who was chief architect of the Monuments Historiques, based in Dijon, and so a colleague of Selmersheim and also of Anatole de Baudot.

Château de Thoury, near Moulins (Allier), restored 1890-1891.
Architect: Paul Selmersheim.
1. View at the present time.
2. Restoration design. Watercolour by Selmersheim.
3. View of the staircase.

3

1

Château de Haut-Koenigsbourg (Vosges),
restoration completed in 1908.
Architect: Bodo Ebhardt.

Another interesting reconstruction of this period was that of the medieval castle of Haut-Koenigsbourg in Alsace (then part of the German Reich), carried out from 1908 on at the personal behest of Kaiser Wilhelm II by the German architect Bodo Ebhardt. The guiding purpose here was to restore to something like its original splendour one of the finest examples of the great medieval halls of the fifteenth century. The hall of Haut-Koenigsbourg was analysed by Viollet-le-Duc in his *Dictionnaire de l'Architecture* (s.v. Construction), in which he also analysed its defences (s.v. Château).[22] But in all this work there is something naïve and touching about the exaggerated concern for "authentic" detail, the misguided search for a "colourful" medievalism, which in the end defeats all the scholarship and skill that went into these restorations. Between the architect and his patron, there was an unconscious complicity in keeping up the sham and turning the historical evocation into something almost hallucinating, for their vision of the past was, inescapably, the vision of 1900. These "historic castles" were the fruit of an imagination which one is tempted to describe now as surrealistic. They are one more of the illusions endemic in the Belle Epoque.

2

1. Restored view from the south and castle ruins before restoration. Drawing by Bodo Ebhardt.
2.4. Inauguration in 1908 in the presence of Kaiser Wilhelm II.
3.5. Views of the castle at the present time.

3

4

5

Winter on the Riviera

1

The "Grand Hotel" is a feature of the Belle Epoque, particularly on the French Riviera where the international set spent the winter, at Cannes, Nice, Monte Carlo. Catering for this clientele, the big hotels continued to be built and rebuilt up to the First World War, each vying with the other in its sumptuous interior arrangements, with decorations commissioned from well-known artists.

The design of the grand hotel is unlike that of any other building: an endless alignment of individual rooms, which meant over-large corridors and repetitive façades (in other words, a barracks architecture, more or less enriched); and a monumental enlargement of lounges and saloons, to give the random collection of wealthy guests an appropriate setting for its entertainments.

The external design, dating from the Second Empire,[23] was that of a gigantic pie, its mass overweighting the environment, the tiered windows somewhat attenuating its impact. By the device of projecting parts and many-sided domes, inspired by French châteaux, an illusion of grandeur was for a long time obtained. Then the apartment building supplied a fresh model: a serried rhythm of bow windows *à la parisienne* (Hotel Carlton, Cannes) was completed with a classical corner rotunda, as in Paul Sédille's Printemps department store in Paris.

This stereotyped shell left the builder a free hand for the magnificent interior settings,[24] like the glazed saloon of the Hermitage at Monte Carlo, the columned lounge of the Regina at Cimiez (Nice), the winter garden of the Gallia at Cannes. A succession of saloons in different historical styles created a spectacular ensemble, whose overall effect depended on a cunning modulation of styles and an ever changing play of light and colour. Here the Beaux-Arts style reached its peak: while Sébastien-Marcel Biasini, who built the Regina at Cimiez (1896) was a pupil of Charles-Auguste Questel and so still belonged to the academic generation of the Second Empire, other men like Charles Dalmas, a pupil of Victor Laloux and builder of the palaces of Henri Rühl (Carlton at Cannes, 1909-1913), or Edouard Niermans, who built the Negresco at Nice, are perfect representatives of the *style pompier* of the Ecole des Beaux-Arts, whose stereotypes they repeated again and again–not without a certain pungency, it must be admitted.

2

1. Nice: Hôtel Negresco, 1912. Architect: Edouard Niermans. Poster by V.M. Lorant.
2. Nice: Hôtel Excelsior Regina at Cimiez, 1896. Architect: Sébastien-Marcel Biasini. Entrance hall.
3. Cannes: Hôtel Carlton, 1909-1910 and 1912-1913. Architect: Charles Dalmas.

3

4. Monte-Carlo: Hôtel
Architecte: Jean.
Dining-room.

Floating palaces

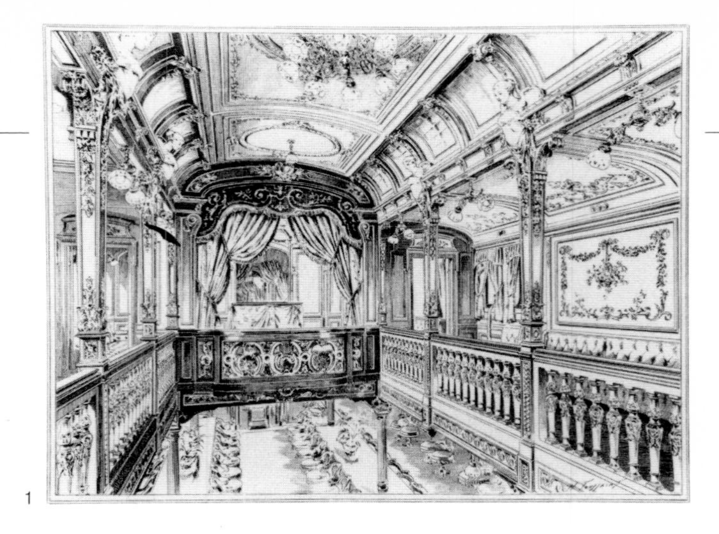
1

The weekly crossings of the great transatlantic liners[25] offered a life very much like that of the fashionable spas. During the week at sea the first-class passengers lived a life of ease and evening entertainments in a setting hardly distinguishable from that of the grand hotels–if anything, even more sumptuous, to compensate for the narrow confines of the sea-bound liner.
The "France," launched in 1912, accommodated 2,526 persons, including a crew of 500, 800 steerage passengers and 534 first-class passengers. The "Fürst Bismarck," launched at Hamburg in 1914, could accommodate 3,145. The differences in comfort from one class to the other were very marked. A self-contained world in itself, the liner offered a cross-section of civilization. It had everything on board: an engine-room as big as a factory, where the bunker-hands fed coal day and night into overheated boilers; stables and poultry-yards, penning in the live animals that went to feed the passengers; immense kitchens and immense sleeping cabins where steerage passengers were huddled together; and the sumptuous midship saloons and staterooms and promenade decks reserved for first-class passengers, secured from intrusion by padlocked bars and grating.
The empire of luxury and its pampered guests occupied the centre of the liner, whose immense flanks enclosed the stately, imperial staircases giving access to the dining room, the smoke-room, the rotunda of the music room, the indoor swimming pool. Marble and stucco covered the floors, walls and ceilings, giving the illusion of a castle interior, which might be of the Louis XVI period, as in the elegant rotunda of the "France," or in the Rococo style, as in the dining room of the "Fürst Bismarck," whose essential role however remained the same: to set a standard and provide an aperçu and epitome of European culture for the liner's international clientele.

2

3

4

5

1. Internal appointments of the French liner "Le Chili." Architect: Girette. *La Construction Moderne*, 1895-1896.
2. The Hamburg-American liner "Fürst Bismarck," 1914. The dining-room.
3. The French liner "France," 1912. Dome of the three staircases leading to the first-class dining-room.
4. The White Star liner "Celtic," 1902. First-class Saloon.
5. The French liner "La Gascogne." Saloon.

An art patron's villa

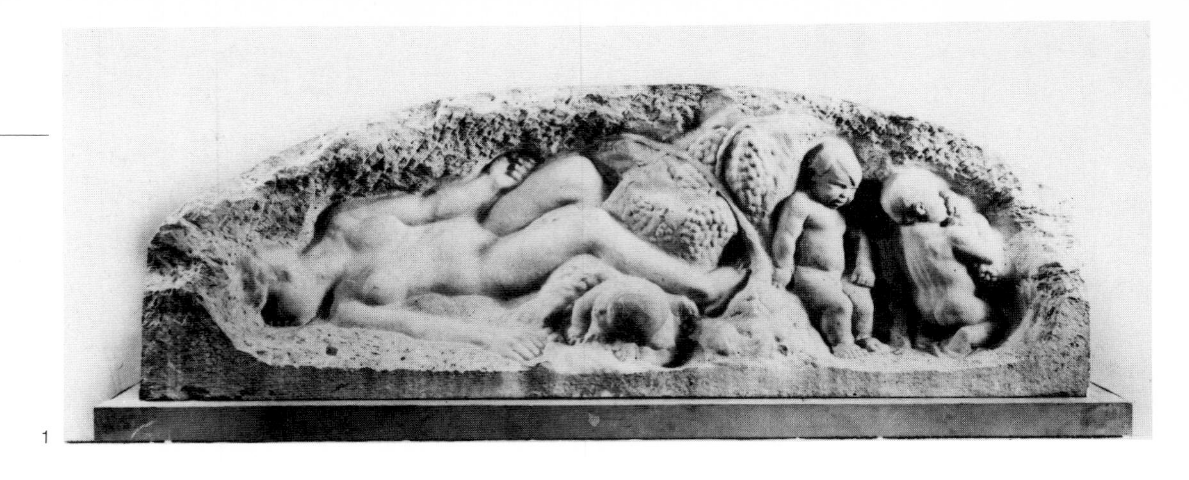

1

In its oddities, and the eye-filling redundancy of its ornamentation, the art of 1900 was an extension of certain marginal experiments of the previous generation. Only a public of connoisseurs was capable of recognizing the stylistic quotation made at a second remove, the incoherent continuation of a sequence, the hidden discordance of the artist's intentions. Begun in 1892 for Baron Jonas Vitta, a wealthy Lyonese banker, the Villa La Sapinière at Evian, on the French shore of the Lake of Geneva, was continued after his death by his son Joseph Vitta, who commissioned its interior decoration from Jules Chéret, Félix Bracquemond, Alexandre Charpentier, Auguste Rodin and Albert Besnard.[26]
The architect was Jean-Camille Formigé,[27] who had collaborated with Ballu on the Hôtel de Ville in Paris and designed the Columbarium in the Père-Lachaise Cemetery (1889-1907). It was Formigé, too, who later built the greenhouses of the Fleuriste Municipal in Paris (1899-1901) and designed the ornamentation of the overhead Métro viaducts. He also had a busy career as architect of historic monuments in France (restoration of Saint-Denis and the Roman theatre at Orange).
The design of La Sapinière is one of skilfully contrived incoherence, built up around a Palladian structure distorted by the independence and non-correlation of the façades–a conglomerate of Louis XIII and Florentine styles, with a bell-turret taken over from the Villa Medici in Rome, a heavy outlay of ornament and bays in some cases out of scale (each rupture expressing a functional element of the plan).
The interior decoration is the fruit of an incongruous combination of artists: Chéret and Bracquemond, with Falguière (for the busts on the front) and Rodin (for the doors of the entrance hall, whose pediments emerge painfully from a mass of white stone), together with the unlikely presence of Albert Besnard. Formigé's classicism might have been expected to clash with the modern taste of Baron Vitta. It did, and the friction between them created the not unpleasing duality of the final outcome. What dominates is contradiction, the clash of opposing temperaments. No positive message is anywhere to be found: art here is its own undoing, weighted down by forms whose aestheticism is as refined as it is inaccessible.[28]

2

3

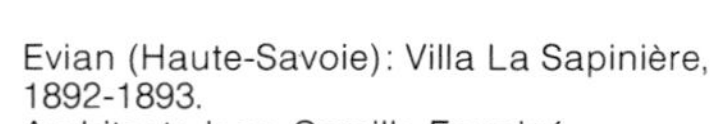

Evian (Haute-Savoie): Villa La Sapinière, 1892-1893.
Architect: Jean-Camille Formigé.
1. *Autumn.* Pediment frieze by Rodin for one of the doorways.
2.3. Terracotta reliefs by Alexandre Falguière.
4. West front.

4

5

5. Decoration by Jules Chéret
for the billiard room, 1897.

The nineteenth century had been the century of history–a backward sweep through time made necessary by an upheaval so far-reaching as to shake the cultural structures that had stood for ages. The twentieth was to be the century of modernity unfolding at a headlong pace as one avant-garde "ism" succeeded another, each quickly overtaken by a new and still more radical stance. This artistic "escalation" was already in full swing in the first decade of the century and the rhythm of change grew faster and faster.

In the debate between art and history, the gap between them steadily widened. On the one hand, pastiche and imitations of the past,[1] some of them tantamount to forgery, even reproducing details of patina and weathering. On the other, an aggressive modernity, a deliberate refusal of history and culture.

Since the romantic age, the controversy over architectural design had developed on the lines of an ideological dualism, opposing decorative historicism first to classical rationalism, then to Gothic and subsequently to other styles–until the day came when, by a surprising reversal, academicism arose out of a rigid adherence to archaeology, while the appeal to history as a cultural patrimony opened the way to a new art untrammelled by imitation.

But this trend had not worked itself out. From Art Nouveau itself sprang that decorative formalism which enabled men like Hankar, Wright, Van de Velde, even Sauvage, to go beyond Art Nouveau, in a current of internal opposition which led some of the great builders of the period to review their work and aims in a radical spirit of self-criticism.

Modern times

Modernity might have seemed the natural outcome of this long debate between art and history. To suppose so, however, is to forget two things. First, the fact that down to the mid-twentieth century the chief works of architecture continued to stem from a historicist tradition increasingly impoverished and barren.[2] Secondly, the conflict which during that same period steadily opposed the upholders of modernism to the upholders of culturalism (essentially regionalist).

As the gap between them widened, the dialogue between art and history became more difficult and more complex; it could not be otherwise between a multitude of contradictory attitudes. The twentieth century is the century of ideological warfare, of a ceaseless clash between artistic factions, each committed to a position and programme often more political than artistic. When architecture, rather than ethical, became militant, it reflected all the shades of the political spectrum, which it transposed metaphorically in terms of style. Thus the conflict between past and present was turned into the conflict between left and right.[3]

Twentieth-century architecture experienced the ordeal of a war of styles: politically, when the neo-classicism of Albert Speer confronted the modernism of Erich Mendelsohn; socially, when the avant-gardism of Le Corbusier encountered the popular blandishments of Art Deco or the conventional regionalism of a seaside resort (sometimes scarcely regional at all, so marked are its stereotypes). Many different kinds of regionalism (from Antoine Pompe to Clemens Klotz, from the suburban workers' homes in Brussels to the Ordensburgs of Hitler's Germany) stand opposed to many different kinds of modernism (those, for example, in Paris alone, of Le Corbusier, Perret, Sauvage, Roger Expert and Michel Roux-Spitz,[4] which can scarcely be said to belong to the same movement). And to these dualities can be added others, like that between regionalism and Art Deco.

The ideological war thus begins with the problem of modernism as an architectural axiom. It was crystallized around the two issues of social housing and the relation to industry. In the first, the cultural preoccupation remained very much alive (most obviously in the general distaste for modernity).[5] In the second, the machine aesthetic prevailed, with the result that once again, for half a century, architecture found itself in the deadlock of formalism. In other words, the debate between art and history is still undecided.[6]

Architecture on the art market

1

At the end of a long evolution, which had carried him far from his initial role as a master mason, the architect stood on an equal footing with the men of the other liberal professions, as a specialist in both the artistic demands of his job and the day-to-day supervision of the buliding site. By the beginning of the twentieth century, the architect was at the same time an inspector, controlling the building site financially and technically in the interest of his client, and an artist in the noblest sense of the term. His was thus an ambiguous position, and he did not gain by it. As a social actor, he always tended to emphasize his role as an artist, enjoying the favourable image attaching to that role, while in real economic terms his position has been that of a superintendent. His professional status links him rather with the tradesman dependent on a circle of customers; to create or widen that circle, his image as an artist is useful and necessary to him.

The artist-architect made his professional breakthrough in France at the end of the nineteenth century, after a century of gestation in the schools among the painter-architects trained by the revolutionary Academy, or among the amateurs, antiquaries and collectors of the romantic period. Present from the start in the annual Paris Salons, he now entered the art galleries where he exhibited and sold his designs. He had long been a practising engraver, both as a means of diffusing his projects and of producing an œuvre of his own, in the way initiated by Piranesi in the eighteenth century. Building was only a part of his architectural activity. The project, the counter-project, and the private dream became as important for him as building, for the idealized image of the design was better suited than the building itself to the selective diffusion of the media (at least until photography came of age as an interpretative instrument).

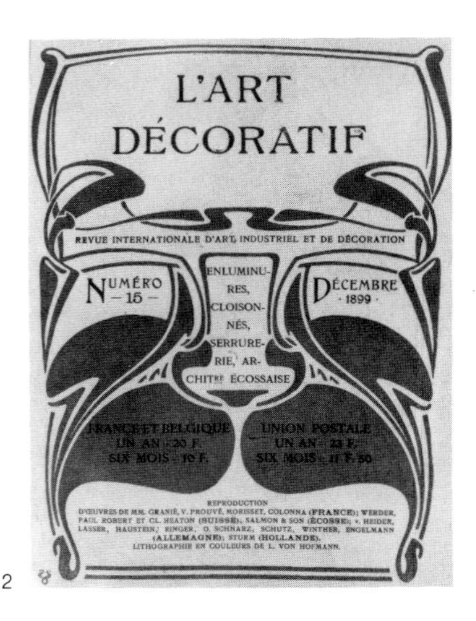

2

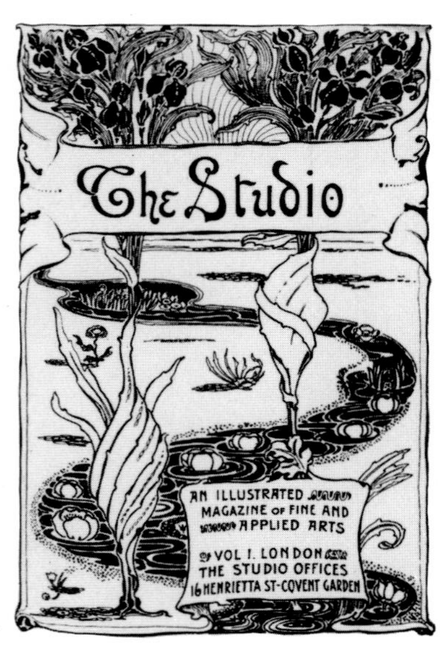

3

As an image-maker, the architect exhibited and sold his designs –Van de Velde at "La Libre Esthétique," Hankar at "Le Sillon," Sauvage and his friends of the Atelier Pascal at the Le Barc de Boutteville gallery. The dealers and places of exhibition were the same ones that catered for the Post-Impressionist painters.[7] Samuel Bing, the great promoter of Japanese art, who called his Paris gallery the "Salon de l'Art Nouveau," specialized in the diffusion of architecture and interior decoration; the building[8] in which, alongside works of applied art, he exhibited the designs of Selmersheim, Plumet and Van de Velde, was remodelled for him in 1895 by Louis Bonnier.

The close connection between the promotion of Art Nouveau and the promotion of architecture, in the galleries and art magazines, was due to the total character of designs which, in one and the same project, embraced object, furniture, building and city. So it is not surprising to find architects taking a prominent part in the activity of the Brussels art galleries in the 1890s, then in the galleries of Paris, Berlin and Vienna. Collaboration was sometimes

1. Cover of *Deutsche Kunst und Dekoration*, Darmstadt, 1900.
2. Cover of *L'Art Décoratif*, Paris, 1899.
3. Cover design for *The Studio*, London, 1893.
4. Poster by Félix Vallotton for the Art Nouveau exhibition at the Bing Gallery, Paris (opened in 1895).

4

very close and personal. Thus Louis Majorelle became a priviliged client of Henri Sauvage after their common experience of the Café de Paris in 1899; Sauvage built two villas for him, at Nancy and Compiègne, before designing the main office building of Majorelle's firm in Paris in 1913 (in an austere style contrasting with the notion one usually has of the style cultivated by the School of Nancy).
Architecture was diffused through the international art magazines: *The Studio* in London, *Dekorative Kunst* in Munich, *Deutsche Kunst und Dekoration* in Darmstadt (with its foreign-language editions, *Arts décoratifs modernes* in France and *Arte decorativa moderna* in Italy), and *Art et Décoration* in Paris. All these magazines carried reports on contemporary architecture, often featuring the products of Art Nouveau; the latter, on the other hand, is not well represented in the specialized architectural magazines of the period.

5. Paris: Majorelle Office Building, 1913.
Architect: Henri Sauvage.
Assistant: Charles Sarazin.
Detail of the front.

5

1

2

The latest and most effective means of familiarizing the public with contemporary architecture were the great international exhibitions. The organizers now turned to architects for all matters connected with interior decoration (hitherto reserved, as Hankar put it with wry humour, for "upholsterers" alone). At the Brussels World's Fair of 1897, Paul Hankar headed the group of architects, including Serrurier-Bovy and Van de Velde, who were asked to design and instal the galleries of the colonial section at Tervueren. The success he scored here ran counter to the then triumphant international "Beaux-Arts" style, a triumph sarcastically commented on by Frantz Jourdain: "I leave to others the patriotic but painful task of praising to the skies the incongruous heap of buildings in plaster, pasteboard, papier mâché and sham-sublime which go to make up the Exposition Universelle of 1900 [in Paris]. This sugar-candy and wedding-cake architecture is shameless in its cynicism, it is an insult to both good taste and common sense." [9]

3

4

It was a contradictory situation indeed, when official art could display such a sorry regression, while the architecture of the future was being promoted in priviliged circles. At the Paris Exposition of 1900, Art Nouveau was only represented by a few isolated buildings, like that of Loie Fuller or that of Louis Majorelle designed by Sauvage, or the Pavillon Bleu restaurant designed by Serrurier-Bovy[10] (Art Nouveau, as a popular style then in fashion, being considered acceptable for a restaurant). The triumph of Art Nouveau only came a couple of years later at the International Exhibition of Modern Decorative Art in Turin in 1902; and in fact the aesthetic tendencies manifested here amounted to a radical critique of the decorative excesses which in France had just been dubbed *le style nouille* (noodle style).

Art Nouveau was seen at the time as the offspring of a momentary alliance between the expanding international art market and the prevailing taste for a certain formula of commercial architecture–a formula embodied by big department stores and luxury shops. This alliance accounted for its immediate success, but confined it within the limits of a passing fashion and a decorative frivolity which at its best it far transcended. Some architects persisted in developing it (Horta and Guimard); others veered away from it (Sauvage and Wagner). The fact is that its commercial success was

1. Brussels: World's Fair of 1897. Colonial section at Tervueren. Ethnographic gallery designed by Paul Hankar.
2. "Paul Hankar, architect," 1894. Poster by Adolphe Crespin. Colour lithograph.

Paris: Exposition Universelle, 1900.

3. Stained-glass window by Georges de Feure for the Bing Art Nouveau Pavilion. *L'Art Décoratif*, 1900.
4. The Blue Pavilion Restaurant designed by Gustave Serrurier-Bovy. *Le Panorama*, 1900.
5. Design for an exhibition pavilion for the firm of Majorelle. Watercolour drawing by Henri Sauvage.

5

fatal to the message that Art Nouveau was intent on delivering; and the architects, catering for a consumer society whose workings they did not understand, were caught in the trap of their own success.

So it is that Art Nouveau represents but a brief moment in the work of men whose achievement is unquestionable. The career of Hector Guimard, which began in 1895 with his trip to Brussels and the Ecole du Sacré-Cœur in the Avenue de la Frillière, culminated in 1897 with the block of flats in Paris known as Castel Béranger and practically ended in 1909 with the Hôtel Guimard in the Avenue Mozart. And in fact by 1903-1904 he had turned away sharply towards a formula whose somewhat Gothic elegance owes much to Plumet and Selmersheim.

1

2

3

4

Paris: The Castel Béranger
apartment building, 1894-1897.
Architect: Hector Guimard.

1. Offices of Hector Guimard.
2. Detail of the front.
3. Front on the Rue de la Fontaine.
   Lithograph.
   Le Castel Béranger, 1899.
4. Entrance hall and door.

1

2

If Henri Sauvage showed more stamina than Guimard, the reason is that, starting from Nancy under the influence of a School of Applied Arts dominated by Emile Gallé and Victor Prouvé, he succeeded in overcoming the determinism of the Art Nouveau style by gradually imposing his own ideas on his client. Sauvage was not a native of Nancy; he began his career in his father's firm, designing wallpaper for the Castel Béranger. It was through Jacques Majorelle, his fellow student at the Ecole des Beaux-Arts, that Sauvage met the latter's brother, Louis Majorelle, a well-established decorator and furniture designer at Nancy, and was commissioned to build a villa for him. The style created by this association of architect and decorator, one of great expressive power, gave its true meaning to the architectural output of the School of Nancy,[11] and shaped the evolution of Emile André and Lucien Weissenburger for a decade to come; whereas Sauvage himself, after a long period of critical reflection on decorative style (worked out in tectonic designs intended for the book *Eléments d'Architecture Moderne* of 1910, but not published), turned towards a more systematic rationalism.

3

4

5

1. Portrait of Emile Gallé, 1892.
   Painting by Victor Prouvé.
2. Nancy (Lorraine): Huot House, 1903.
   Architect: Emile André.
   Carriage entrance.

   Nancy (Lorraine): Louis Majorelle House, 1901-1902.
   Architect: Henri Sauvage.
   Furniture and wrought iron designed by Louis Majorelle.
   Painter-decorator: Victor Prouvé.
3. Overall view.

5.6. Details.

4. Drawing by Sauvage for *Eléments d'Architecture Moderne* by Henri Sauvage and Charles Sarazin (1910), unpublished.

6

Art Nouveau was by no means confined to France. With Japanese overtones it was cultivated in Germany by August Endell in his Elvira Photo Studio in Munich (1899-1900), where he gave free rein to his decorative extravagance (on themes whose fanciful aspect is literary, while the formal means are purely theatrical). It is exemplified by two major works by Otto Wagner in Vienna: the Stadtbahn station in the Karlsplatz (1898) and the Majolika Haus (1898-1899). The Karlsplatz metropolitan railway station, with its ironwork and polychrome fillings, owed something to Formigé's buildings at the 1889 Exposition Universelle in Paris, also to the skyscrapers of Sullivan and the recent exhibition at Tervueren (Brussels) which, for Wagner, had been a revelation. He remained in fact very close to Paul Hankar, in particular to the latter's Ciamberlani House; the latter's black-and-white work façade influenced the façade design of the Majolika Haus. Only the details of this house in Vienna take over the forms of Art Nouveau and its whiplash line.

1

2

3

4

5

1. Munich: Door in the "Room of an Art Lover."
   Architect: Richard Riemerschmid.
   Deutsche Kunst und Dekoration, 1900.

   Vienna: Karlsplatz city railway station, 1898-1899.
   Architect: Otto Wagner.
2. Perspective views.
   Watercolour drawing by Wagner, 1898.
3. Detail of the entrance.
4. Munich: Elvira Photo Studio, 1899-1900.
   Architect: August Endell.
   Hall.
   L'Art Décoratif, 1900.
5. Düsseldorf: Dwelling house with shops, 1901.
   Architect: G. Wehling.
   Die Architektur des XX. Jahrhunderts, 1901.

Comparison of Wagner's buildings with what was being done in Germany (for example, the vaguely Hankarian apartment house of G. Wehling, Düsseldorf, 1901) shows the extent to which both Wagner and Hankar took a critical view of Art Nouveau,[12] avoiding the facile decorative effects which so many others indulged in. And this accounts for the fact that, after Hankar's death in 1901, the Viennese movement assumed the leading role well attested by the illustrations in *Ver Sacrum*, the periodical of the Vienna Secession. (The one reproduced here is by Koloman Moser, the sculptor who collaborated with Otto Wagner.)
The way forward was more difficult for those interior decorators who wished to be more than "upholsterers." Such was the case with those Art Nouveau artists who realized that its decorative style was merely one more aspect of the current style of their time, against which they were led to react in one way or another. One of those most painfully aware of the vulgarity of their time was Henry Van de Velde, a versatile artist from Antwerp. Trained as a painter,

Brussels: House of the painter Ciamberlani, 1897.
Architect: Paul Hankar.
1. Detail of the front.
2. Design for the front. Drawing by Hankar.

1

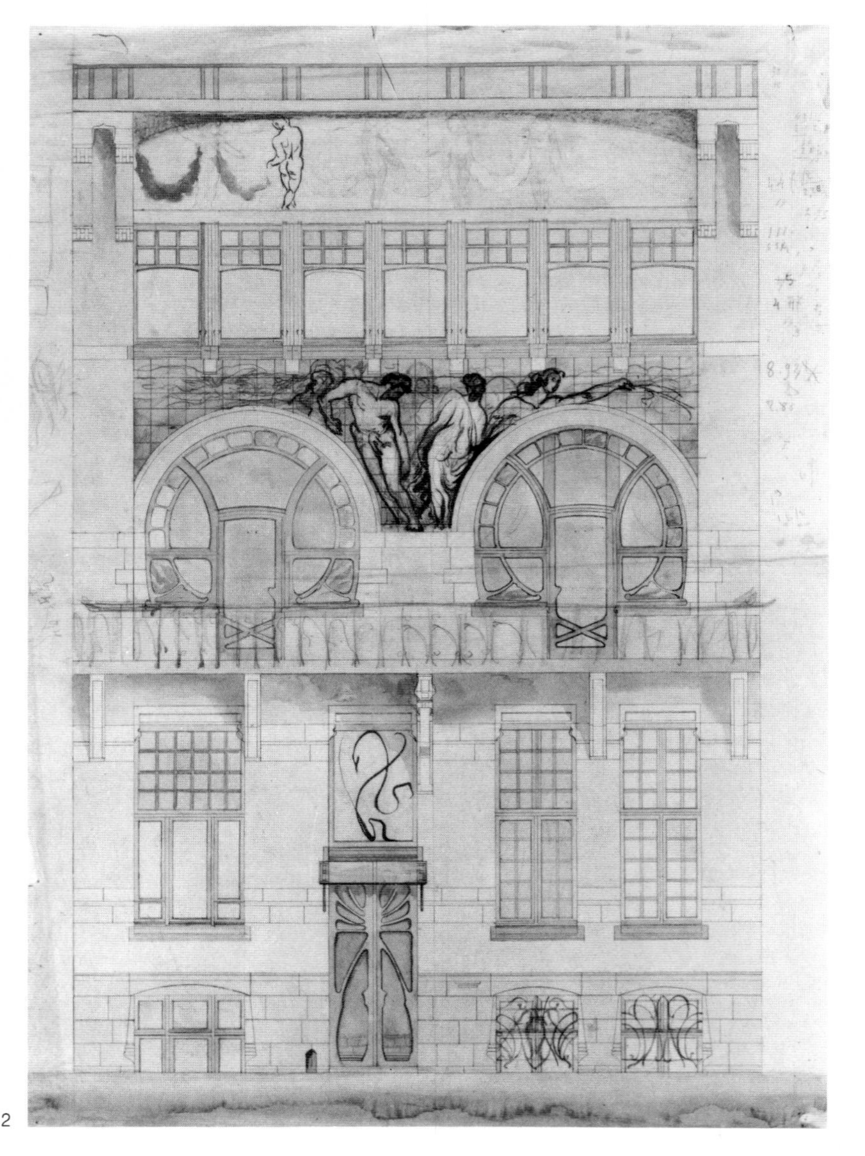

2

3

Vienna: Majolika Haus, 1898-1899.
Architect: Otto Wagner.

3. Detail of the cornice.
L'Architecte, 1906.
4. Front at the corner.
5. The Dance, 1903.
Woodcut in black and gold
by Koloman Moser for *Ver Sacrum*, Vienna.

4

5

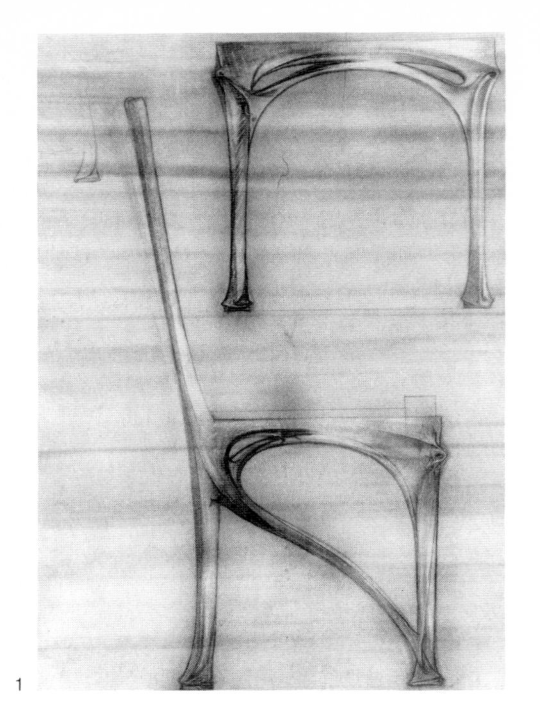

he only turned to architecture after his marriage when, in 1895, he built his own home, Villa Bloemenwerf, at Uccle near Brussels. In his autobiography,[13] he said of himself: "The decline of architecture and the general corruption of taste struck him as something peculiarly repellent. It was as if an infection had put its blight on everything that met his eye. At all costs he felt bound to protect the woman who had consented to share his life and the children that might be born to them, for ugliness is as corrupting to the soul and spirit as it is to the eyes."
Van de Velde's outlook was avowedly messianic. It was this personal factor that enabled him to escape many pitfalls by maintaining a high standard of exactness in the design and economy in the means of carrying it out; indeed exactness and control are the watchwords of his whole achievement and facilitated his transition to the language of modernism. His furniture, built in the semi-industrial workshops which he founded at Uccle-Brussels, have a rustic energy of design contrasting with the refinement and elegance of Guimard's furniture; it shows less talent, perhaps, but greater force and also the courage of his conviction that in simplicity lay the answer to the modern predicament.

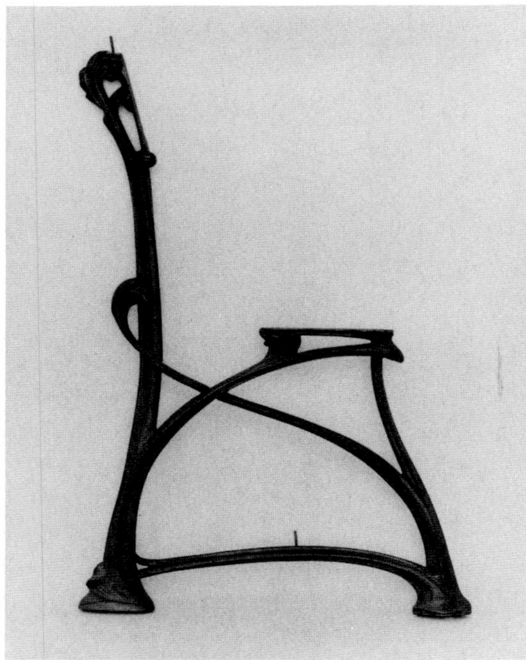

1. Chair design by Hector Guimard, c. 1899.
2. Cast-iron frame of a garden bench by Hector Guimard.
3. Design for wall tiles by Henry van de Velde. *L'Art Décoratif*, 1898.

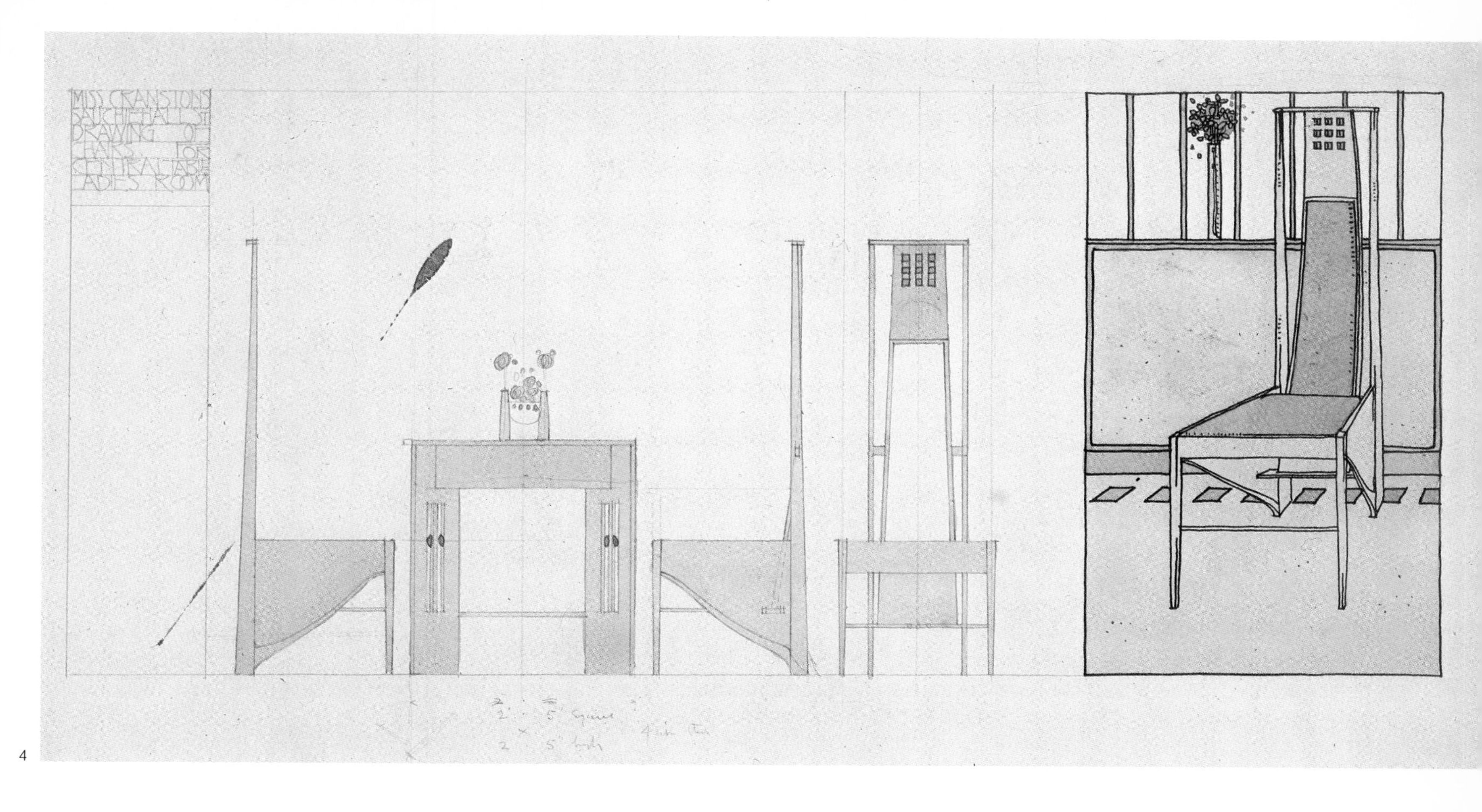

4

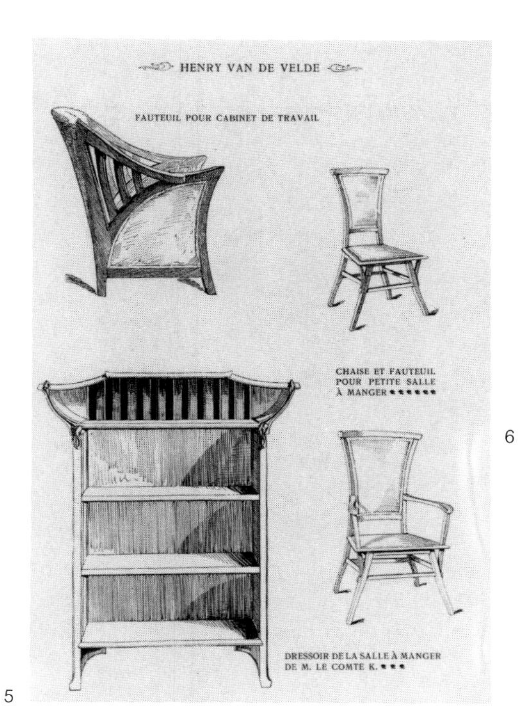

5

6

4. Design for table and chair with high back for the Willow Tea Rooms, Glasgow, by Charles Rennie Mackintosh. Watercolour, 1903.
5. Furniture designs by Henry van de Velde. *L'Art Décoratif*, 1898.
6. Bedroom by Henry van de Velde exhibited at the Arts and Crafts Salon, The Hague, 1898. *L'Art Décoratif*, 1898.

The Glasgow School carried this formal purism to its extreme limits. The furniture designed by Charles Rennie Mackintosh,[14] at once exquisite and austere, based on the straight line and right angle, is wholly in keeping with the Arts and Crafts movement with which Van de Velde also claimed allegiance. The formal means are not the same, Mackintosh clinging to the line, Van de Velde to the plane, but the intention was similar. Never were facile solutions more clearly condemned than in the work of these two men (even though, in some works, Mackintosh's stylization may now seem mannered).

The reconquest of the city

L'ART DE BATIR LES VILLES

VERONA, Piazza Erbe

NOTES ET RÉFLEXIONS D'UN ARCHITECTE

PAR

CAMILLO SITTE

LIBRAIRIE RENOUARD
H. LAURENS, ÉDITEUR
Rue de Tournon, 6 PARIS

GENÈVE
ÉDITION ATAR
Rue de la Dôle, 11

1

The controversy over form running through the work of the early 1900s shows that rationalist thinking was by no means moribund, that it was again trying to gain control of architectural design and stamp it with a formal coherence in keeping with the logic of its intellectual requirements. But the rationalist view was soon to lose out, for other more vital necessities were at stake, touching both the social role of art (in its most characteristic locus: the city) and its means of production, threatened by the tentacular spread of industry. The positions Van de Velde continued to defend at the Deutscher Werkbund exhibition (Cologne, 1914) were contested on behalf of the younger generation by Walter Gropius. In France, Tony Garnier's Industrial City came as the implicit, and irrefutable, condemnation of Camillo Sitte's ideas on town planning (set forth in *Der Städtebau*, Vienna, 1889).

As Le Corbusier wrote, summing up the modernist view: "The demonstrations of Sitte... were based on the past. Indeed, they *were* the past, and the past on a small footing, the sentimental past, the rather insignificant flower by the wayside."[15] It is true that Sitte's book of 1889 represented a point of view quite opposed to functionalism. Writing in the Viennese context of his day, Sitte was protesting against the taking over of the townscape by engineers, at a time when the Ring was being built on the old fortifications. He called for empty spaces forming an integral part of the city architecture, planned with the same care as the buildings. He showed that alignment in itself was no answer to the plastic problem of handling urban spaces; that a discipline was involved whose importance had been overlooked.

In his book, furthermore, Sitte traced out a historical survey of unusual insight, covering such themes as the relation of monumental buildings to their surroundings, the central square and the rectilinear street. For the latter, taking the example of the Rue de la Régence in Brussels, he wrote: "While the wavy line is more picturesque, the straight line is more monumental; but we cannot make do with monumentality alone." He accordingly emphasized the variety and correlation required of the different types of urban forms set within an organic whole. Sitte's pragmatic approach was dismissed by the modern-minded theorists, keen on abstract models. But it was not lost on everyone. Charles Buls, the mayor of Brussels, intelligently applied its principles to his city in the last two decades of the nineteenth century, and Laprade and Lyautey subsequently followed them in their planning of Moroccan towns.

Around the turn of the century several books appeared on the aesthetics of the city (by Charles Buls, Emile Magne and August Endell) and of the street (for example, *L'Esthétique de la Rue* by Gustave Kahn). All bear the mark of Sitte's views, whose influence

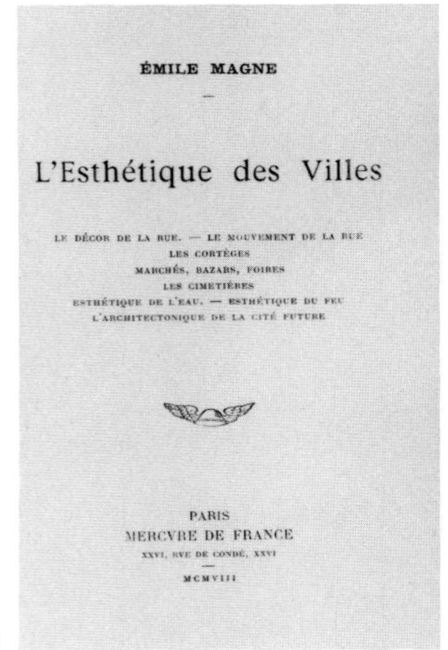

ÉMILE MAGNE

L'Esthétique des Villes

LE DÉCOR DE LA RUE. — LE MOUVEMENT DE LA RUE
LES CORTÈGES
MARCHÉS, BAZARS, FOIRES
LES CIMETIÈRES
ESTHÉTIQUE DE L'EAU. — ESTHÉTIQUE DU FEU
L'ARCHITECTONIQUE DE LA CITÉ FUTURE

PARIS
MERCVRE DE FRANCE
XXVI, RVE DE CONDÉ, XXVI
MCMVIII

2

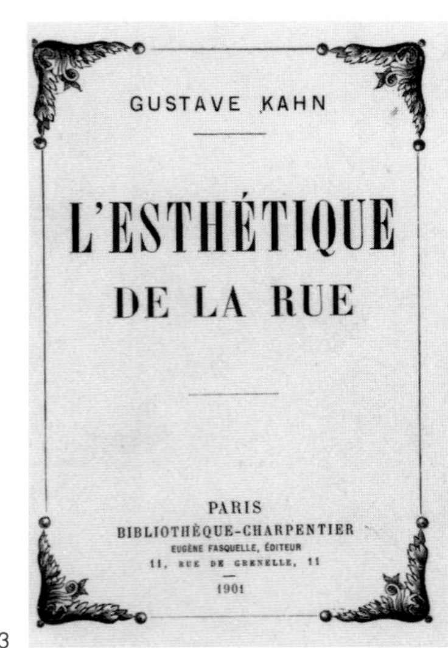

GUSTAVE KAHN

L'ESTHÉTIQUE DE LA RUE

PARIS
BIBLIOTHÈQUE-CHARPENTIER
EUGÈNE FASQUELLE, ÉDITEUR
11, RUE DE GRENELLE, 11
1901

3

bore not only on architects but on historians as well. Take Marcel Poëte, professeur of the history of Paris at the Bibliothèque Historique de la Ville de Paris from 1903 on, who was instrumental in setting up the Institut d'Urbanisme in 1924: his whole career was founded on the conception of an organic link between history and urban form; he combined Sitte's shaping observation of urbanism with a historian's and sociologist's approach (in the manner of Patrick Geddes in Britain).

4

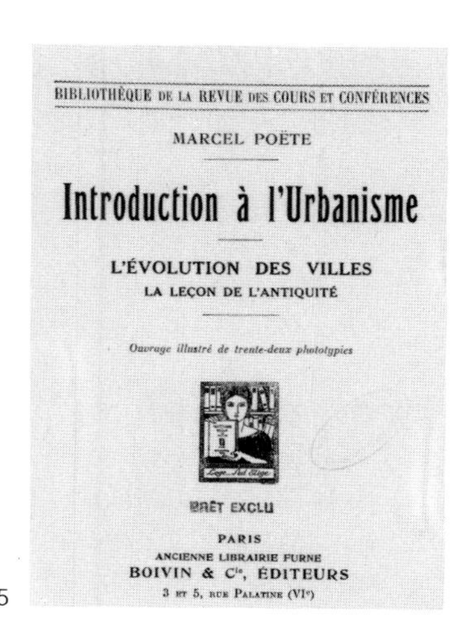

5

6

Title pages:

1. Camillo Sitte, *L'Art de bâtir les villes*, Geneva and Paris, 1918 (French edition of Sitte's *Der Städtebau*, Vienna, 1889).
7. Illustration of a Brussels street.
2. Emile Magne, *L'Esthétique des Villes*, Paris, 1908.
3. Gustave Kahn, *L'Esthétique de la Rue*, Paris, 1901.
4. August Endell, *Die Schönheit der grossen Stadt*, Stuttgart, 1908.
5. Marcel Poëte, *Introduction à l'Urbanisme*, 1929.
6. New type of boulevard with house-fronts alternating with tree-planted courtyards. Illustration in Eugène Hénard, *Etudes sur les transformations de Paris*, Paris, 1903-1909.

7

1

The interest taken by artists in the townscape was a key factor in the nascent theory of town planning. Even Eugène Hénard–who in his *Etudes sur les transformations de Paris* (1903-1909) laid down some town-planning principles which anticipate those of Le Corbusier–aimed in his projects at respecting the plastic unity of the urban form. His interest was always focused on actual sites. Thus his *boulevard à redans* (lined, that is, with building units alternately brought forward and set back) was designed as a continuation of the Boulevard Raspail; his *carrefour à giration*, a large roundabout, was meant to complete the Boulevard Haussmann. It was Eugène Hénard too who, overcoming all opposition, contributed most to the construction of the Pont Alexandre III and the Avenue Alexandre III, now recognized as among the most admirable features of post-Haussmannian Paris.

The simplified layouts of the early town planners are now of merely didactic interest. Since Charles Garnier, the major preoccupation has remained the overall treatment of the urban space. So it would

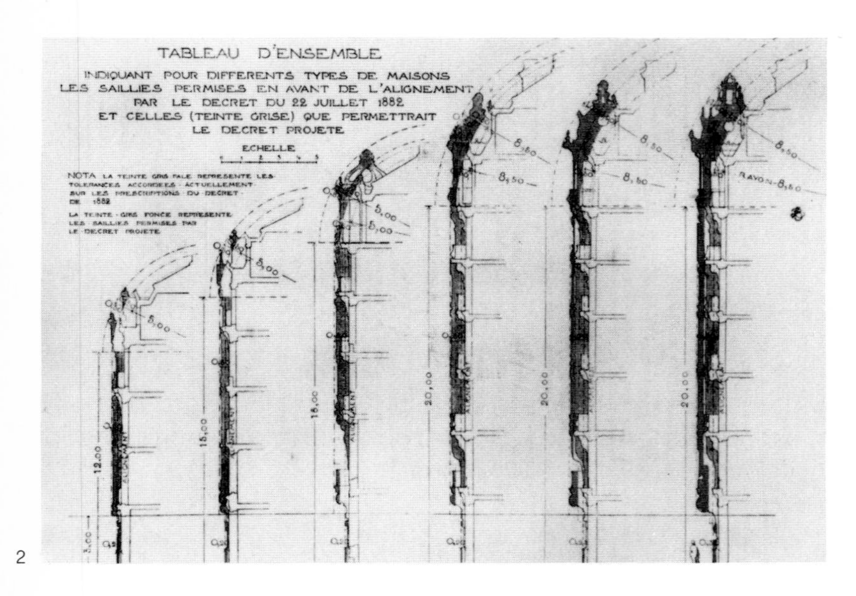

2

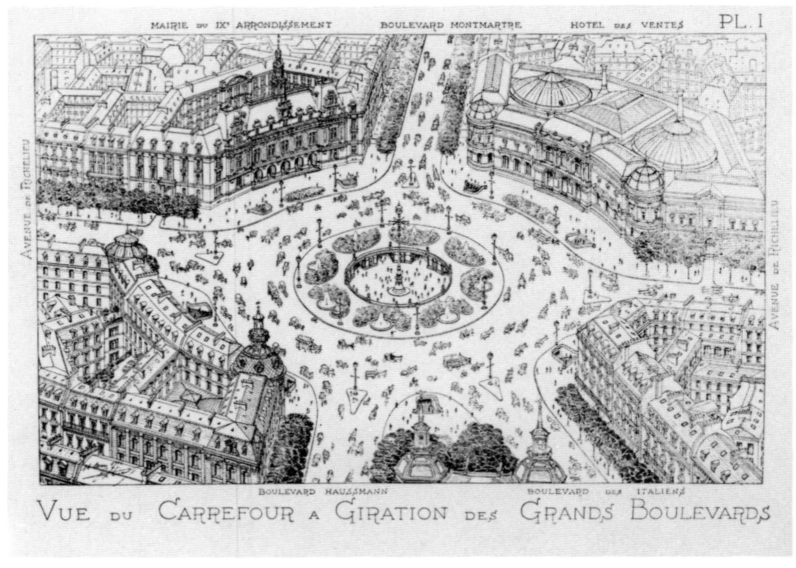

3

1. Paris: Buildings on the Boulevard des Italiens. Architect: Edouard Arnaud. *L'Architecte*, 1913.
2. Illustration for a lecture by Louis Bonnier on his 1899 project incorporated in the Paris building regulations of 1902. *L'Architecture et la Construction dans le Nord*, 1899.

4

3. Proposed roundabout in Paris. Illustration in Eugène Hénard, *Etudes sur les transformations de Paris*, 1903-1909.
4. Paris: Apartment house, Boulevard Raspail and Rue de Sèvres, 1913. Architect: Louis Sorel. *L'Architecte*, 1914.

be a mistake to consider Hénard's ideas apart from those of Louis Bonnier, who drew up the fundamental "regulation of 1902" for Paris which, continuing a century-old town-planning tradition, defined the style and outline of the post-Haussmannian buildings so characteristic of the peripheral *arrondissements* of Paris.
The urban architecture of Paris between 1900 and 1930 was the outcome of ideas worked out in the closing years of the nineteenth century, by way of the façade competitions sponsored by the city authorities and the regulatory projects set on foot to correct some of Haussmann's faulty alignments–the prevailing concern being to maintain architectural unity. The large apartment buildings of Louis Sorel (7, Rue Le Tasse, 1905; Boulevard Raspail and Rue de Sèvres, 1913), of Auguste Bluysen (48, Avenue du Président-Wilson, 1908), of M. P. Du Bois d'Auberville (1-5, Avenue Mozart, 1907-1908) and many other architects of the early 1900s are a remarkable synthesis of the set formula, with their roomy cambered attics (whose luxurious flats, embellished with loggias or terraces, are accessible by lift) and their fine ashlar fronts, generally overlaying a reinforced concrete frame (hence the many terrace roofs, like those of Bluysen's building in the Avenue du Président-Wilson and the Hôtel Lutétia in the Rue de Sèvres).

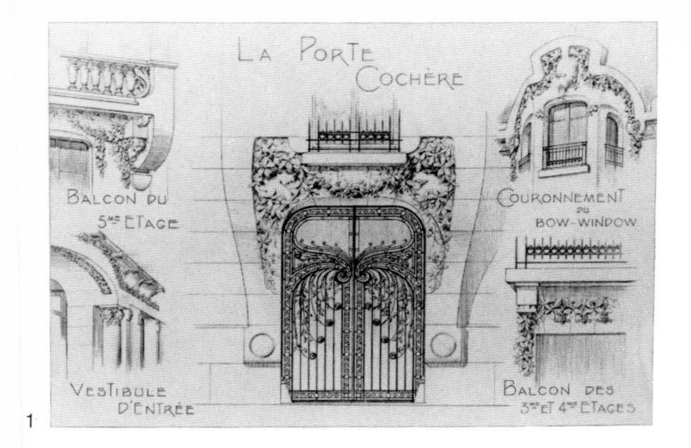

Profiting from earlier experiments (like the Rue Réaumur), the post-Haussmannian building types allow equally well for the small-scale constructions of the periphery (Charles Plumet, artist's studio, 21, Rue Octave-Feuillet, 1908) and for the big office buildings (E. Arnaud, Rue and Boulevard des Italiens, 1913). Never had *regulation architecture* been better suited to its purpose, thanks to the consensus then reached in Paris on the problem of urban form, a consensus from which the modernists were soon to depart, not without disruptive consequences. Even so advanced an architect as Henri Sauvage was able to set side by side in the Rue Vavin a typically post-Haussmannian apartment building–on the corner, harmonizing with the design of the Boulevard Raspail–and a "tiered" apartment building;[16] the latter fails to comply with the 1902 regulations, but because it is set back unobtrusively from the main alignment it does not jar with the rest.

The search for a harmonious pattern of urban building style and layout was by no means specifically French. Another example is provided by the extensions made to Amsterdam, planned by H. P. Berlage on the basis of similar concepts. But the example of Paris is of particular interest as covering the whole field of construction, including the problem field of social housing. Of this, it is worth saying something more.

Paris: Apartment building,
48, Avenue du Président-Wilson,
1908.
Architect: Auguste Bluysen.
1. Carriage entrance.
2. Front.
L'Architecte, 1908.
3. Paris: Artist's studio,
21, Rue Octave-Feuillet, 1908.
Architect: Charles Plumet.
L'Architecte, 1908.

4

5

6. Paris: Apartment building, 19, Rue Octave-Feuillet, 1910. Architect: Maurice-Paul Du Bois d'Auberville. Detail of the front.

6

4. Paris: Apartment building, 7, Rue Le Tasse, 1905. Architect: Louis Sorel. Detail of the front.
5. Paris: Apartment building, 1-5, Avenue Mozart, 1907-1908. Architect: Maurice-Paul Du Bois d'Auberville.

1

The low-cost residential building known as *habitation à bon marché*, the famous H.B.M.'s of the outer Paris boulevards, erected in the 1930s, answer to a type worked out at the beginning of the century: reinforced concrete frame and brick construction; apartment blocks[17] set round large, tree-planted courtyards; oblique perspectives, and embellished attics and roofs. The Cité l'Argentine, built by Henri Sauvage about 1903, may be taken as the archetype, and its main features go back to the theoretical designs of Viollet-le-Duc (its direct ancestor being the project for an iron-frame apartment building which concludes Viollet-le-Duc's *Entretiens*).

Defined here was the architectural model of what in France is called hygienic housing *(logements hygiéniques)*. It remained to work out an effective urban model, and the key to this lay in the principle of the city block, a breakaway from the traditional separate plot in favour of an overall concept suitable to an entire neighbourhood. In 1905 the competition sponsored by the Fondation Rothschild[18] brought forward some cogent examples of this concept. The most brilliant design was that of Tony Garnier, whose project announced all the main features of the type, as fully

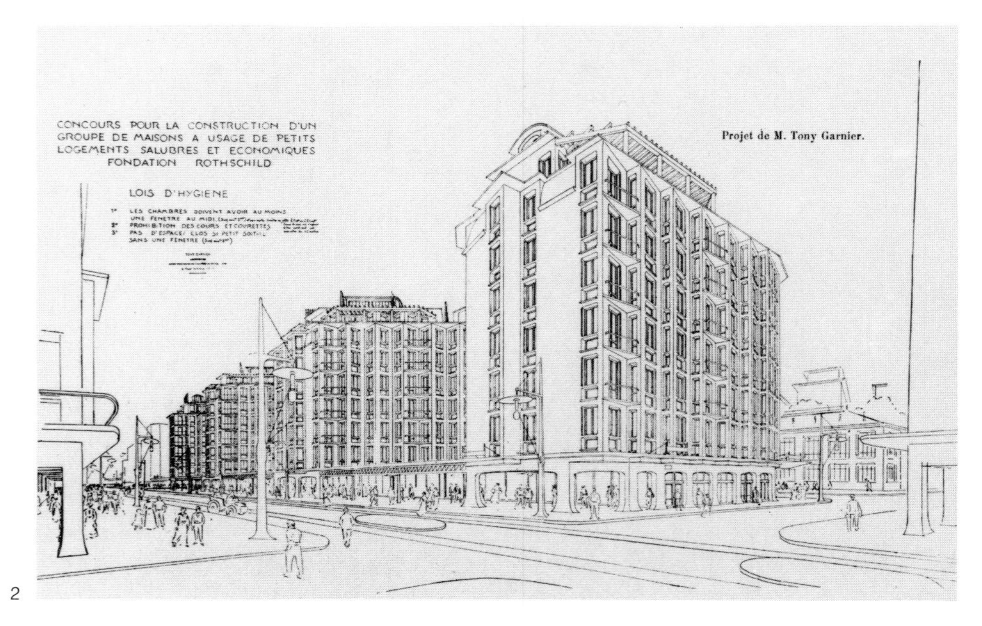

2

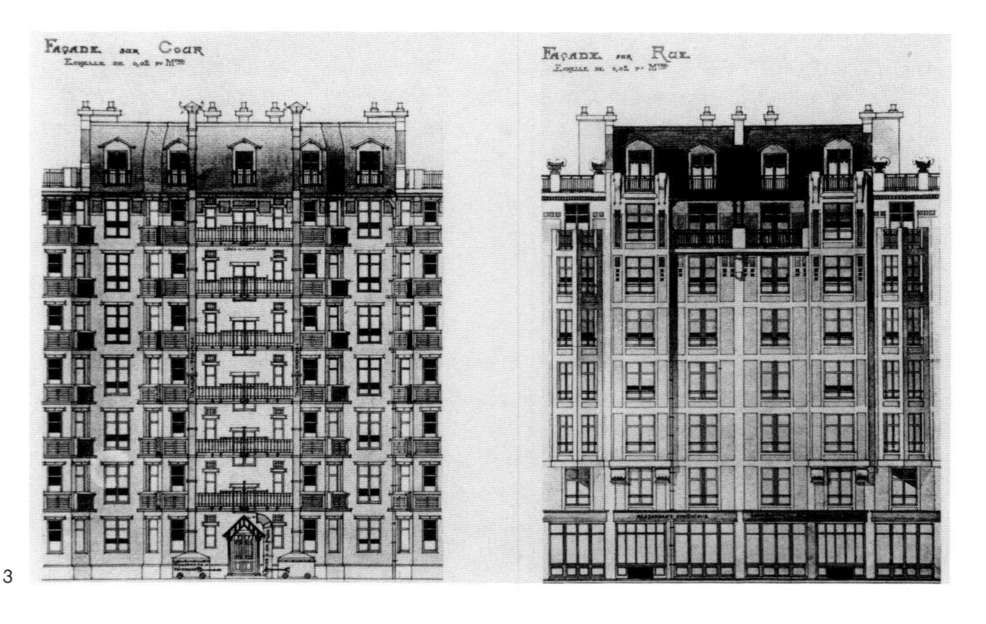

3

Competition of the Rothschild Foundation, Paris, 1905.

1. Project of Adolphe-Augustin Rey. Detail of house-front on the Rue de Prague. *Les Concours publics d'Architecture*, 1906.
2. Project of Tony Garnier. View of the Rue de Prague. *La Construction Moderne*, 1907.
3. Project of Henry Provensal. Details of house-fronts. *Les Concours publics d'Architecture*, 1906.

4

5

4. Paris: The Cité l'Argentine apartment building, 111, Avenue Victor-Hugo, c. 1903. Architect: Henri Sauvage. Bow window.
5. Paris: Hostel for single men (now Palais de la Femme), 94, Rue de Charonne, 1909. Architects: A. Labussière C. Longerey. *L'Architecte*, 1911.
6. Brussels: Project for workers' dwellings, Rue Blaes. Elevation at the back, 1912. Design by Emile Hellemans.

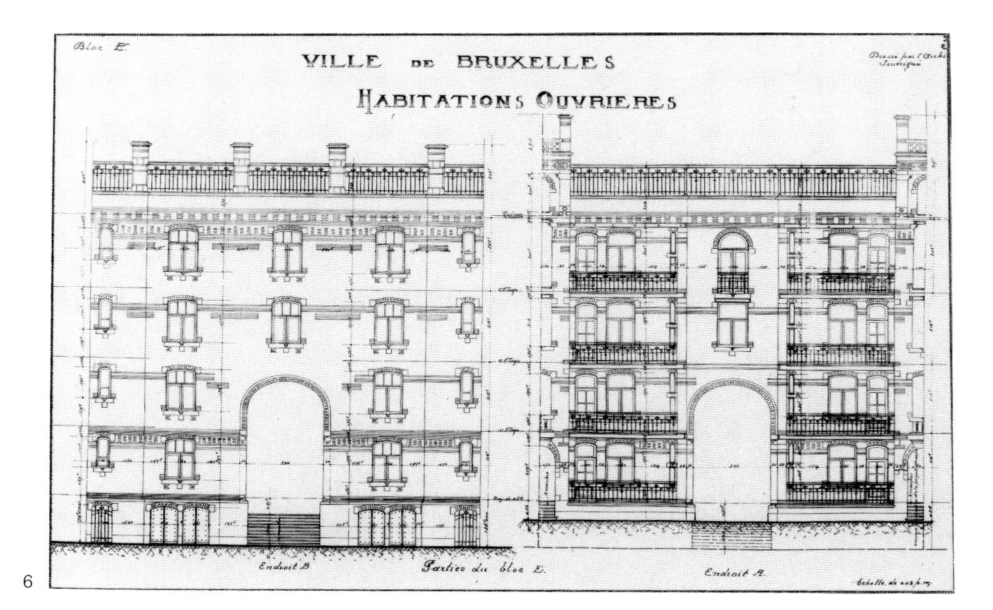

6

developed in his *Cité Industrielle* (conceived in 1902-1904, not published till 1917).

Social architecture proceeded from these definitions, both in Paris (hostel for single men, 94, Rue de Charonne, by A. Labussière and C. Longerey, 1909) and in other European cities (workers' houses, Rue Blaes, Brussels, by Emile Hellemans, 1912). The generic model could be adapted to specific needs, and it was this model that inspired the Amsterdam School after 1910, the work of Michael De Klerk in particular.

Emphasis here has been laid on the urban pattern as the major problem of early twentieth-century art, disregarding the often fierce criticisms levelled against this approach in the name of a strictly functional definition of the urban organism. Disregarding them, the better to bring out the all too often unrecognized originality of this solution which, in order to regain the lost unity of the city, first marshalled all the resources of urban planning.

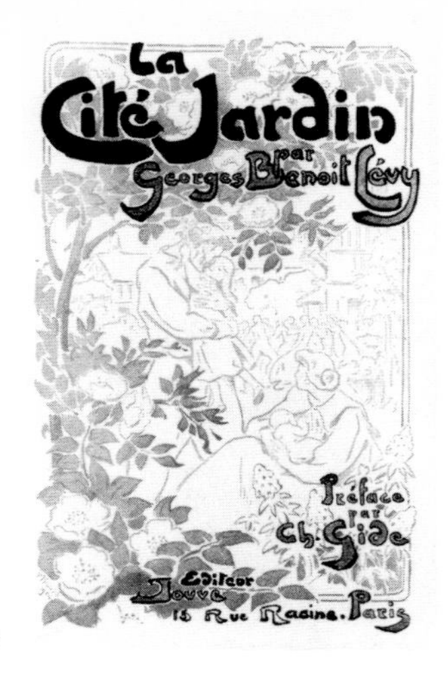

1

This approach is the reverse of the Anglo-Saxon approach, which is in effect a *de-urbanization*–an escape from the metropolis and a return to the village as the urban type. It needs to be added that the condemnation of the city by English theorists is in fact purely formal, its purpose being to put across the counter-project set up in opposition to the city. More real is the difference of life-style implied by the individual house of the English city and the apartment building of the French one. Here is an essential difference of definition; on the one hand, the city as a purely urban entity of high density, based on close and interacting exchanges; on the other, the city as a binary organism divided between centre and periphery, its essential features deriving from this distinction (and so implying, both in architectural and urban terms, the existence of two distinct building patterns).

The garden city is not the whole answer. It is one-half of the answer to the problem involved. Where the French mind sees the urban pattern and the city centre as the heart of the matter, the English

1. Cover of Georges Benoît Lévy, *La Cité Jardin*, Paris, 1904.
5. "A street at Port Sunlight." Illustration in *La Cité Jardin*.

2

3

4

2. London: Bath Road, Bedford Park, 1876-1886. Architect: Richard Norman Shaw. Lithograph by B.F. Berry, 1882.
3. Hampstead: Garden suburb.
4. Letchworth: Garden city. Illustrations from Raymond Unwin, *Town Planning in Practice*, London, 1909.

5

mind looks rather to the question of housing structures on the periphery. Yet it would be a mistake to suppose that the garden city is a purely English conception. It was already defined in the workers' city of Frédéric Le Play and also in peripheral residential complexes like those of Le Vésinet (1856-1875) in the west suburbs of Paris and Bedford Park (1876-1886) in London.
The real issue, still alive today, is that of popular housing both in the city and in the suburbs. The early 1900s offered the inexpensive models which amounted to something more than an impoverished version of the middle-class home. City-block housing came as one response, the garden city as another.
The idea of the garden city was put forward by Ebenezer Howard in 1898 in his book *Tomorrow: A Peaceful Path to Social Reform* (republished in 1902 as *Garden Cities of Tomorrow*). It was put into practice at once, notably by Raymond Unwin and Barry Parker, who in 1903 began the first garden city at Letchworth in Hertfordshire, some thirty miles from London. It soon spread not only to the continent, to Holland, Belgium and France,[19] but also to North America. Once again the whole point of the idea lay in the fact that it offered a complete answer to the problem involved: it offered a set of architectural types, a model of urban space and a system of economic and social organization. Each country was free to adapt it to its own culture and needs, often departing very markedly from the Anglo-Saxon conception as stamped by the influence of Richard Norman Shaw and Charles F. Annesley Voysey.

Socialism or modernism?

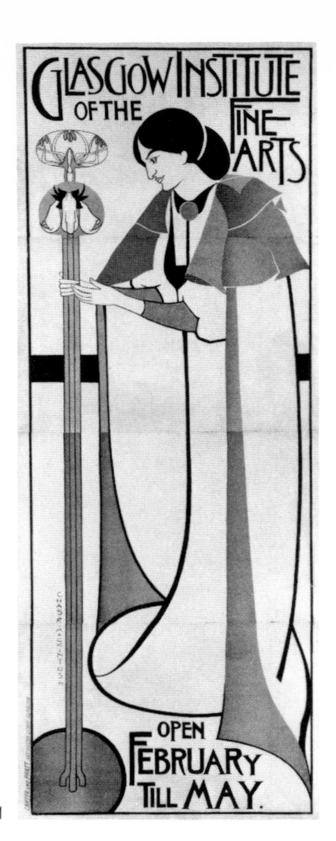

1

In the field of social architecture, Art Nouveau found an outlet for its decorative formalism, and here it shows how strong an influence was exerted on both architecture and the applied arts by the ideas of William Morris. The internal debate among architects was able to achieve results only by being transposed to another plane, that of the social role of architecture. Only by facing this issue, in the technical and economic context of his time, was the architect able to define his mission and his language.

As always, the best artists ignored the politics of fashion,[20] the systematic promotion of this or that avant-garde. Taking over and adapting the tradition of the English Arts and Crafts movement, they were able to design forms which were not only the expression of luxury and refinement, but also answered to a genuine popular demand, and one (as they well realized) that was being extended under the impact of social changes.

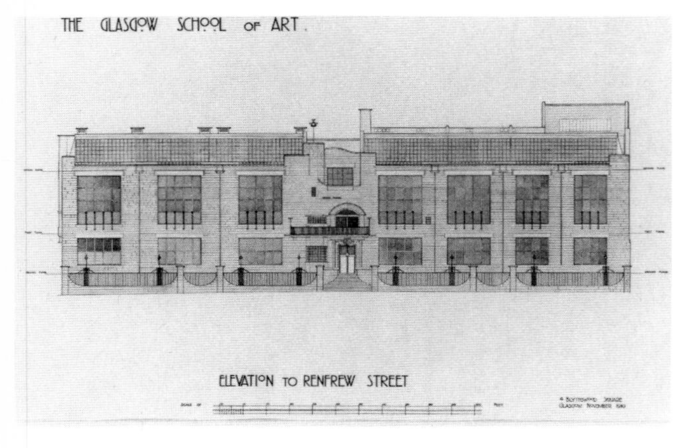

2

All this involved the breaking down of the old professional hierarchy of the arts and crafts–just what Ruskin had called for half a century earlier, and what William Morris had consciously practised. From the collaboration between artist and craftsman, from the creation of professional "guilds" facilitating the exchange between artists and technicians, there arose a new spirit, a new unity of artistic and craft skills, over and above sociological divisions.

In 1919 Walter Gropius could write: "There is no difference in nature between artist and craftsman. The artist is only an inspired craftsman. There are rare moments of illumination, when by heaven's grace, independently of his will, his handiwork becomes art. But every artist must possess technical skill. In that skill lies the true source of the creative imagination. Let us therefore form a corporation of a new kind, one without that class separation which sets up a wall of disdain between craftsman and artist."[21]

These statements from the Bauhaus programme of 1919 show the underlying unity of aim connecting the new school of design with the old one, the Kunstgewerbeschule (School of Applied Arts) founded in Weimar in 1907 by Henry van de Velde, who now passed on the torch to Walter Gropius, his opponent in the debate over art and industry which had marked the Sonderbund exhibition in Cologne five years before.

3. Weimar: School of Applied Arts (Kunstgewerbeschule), 1908-1911. Architect: Henry van de Velde.

3

The schools of applied arts were the focus of this exchange between artist and craftsman which did so much to renew artistic culture, bringing to the fore a whole generation of "art craftsmen" whose exceptional skills were revealed in the 1920s and '30s by a particularly lively production, extending even to provincial centres. The unity of style marking this production was due to the permanent exchanges and reciprocal respect prevailing between the many artists concerned.

4

1. Poster by Charles Rennie Mackintosh for the Glasgow Institute of the Fine Arts, c. 1895. Colour lithograph.

Glasgow: School of Art, 1898-1899. Architect: Charles Rennie Mackintosh.
2. North elevation showing attic storey.
4. View of the main front.

The architecture of certain schools, together with the many exhibitions which they sponsored, testify to the vitality of this art. The Glasgow School of Art built by Charles Rennie Mackintosh (1898-1899) is worth comparing with the Weimar Kunstgewerbeschule built by Henry van de Velde (1908-1911). They are alike in their sober grandeur, their clear, rational forms, the quiet effectiveness of their decorative elements.

Similar aims underlie another major creation of the early twentieth century: the art colony on the Mathildenhöhe in Darmstadt,[22] where the first house was built in 1901 by Joseph Maria Olbrich, a pupil of Otto Wagner and the founder, with Josef Hoffmann, of the Vienna Secession (1897). Alongside Olbrich, other artists worked on the Mathildenhöhe, including Peter Behrens, Hans Christiansen, Patriz Huber and Emanuel Josef Margold.

Created in 1899, the Darmstadt art colony centred on a group of seven artists who lived and worked there for the next four years. It got a new lease of life in 1907 when Jacob Julius Scharvogel opened his pottery works there. A place of production rather than schooling, the Darmstadt colony acted in effect as a permanent showplace of architecture and applied arts, each artist building and fitting out his own house in his own style; such are the admirable Behrens House (1901) and the two-family Glückert House by Olbrich (1900-1901). The work of the Darmstadt Künstlerkolonie was present at all the big international exhibitions, notably at the 1904 World's Fair in St Louis, where Olbrich exhibited his "Summer House of an Art Lover."

2

1

Darmstadt: Artist's house built for the exhibition of the Mathildenhöhe artists' colony of the Grand Duke Ernst Ludwig of Hesse-Darmstadt, 1901.
Architect: Peter Behrens.
1. North front.
3. North-south cross-section.
5. Mosaic pavement.
Deutsche Kunst und Dekoration, 1902.

2. Darmstadt: Wall hanging for the New Palace of the Grand Duke of Hesse-Darmstadt. Design by Joseph Maria Olbrich, 1903-1904.

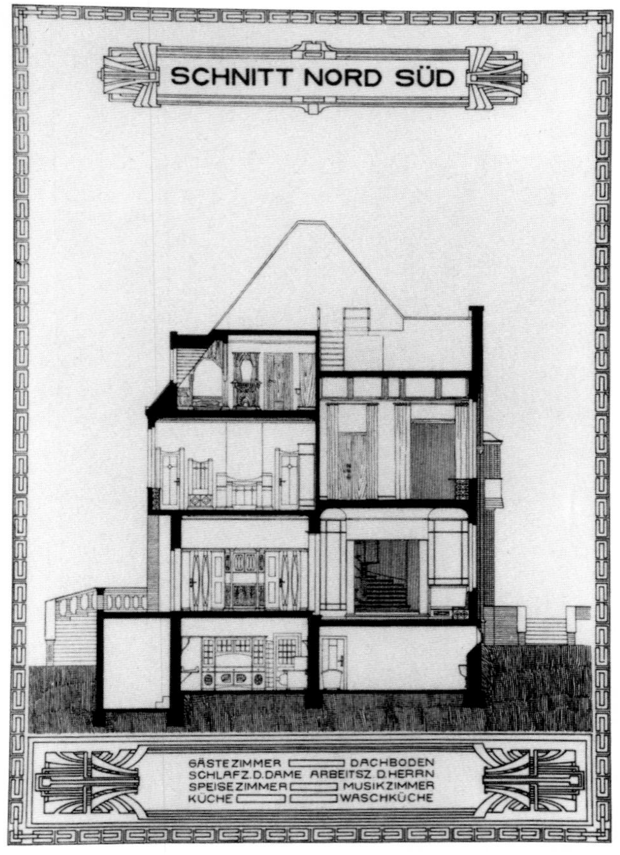

3

4

4. "Summer House of an Art Lover"
   designed by Joseph Maria Olbrich
   for the St. Louis World's Fair, 1904.
   The Tea Room.
   Watercolour by Olbrich, 1903.

Darmstadt: Glückert House, 1900-1901.
Architect: Joseph Maria Olbrich.

6. West and north fronts.
7. Cross-section of the entrance hall.
   Drawings by Olbrich.

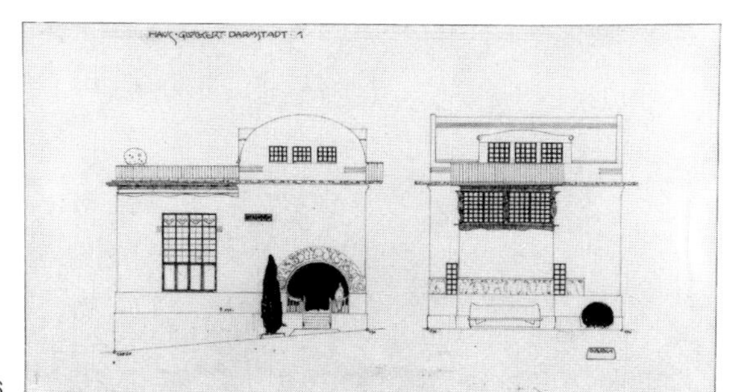

6

5

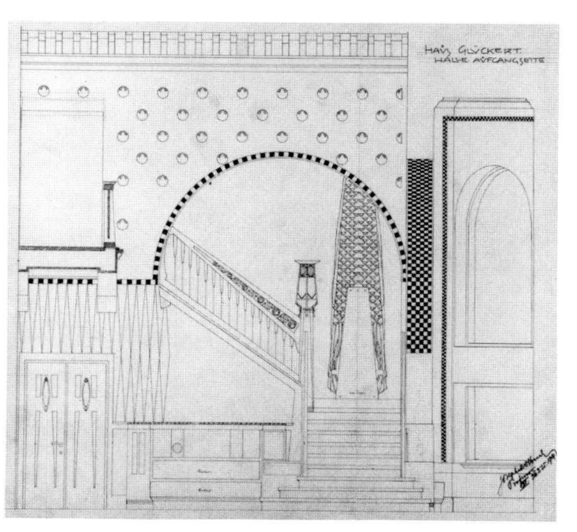

7

1

1. Vienna: Ideal design of the 22nd district, 1910-1911. Bird's-eye view. Design by Otto Wagner.
2. Brussels: Palais Stoclet, 1906-1911. Architect: Josef Hoffmann.
3. Vienna: Post Office Savings Bank, 1904-1906. Architect: Otto Wagner. Perspective section. Watercolour drawing by Wagner, 1903.

The spirit of the Vienna Secession entered very much into the later work of Otto Wagner, as also into that of Josef Hoffmann. Wagner's great urban projects (like that for Vienna's 22nd Bezirk, 1910-1911), together with his actual constructions (the Am Steinhof church and above all the Post Office Savings Bank in Vienna, 1904-1906), aim at stripping architecture of all decorative formalism by exploiting the beauty of the materials (steel, aluminium, marble, glass) and the harmony of their combination (creating a surface animation in the lines of the Majolika Haus), and by giving prominence to chosen monumental elements (architectural details or sculptured emblems) which form the strong points of the overall design.

2

3

This movement continued the critique of Art Nouveau sketched out in the last years of the nineteenth century. It resulted, with Adolf Loos, in a style of uneasy austerity; with Josef Hoffmann, in a wayward elegance compounded of indirect allusions. The distinction between individual temperaments and manners made no difference to the prevailing spirit: with Wright, with Berlage, in Vienna, in Paris, we find similar preoccupations. Thus the interest taken by Henri Sauvage in large architectural forms (his tiered houses are one example) is peculiar to him, while Auguste Perret was chiefly concerned with the problem of the relation between structure and facing (between the concrete frame and the covering chosen for it). The problem was raised at once in his Rue Franklin

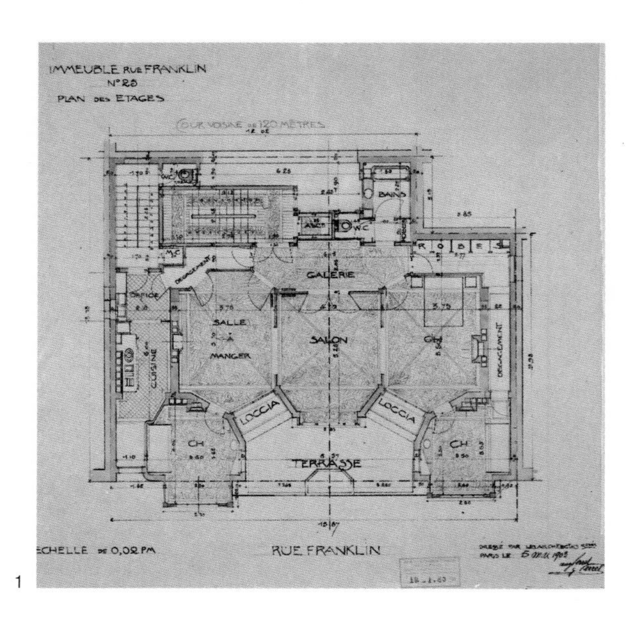

1

Paris: Apartment building and Perret Office.
25 bis, Rue Franklin, 1903-1904.
Architects: Auguste and Gustave Perret.

1. Plan of the storeys.
2. Doorway on the right side.
3. Front.
   Elevation and cross-section.
   Watercolour drawings by A. and G. Perret, 1903.
4. View of a loggia.

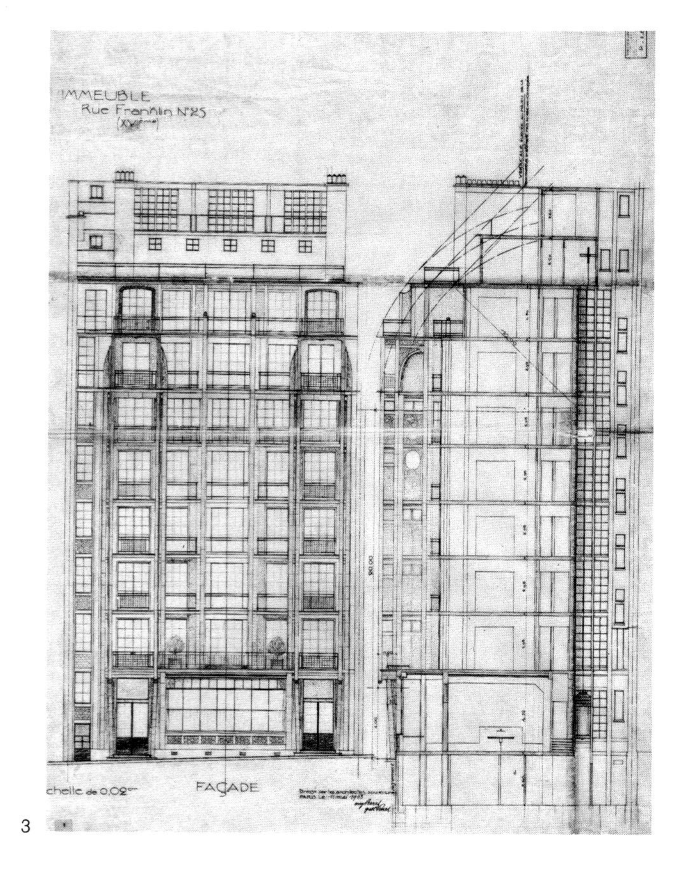

3

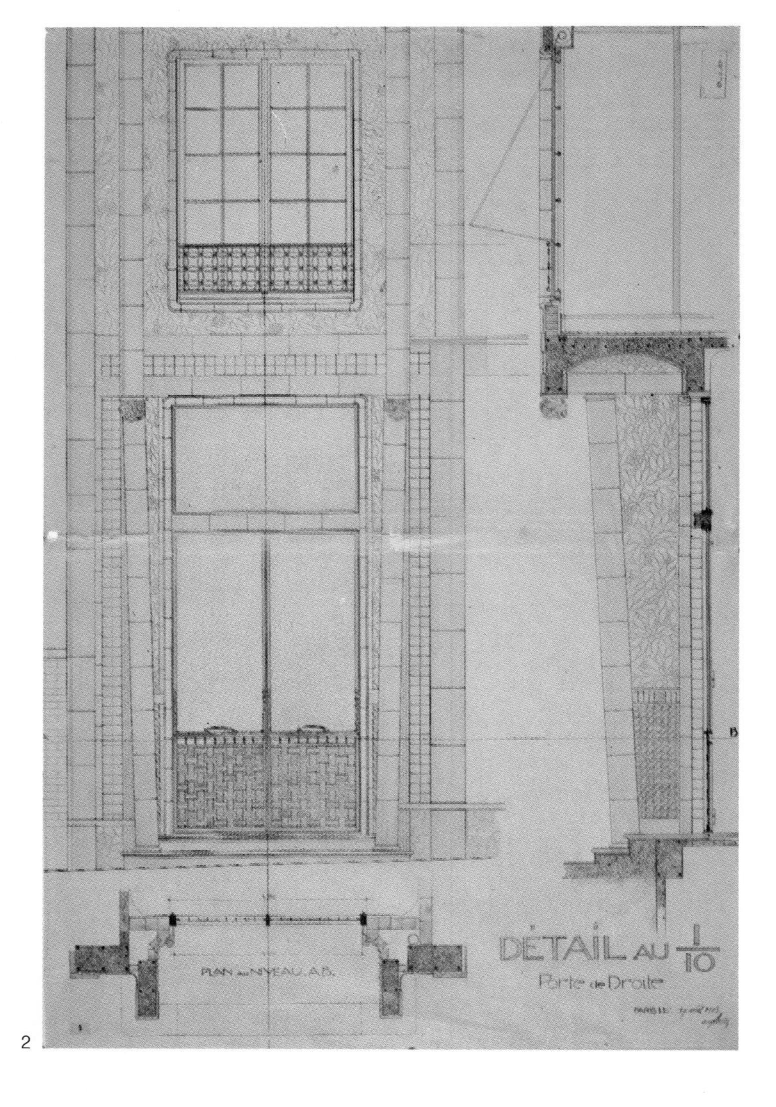

2

4

5. Paris: Ponthieu-Automobile Garage.
51, Rue de Ponthieu, 1906-1907. Demolished 1970.
Architects: Auguste and Gustave Perret.
L'Architecte, 1908.

6. Paris: Hôtel Carnot, Avenue Elisée Reclus,
1907. Demolished.
Architect: Paul Guadet.
L'Architecte, 1908.

5

6

apartment house (1903-1904), where the visible framework is filled in with a concrete facing inset with stoneware, whose floral arrangement is in the Japanese style (a principle deriving from the work of Anatole de Baudot). And the problem was treated systematically in his Ponthieu garage (1906-1907, demolished), which was entirely faced with glass, in accordance with his programme. Perret's attitude was the reverse of that of a man like Paul Guadet (Hôtel Carnot, Avenue Elisée Reclus, Paris, 1907, demolished), who faced the entire façade with stoneware tiles in Prussian blue; or that of Henry van de Velde who, for the Théâtre des Champs-Elysées,[23] designed the façade as a wall of sculptured marble (a device further emphasized by Bourdelle in the final projects).

The problem of the wall as a dialogue between skeleton and filling was by no means new. It preoccupied Viollet-le-Duc as much as Sullivan, Baudot as much as Wagner. But now the answer given to it was more unequivocal. If the wall was faced, the nature of the facing was undisguised.[24] If the emphasis was laid on the structural framework, the repetition of the facing panels went to create a rhythm of solids and voids (the skeleton setting the pattern of the design). Finally, when broad spans turned this skeleton into a megastructure, the dialogue with the outer shell determined the whole architectural scheme; hence the large vertical slits admitting light in the stepped-roofing system adopted by Tony Garnier for the abattoir of La Mouche in Lyons (1909-1913) and Hans Poelzig for the Posen water tower (1911).
The straightforward affirmation of structural principles came to overshadow decorative problems, and architects lost much of their interest in the latter. Architectonic concerns tended to prevail, in reaction against the ornamental excesses of the previous generation, and the trend was set towards a monumentalism, sometimes inordinate, sometimes grandiose, whose austere lines allowed the masses to speak for themselves in all their sculptural power.

1. Posen (Poznan): Water Tower erected by Hans Poelzig for the East German Exhibition of Applied Art, Industry and Economy, 1911. View of the interior.
Lyons: Cattle Market and Slaughterhouse of La Mouche, 1909-1913. Architect: Tony Garnier.
2.3. Main hall. Interior and exterior views.

1

2

3

With Peter Behrens, one of the masters of the Darmstadt art colony, this reaction against the decorative art of the 1890s assumed a systematic character whose variations involved certain risks. By calling on the artist to take his due place in industrial society and not to ignore it, by seeking through the Deutscher Werkbund, an association of both industrialists and artists, to work out a policy of design for industrial objects, Behrens did indeed open the way for twentieth-century industrial design; but at the same time he opened it to that celebration of industry, that cult of industrial power, which led to an inhuman machine aesthetic.

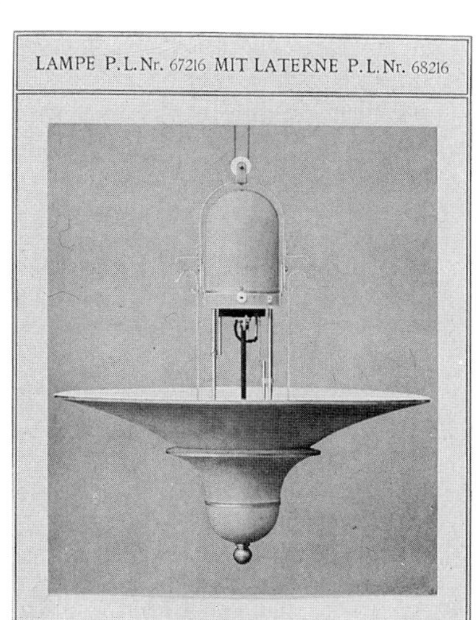

LAMPE P.L.Nr. 67216 MIT LATERNE P.L.Nr. 68216

5

4

Berlin: AEG Factories (General Electricity Company), 1907-1914.
Architect: Peter Behrens.

4. View of the High Tension Factory. Watercolour by Behrens, 1909.
5. Arc lamp. Design by Peter Behrens, 1907.

1

The outlook, the world-view, defined for his generation by Robert Musil was at once top-heavy with culture, pessimistic and overtly Pavlovian. It was imagined that some form of human engineering could be applied to man's body and eliminate its defects–imagined with a sangfroid that sometimes reveals a hatred of the body. "The human body stands in need of revision at birth," wrote Henri Sauvage in 1923. "Why not, once and for all, get rid of the appendix, the prostate gland, the foreskin, the tonsils, the bridle of the tongue, etc. At fifteen we should have our teeth out. At twenty we should have superfluous hair removed. Think of the time that would save later on!"[25]

This engineering view of man and life occurs again and again in architectural writings and designs around the time of the First World War. It deliberately enslaves man to the machine. It provides for buildings and spaces often of great beauty, but quite inhuman. When Tony Garnier designed the blast furnaces of his Industrial City (1901-1904), he pictured them with the same diligent realism, the same freakish fancy, that we find in comic strips, welcoming and invoking industrial society just as it was taking over the world and subjecting man to its law. Likewise, the futuristic skyscrapers of Mario Chiattone's modern metropolis (1914) are a lyrical prefiguration of the space models of today.

Machine worship has wrought havoc in the arts. If European culture has been brought low, it is industry that has done it, leaving today a retrospective impression of the twentieth century as an age of oppressive barbarism. True, the purely aesthetic image conveyed by artists in the past also lent itself to exploitation of various kinds which they were powerless to control. But as things stand, it must be recognized that the industrial economy now at full maturity has revealed its totalitarian character: it has destroyed art, as it has destroyed so many other values, for its own profit.

1. The blast furnaces, 1901-1904. Design for *La Cité Industrielle* by Tony Garnier, published 1917.
2. Design for a modern Metropolis, 1914. Watercolour drawing by Mario Chiattone.

2

Turin 1902

1

Remembered chiefly for the buildings designed by Raimondo d'Aronco, the Turin exhibition appears in retrospect as the belated triumph of Art Nouveau. That indeed it was is shown by the fact that so large an international exhibition could be mounted around the theme of decorative art. Of this Europe-wide movement of style and taste, the conclusion came in 1925 with the great Exhibition of Decorative Art in Paris.

But the Turin exhibition was seen even at the time as the swansong of Art Nouveau. Contemporary accounts have little to say about d'Aronco's very formal pavilions and merely mention (without setting any store by it) Horta's participation in the Belgian pavilion; curiously, they put Horta on the same plane as Govaerts, whose designs seem to us much less coherent. But the only radical break was made by the Germans and by other Belgians. Outstanding was the great hall designed by Peter Behrens, in spite of its rather cryptic character; the form was no longer self-sufficing, being overlaid with a literary content (based here on the idea of archaism and incompleteness) which is closely akin to the work of Gaudí at about the same time.

On the Belgian side, the reaction against Horta came out clearly in the pupils of Paul Hankar, who dedicated their work to his memory. The young Antoine Pompe (using the pseudonym Georges Hobé) exhibited some furniture of a fine severity of design, while Léon Sneyers and Adolphe Crespin cultivated a geometric style close to that of the Vienna Secession; this was also true of the Ghent artist Oscar van de Voorde. There was an obvious kinship between this new decorative formula and the work in the Scottish section by Charles Rennie Mackintosh, his wife Margaret Macdonald, and Herbert MacNair. All this showed that Art Nouveau had had its day as a decorative style.

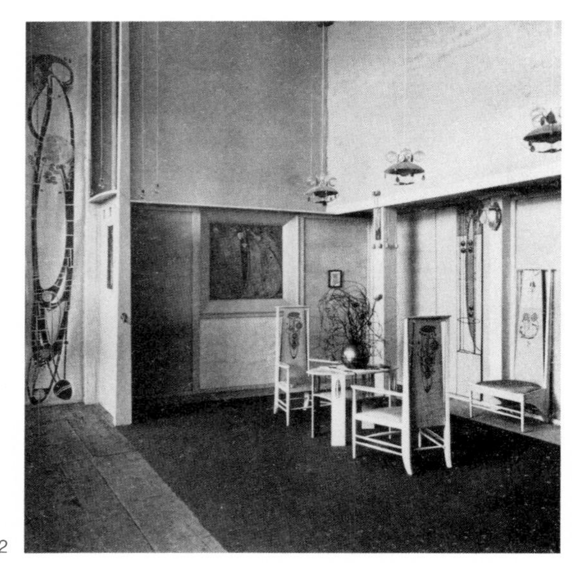
2

Turin: First International Exhibition of Modern Decorative Art, 1902.

1. Exhibition poster by Leonardo Bistolfi.
2. Scottish section.
   "The Rose Boudoir."
   Designers: Charles Rennie Mackintosh and Margaret Macdonald-Mackintosh.
   Deutsche Kunst und Dekoration, 1902.
3. German section.
   Hall.
   Architect: Peter Behrens.
   The Studio, 1902.

3

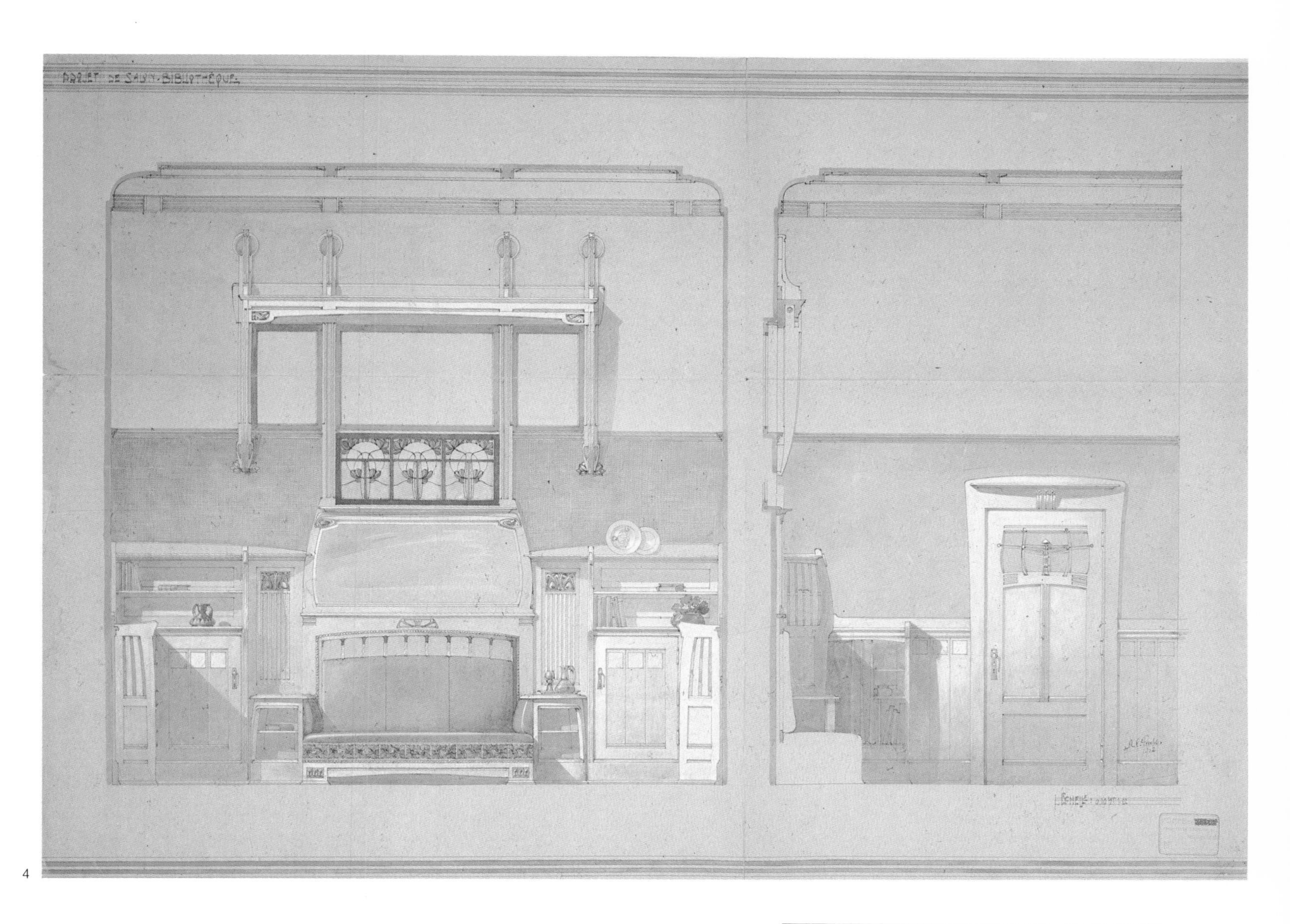

4

5

4. Belgian section.
   Preliminary design for the Studio of Hobé.
   Elevation and cross-section.
   Watercolour drawing by Antoine Pompe.
5. Prussian section.
   Kaiser Wilhelm Room.
   Architect: Bruno Möhring.
   Deutsche Kunst und Dekoration, 1902.

The tiered apartment building of Henri Sauvage

The builder in 1903 of the Habitation Hygiénique à Bon Marché ("Low-cost Hygienic Housing") in the Rue Trétaigne in Paris, Henri Sauvage centred his work on housing for one-third of a century. The Rue Trétaigne building[26] included a "consumers' cooperative," a people's university, a restaurant and shower baths, and a hanging garden on the concrete terrace roof. Together with Frantz Jourdain, Sauvage worked out a new conception of social housing, one that challenged the standing type of Parisian apartment building dating from Haussmann's time. His new type of tiered house made its first appearance in the Rue Vavin, Paris.

Sauvage sketched out his plans for the Rue Vavin building in 1909. When in 1912 he applied for the construction permit, it was refused on the grounds that his design would over-occupy the available terrain and rise too high. A second application being accepted, the building was erected in 1912-1913.

The principle of the tiered construction is best seen in cross-section. By the setting back of each storey, it avoids the corridor-street and opens up the lower levels to light and sun, even in the case of a high building. By the use of reinforced concrete, the shifting of loads caused by the set-back façade could be borne without ill consequences. As for the loss of internal volume which the tiering involved, it was compensated by the uses to which the tiers could be put (stocking, business, studios, circulation, ventilation shafts, etc.).

The Rue Vavin building demonstrated the soundness of the design, and Sauvage installed his offices on the ground floor. In an effort to publicize the town-planning advantages of his architectural model, he published a series of comparative illustrations of the successive types of street design: the medieval street, the modern street (a darkened corridor), the tower building (a negation of the city) and the tiered apartment building–only the last affording sunlight, greenery and urban continuity. After the First World War, in 1922, Sauvage built a low-cost housing block in the Rue des Amiraux (Paris XVIIIe), whose tiered design enabled him to include a large swimming pool. He also submitted many proposals for the opening up of a "triumphal way" in Paris (c. 1920) and for the rearrangement of the Porte Maillot (1931). More effectively than the principles laid down by Le Corbusier, the designs of Henri Sauvage would have reconciled the maintenance of an urban pattern with the necessities of improved sanitation in a city too densely built and populated.

Four drawings illustrating the advantages of tiered houses, from Henri Sauvage, *Les avantages des constructions à gradins*, 1914.

Paris: Tiered apartment house (Maison Sportive) designed by Sauvage at 26, Rue Vavin, 1912-1913. Detail of the front.

Imperial Hotel, Tokyo

1

The outstanding American architect of his day, and the only one who survived the shipwreck of the "international style," Frank Lloyd Wright[27] crowned the first part of his career by building the large Imperial Hotel in Tokyo (1915-1922, now demolished).
Wright conceived the hotel as a complex of low buildings in brick and concrete, designed to resist earthquakes. By means of gardens and sheets of water, he achieved that interpenetration of architecture and nature by which he set so much store, following the formulas worked out in his "prairie houses" of the Chicago region and adapted here to the Japanese tradition (after careful study of many Japanese buildings and early prints of them). Wright gave free rein to his decorative style, amplifying the repertory of the Chicago School, of Louis Sullivan in particular, whose chief collaborator Wright had been. But he now associated that style with his double passion for Maya and Japanese art. The result was neither eclecticism nor historicism, for Wright recast all he took. Forms are sober and powerful, the grid-plans distinctively his own. Motifs are monumentalized or drastically reduced, in a subtle interplay of scales which subsequently inspired the Dutch "De Stijl" movement.
The Imperial Hotel stands out as a remarkably inventive exercise in early twentieth-century modernity; its only rivals are the finest works of Behrens, Berlage and Van de Velde. It exemplifies all the wealth of a personal culture at once extensive and refined. Wright always refused to turn his back on the past for the sake of the future, and it was this solid grounding in history that enabled him, twenty years later, to regain the leadership of the modern movement and give it some hope of overcoming its liabilities.

2

Tokyo: Imperial Hotel, 1915-1922.
Demolished.
Architect: Frank Lloyd Wright.
1.2.4. Details of the interior and exterior.
3. Interior view.
L'Architecture Vivante, 1930.

3

4

Notes and bibliographical references

Introduction
(pages 6-7)

[1] This book may seem "very French": I realize this but do not think it matters, for the major themes of the 19th century have nothing national about them and parallel examples can always be found from one country to another. I have preferred to deal with those most familiar to me: an encyclopaedic approach, necessarily covering unfamiliar ground, is only too liable to result in caricature or confusion. I feel that, while the theories of Heinrich Wölfflin, for example, apply to the whole of classical production, they cannot be transposed and made to fit the original culture of this or that European country. Emil Kaufmann (*Architecture in the Age of Reason*, 1955) was commendably prudent in his approach, giving parallel accounts of three distinct countries, England, Italy and France. But this fails to work for the 19th century, when the geographical field of culture widens and new entities appear, like Germany, the United States, Russia. The linear character of my account called for one national culture as a guide-line and reference point in constant relation to parallel developments elsewhere. This book does not pretend to be exhaustive. It is not a catalogue. On the contrary, it is an attempt to get away from the usual "cataloguing" of 19th century styles of architecture.

[2] I am chiefly concerned with the mid and later 19th century and the early 20th; the period 1789-1830 is dealt with much more briefly. This treatment is dictated by the international development of industry.

[3] For a closer definition of eclecticism, see Chapter 3 (also Chapter 4, note 16). Though widely used, the term remains imprecise. Starting from its broadest acceptation, I have tried to narrow it down progressively.

Chapter I
Planning the landscape 1789-1830
(pages 11-37)

[1] Pompeii and Athens were rediscovered by artists in the late 18th and the 19th century. This rediscovery, as illustrated by the works sent back to Paris by French architects, prizemen of the Academy competition, was the theme of two exhibitions at the Ecole des Beaux-Arts, Paris: *Pompéi. Travaux et envois des architectes français au XIXe siècle*, 1981 and *Paris-Rome-Athènes. Voyage en Grèce des architectes français aux XIXe et XXe siècles*, 1982. The catalogues of these two exhibitions provide the most up-to-date survey of the archaeological sources of the return to the antique and its impact on the schools.

[2] In relying on the surveys of Delagardette rather than those of Labrouste, Quatremère de Quincy revealed his attachment to classical harmony. See Louis Hautecœur, *Histoire de l'architecture classique en France*, Paris, 1955, Vol. VI, p. 231.

[3] This view was put forward by Sigfried Giedion in *Space, Time and Architecture*, Cambridge, Massachusetts, 1941.

[4] The problem of the unity of the whole and the independence of the parts, in the doctrine of Leon Battista Alberti which forms the basis of the classical spirit, was brilliantly elucidated by Emil Kaufmann, *Architecture in the Age of Reason*, Harvard University Press, 1955. My own approach to the 19th century is largely inspired by Kaufmann's analysis.

[5] Henry Hitchcock, *Architecture: Nineteenth and Twentieth Centuries*, Pelican History of Art, Penguin Books, 1958 (p. 43 of the 1975 edition).

[6] The "regulation" alignments and outlines of Parisian buildings are discussed in a general historical study by Jean-Louis Subileau, "Le règlement du P.O.S. et le paysage de Paris", in *Paris-Projet*, No. 13-14, Paris, 1975, pp. 4-89.

[7] This is the point which, on the basis of my study *Paris XIXe siècle*, A.P.U.R., Mairie de Paris, 1982, I have tried to demonstrate for Pontivy ("L'urbanisme napoléonien à Pontivy," in *Mémoires de la Société d'Histoire et d'Archéologie de Bretagne*, Vol. LVII, 1980, pp. 5-30).

[8] One of the soundest overall studies of this question is Lewis Mumford, *The City in History*, New York, 1961.

[9] Jean-Marie Pérouse de Montclos, taking the example of La Garenne Lemot at Clisson, was the first to draw attention to the picturesque origins of suburban architecture ("La reconstruction de Clisson et le foyer artistique clissonnais dans la première moitié du XIXe siècle," in *Congrès Archéologique de Haute-Bretagne*, Paris, 1968, pp. 241-270, and "De la villa rustique d'Italie au pavillon de banlieue," in *Revue de l'Art*, No. 32, Paris, 1976, pp. 23-36).

[10] See Martin S. Van Treeck, "Inveraray, un exemple d'architecture avancée en Ecosse," in *L'Œil*, No. 158, February 1968, pp. 2-13.

[11] Reinhard Bentmann and Michael Müller, *Die Villa als Herrschaftsarchitektur. Versuch einer kunst- und sozialgeschichtlichen Analyse*, Frankfurt am Main, 1971; *La villa, architecture de domination*, Brussels, 1975.

[12] Much work has been done on this theme, following Michel Foucault, *Surveiller et punir*, Paris, 1975, which deals with prison and hospital architecture in the 19th century.

[13] "The Industrial Landscape" is the title of the exhibition organized by Hans Wieser-Benedetti, Annick Brauman and Pierre Lenain at the Archives d'Architecture Moderne, Brussels, 1975. Since then the term has gained wide currency.

[14] The best documented books on early iron construction (marred, unfortunately, by some errors of detail) are those of Giulio Roisecco, *L'architettura del ferro: l'Inghilterra 1688-1914*, Rome, 1972, *L'architettura del ferro: la Francia 1715-1914*, Rome, 1973, and *L'architettura del ferro: gli Stati Uniti 1776-1914*, Rome, 1980. For Cessart and his work in fields which have not yet been well researched, the indispensable source book remains *La Description des travaux hydrauliques de L.A. de Cessart*, Paris, 1806-1808.

[15] Jean-Marie Pérouse de Montclos, *Etienne-Louis Boullée 1728-1799. De l'architecture classique à l'architecture révolutionnaire*, Paris, 1969; *Etienne-Louis Boullée 1728-1799, Theoretician of Revolutionary Architecture*, London and New York, 1974.

[16] In addition to the book by Johann Friedrich Geist, *Passagen. Ein Bautyp des 19. Jahrhunderts*, Munich, 1969, the Parisian *passages* or covered galleries have been studied by Laura Wodka, "Les passages couverts dans Paris," in *Paris-Projet*, No. 15-16, 1976, pp. 110-151 (followed up by François Loyer, "A propos des passages," *Paris-Projet*, No. 17, 1977, pp. 108-119) and by Bertrand Lemoine, *Les passages couverts à Paris et en France*, Paris, 1980.

[17] Werner Szambien, "Paris néo-classique," supplement to *Bulletin d'Informations Architecturales*, No. 67, Institut Français d'Architecture, Paris, April 1982, summarizes his researches on this neglected subject, on which Szambien is preparing a book.

Bibliographical references

AULANIER Christiane, *Histoire du Palais et du Musée du Louvre*, Musées Nationaux, 1948-1971.

CHOAY Françoise, *The Modern City: Planning in the 19th Century*, New York, 1969.

CHRIST Yvan, "Alexandre Lenoir et son musée" in *Jardin des Arts*, March 1969.

CROOK J. Mordaunt, *The British Museum*, London, 1972.

CROOK J. Mordaunt, *The Greek Revival. Neo-Classical Attitudes in British Architecture. 1760-1870*, London, 1972.

DAVIS Terence, *The Architecture of John Nash*, London 1960.

EL-WAKIL Leila, "Architecture et urbanisme à Genève sous la Restauration" in *Genava*, Vol. 25, 1977.

FISCHER Manfred F., "A Century of Architecture. From Neo-Classicism to Aestheticism" in *Apollo*, No. 117, November 1971.

GANTNER Joseph, *Grundformen der europäischen Stadt. Versuch eines historischen Aufbaues in Genealogien*, Vienna, 1928.

GROMORT Georges, *Histoire abrégée de l'architecture en France au XIXe siècle*, Paris, 1924.
GUTKIND E.A., *Urban Development in Western Europe*, New York and London, 1971.
HUDSON Kenneth, *A Guide to the Industrial Archaeology of Europe*, Bath, 1971.
HUDSON Kenneth, *A Pocket Book for Industrial Archaeologists*, London, 1976.
ISON Walter, "A Show-Place of European Fame" in *Apollo*, No. 141, November 1973.
LANKHEIT Klaus, *Friedrich Weinbrenner und der Denkmalskult um 1800*, Basel and Stuttgart, 1979.
MORACHIELLO Paolo and TEYSSOT Georges, "Città di stato. La colonizzazione del territorio nel primo impero" in *Lotus International*, No. 24, 1979/III.
PEVSNER Nikolaus, *An Outline of European Architecture*, Pelican Books, 1943; Penguin edition, 1963.
PEVSNER Nikolaus, *Studies in Art, Architecture, and Design*, London, 1968.
ROSENAU Helen, *Boullée & Visionary Architecture*, London and New York, 1976.
RUFFINIÈRE DU PREY Pierre de la, *John Soane. The Making of an Architect*, Chicago and London, 1982.
STROUD Dorothy, *The Architecture of Sir John Soane*, London, 1961.
TEYSSOT Georges, "Cottages et pittoresque. Les origines du logement ouvrier en Angleterre. 1781-1818" in *Architecture-Mouvement-Continuité*, No. 34, 1974.
VALDENAIRE Arthur, *Friedrich Weinbrenner: sein Leben und seine Bauten*, Karlsruhe, 1919.
ZIEGLER Ernst, "Vom Leinwandgewerbe im alten St. Gallen" in *Schweiz*, 1/1976.

Exhibition catalogues

The Age of Neo-Classicism, Arts Council of Great Britain, Royal Academy and Victoria and Albert Museum, London, 1972.
Jardin en France, 1760-1820, Caisse Nationale des Monuments Historiques et des Sites, Hôtel de Sully, Paris, 1978.
Glyptothek München 1830-1980, Glyptothek, Munich, 1980.
Karl Friedrich Schinkel, Eine Ausstellung aus der Deutschen Demokratischen Republik, Hamburgische Architektenkammer/Hamburger Kunsthalle, Hamburg, 1982-1983.

Lassus has been studied in a monograph of the Ecole des Chartes: Jean-Michel Leniaud, *Jean-Baptiste Lassus (1807-1857) ou le temps retrouvé des Cathédrales*, Paris, 1980.

7 The philosophy of legitimist neo-Gothic is well brought out by Christian Derouet in the exhibition he organized on *L'œuvre de René Hodé 1840-1870* (published in the review *Les Monuments Historiques de la France*, 1976, No. 4, pp. 49-64, and accompanied by a pamphlet on *Les réalisations rurales des propriétaires terriens entre 1840 et 1870*, C.N.M.H.S., Paris, 1977). This work was followed up by François Loyer, "René Hodé: le néo-gothique 'Troubadour' en Anjou," *Arts de l'Ouest*, 1978, 1, pp. 37-44.

8 Véronique Miltgen, *Touraine néo-gothique*, exhibition catalogue, Musée des Beaux-Arts, Tours, 1978. Further regional studies of this kind are needed to show the diversity of French castle-building in the 19th century. English and German studies here are already much more comprehensive.

9 Ruskin's role was international. In France he was admired and supported by Robert de la Sizeranne (*Ruskin ou la religion de la Beauté*, Paris, 1897, often reprinted up to 1923) and Marcel Proust, who in 1903 published a French translation of Ruskin's *Bible of Amiens* prefaced with a long essay of his own. Curiously enough, Ruskin's ideas made their impact in France at the time of Art Nouveau, while in England of course they had been brought to bear long before. Cf. Kristine Ottesen Garrigan, *Ruskin on Architecture. His Thought and Influence*, University of Wisconsin Press, 1973.

10 On the early railway stations, see the exhibition catalogue *Le Temps des Gares*, Centre Georges-Pompidou, Paris, C.C.I. Edition, 1978, and (better documented than the exhibition itself) "L'espace du voyage: les gares," special issue of the review *Monuments Historiques*, 1978, No. 6.

11 *Hector Horeau. 1801-1872*, exhibition catalogue by F. Boudon, F. Loyer and P. Dufournet, Musée des Arts Décoratifs, Paris, C.E.R.A., 1979.

12 On Brighton see the well-documented article "Der Royal Pavilion in Brighton," *DU*, Zurich, February 1971, and Sigfried Giedion, *Space, Time and Architecture*, pp. 185-186.

13 Most historians confuse the greenhouses of Rohault de Fleury, in the Jardin des Plantes, Paris, with the existing ones, which are a reconstruction after the Prussian bombardments of 1870. On this point see the well-documented study by Marie-Christine Gangneux, Bernard Paurd and Edith Girard, edited by Bernard Marrey and Paul Chemetov under the title *Familièrement inconnues... Architectures, Paris 1848-1914*, Secrétariat à la Culture, Paris, n.d., published for the exhibition of this title in 1976.

Chapter II

The mechanical revolution 1830-1850
(pages 39-67)

1 Before it came to designate the decorative style of c. 1880-1910, the term Art Nouveau ("new art") had been widely used in the 19th century. The well-known report on the Great Exhibition of 1851 in London, drawn up in France by the Comte de Laborde, called for the creation of a new art closely linked with industry–a fundamental theme in the art of the 19th and 20th centuries.

2 The Salford mill, built in 1801 by Boulton and Watt's Soho foundry, is a prototype of the highest interest. Its advanced construction, a "truly extraordinary feat for builders of that date," was pointed out by Sigfried Giedion (*Space, Time and Architecture*, p. 189).

3 Apart from a few remarks of my own (*Architecture de la Grèce contemporaine*, typescript thesis, Sorbonne, Paris, 1966), there has been no research into the technology of cast-terracotta ornaments in Greek and Italian neo-Antique; and this is a pity, for by linking up with an ancient tradition this technology gave academic architecture of the 19th century one of its most effective means of expression.

4 After Lord Clark's remarkable study *The Gothic Revival* (London, 1928, revised edition 1950), little was written on this theme until the appearance of Paul Frankl's *The Gothic: Literary Sources and Interpretations through Eight Centuries*, Princeton, 1962, a most intelligent book which renewed the study of Gothic and opened a fresh field of investigation for medievalists. Since then the most accessible synthesis of the subject is Georg Germann, *Gothic Revival in Europe and Britain: Sources, Influences and Ideas*, London, 1972; see also the exhibition catalogue *Le "gothique" retrouvé*, C.N.M.H.S., Paris, 1979.

5 Viollet-le-Duc's *Dictionnaire raisonné de l'architecture française du XIe au XVIe siècle*, Paris, 1854-1868, 10 volumes, is full of pertinent observations on his restoration of Notre-Dame. See also François Loyer, "Notre-Dame lavée," *L'Œil*, No. 208, April 1972, pp. 12-24.

6 Since the fine article by Bruno Foucart and Véronique Noël-Bouton, "St-Nicolas de Nantes, bataille et triomphe du néo-gothique," in *Congrès Archéologique de Haute-Bretagne*, 1968, pp. 136-181, the personality of

Bibliographical references

BERTSCH Christoph, *Fabrikarchitektur. Entwicklung und Bedeutung einer Baugattung anhand Vorarlberger Beispiele des 19. und 20. Jahrhunderts*, Wiesbaden, 1981.
DAUMAS Maurice, *L'archéologie industrielle en France*, Paris, 1980.
DEVILLERS Christian and HUET Bernard, *Le Creusot. Naissance et développement d'une ville industrielle 1782-1914*, Seyssel (France), 1981.
ETLIN Richard A., "Landscapes of Eternity: Funerary Architecture and the Cemetery, 1793-1881" in *Oppositions*, No. 8, Spring, 1977.
FORTIER Bruno and VAYSSIÈRE Bruno, "Spazio pubblico e società civile. Dalle Saline di Chaux al Foro Bonaparte di Milano" in *Lotus International*, No. 24, 1979/III.
HUPPERTZ Andreas, *Der Kölner Dom und seine Kunstschätze*, Cologne, 1956.
KLINGENDER Francis D., *Art and the Industrial Revolution*, London, 1968.
KUBINSZKY Mihály, *Bahnhöfe Europas*, Stuttgart, 1969.
LENAIN Pierre, "Quand l'industrie laisse des paysages" in *Lotus International*, No. 14, March 1977.
LESUEUR Frédéric, *Le Château de Blois*, Paris, 1970.
LIEB Norbert and HUFNAGL Florian, *Leo von Klenze: Gemälde und Zeichnungen*, Munich, 1979.
MEEKS Carroll L.V., *The Railroad Station. An Architectural History*, New Haven, 1964.
MEYER André, *Neugotik und Neuromantik in der Schweiz. Die Kirchenarchitektur des 19. Jahrhunderts*, Zürich, 1973.
PAYEN Jacques, *Les bâtiments à usage industriel aux XVIIIe et XXe siècles en France*, Paris, 1978.
POËTE Marcel, *Une vie de cité. Paris de sa naissance à nos jours*, 4 vols., Paris, 1924-1931.
PÜCKLER Fürst, "Reise ins Regency" in *Du*, 8, 1980.
PUTTEMANS Pierre, *Architecture moderne en Belgique*, Brussels, 1974.
QUERZOLA Jean, "La naissance de l'usine" in *Technique & Architecture*, No. 314, May 1977.
RATHKE Ursula, *Preussische Burgenromantik am Rhein*, Munich, 1979.
ROBINSON John Martin, *The Wyatts: An Architectural Dynasty*, Oxford, 1979.
SMETS Marcel, *L'avènement de la cité-jardin en Belgique: histoire de l'habitat social en Belgique de 1830 à 1930*, Brussels, 1977.

VIDLER Anthony, "Architettura, gestione, principi etici: progetto di una comunità produttiva alla fine del XVIII secolo" in *Lotus International*, No. 14, March 1977.
VORSTEHER Dieter, "Alta Slesia: nascita di un paesaggio industriale" in *Casabella*, No. 483, September 1982.

Exhibition catalogue

La Représentation du Travail. Mines, forges, usines, Centre National de Recherche d'Animation et de Création pour les Arts Plastiques, Ecomusée de la Communauté, Le Creusot-Montceau, Château de la Verrerie, Le Creusot, 1977-1978.

Chapter III

Industry in its splendour 1850-1870
(pages 71-109)

1 For an understanding of the mentality of the Second Empire, the playwright Eugène Labiche (1815-1888) is as important as Zola, if not more so, for his comedies of character and manners are a direct reflection of contemporary events, while Zola's novels were written later, under the Third Republic. From *Un Chapeau de paille d'Italie* (1851), *L'Affaire de la rue de Lourcine* (1857), *Le Voyage de Monsieur Perrichon* (1860) and *La Poudre aux yeux* (1861) up to *La Grammaire* (1867), Labiche's plays illustrate with comic ferocity the ascension of the French bourgeoisie, with many incidental insights into the role of architecture in everyday life.

2 The term "guerre sociale" is used by General L.P.J.M. Cosseron de Villenoisy in his *Essai historique sur la fortification*, Paris, 1869. Discussing the French siege of Saragossa (1808-1809), he points out that modern warfare is in effect "social warfare" or "guerrilla warfare."

3 Just as George Sand was writing her peasant novels, French ethnography was being born: folk songs and tales were being collected, rural costume and furniture studied. In Brittany the Association Bretonne was founded by the legitimist Henri de la Villemarqué, compiler of the Breton folk miscellany *Barsaz Breiz*: his work has much to tell us about this cultural regionalism and its undisguised political overtones. But the material culture of rural life, its objects and utensils, only began to be seriously studied later on, under the impact of the English Arts and Crafts movement.

4 This expression, familiar to historians of the Roman Empire, seems appropriate to one of the schools of 19th century architecture, in the perspectives opened up by the Atelier Lebas ("La basilique Sainte-Anne d'Auray, monument de l'éclectisme" in *Bulletin de la Société de l'Histoire de l'Art Français*, Année 1977, Paris, 1979, pp. 237-264).

5 The specialization of agriculture, by the single-crop system, is a form of industrialization, only made possible by an exchange economy based on transport. All Western Europe experienced this transformation of tools, methods and products as soon as the industrial economy came into being. It is a mistake to suppose that, while the cities were being renewed, the countryside remained static. On the contrary, the 19th century was a period of sweeping reconstruction of farm buildings, of villages and country towns, of rural churches and monuments, so much so that our rural patrimony of today, like our urban and industrial patrimony, largely dates to the latter half of the 19th century.

6 Unlike earlier industrial plants such as Le Creusot or Port-Brillet, which were located in sites providing water power, river transport, and forests to keep the furnaces burning. The same was true of the Ardennes, along the river Meuse, whose high industrial density was due to the abundant fuel supplied by the upland forests.

7 "Industrial minarets": the term occurs in an article of 1893 by Henri Beyaert in the Brussels review *L'Art Moderne* edited by Octave Maus (and reprinted in *L'Emulation*, the magazine of the Société Centrale des Architectes de Belgique, 1893, column 154): "Our chimneys are our minarets, often much finer than the minarets of Eastern cities described in ecstatic terms by travellers, who are always inclined to be struck in foreign lands by beauties which they do not notice at home." The whole article is a hymn to industrial architecture.

8 On these early brick chimneys, see the fine illustrated book by J. Lacroux and C. Détain, *La brique ordinaire au point de vue décoratif*, Paris, 1878.

9 Christian Beutler, *Weltausstellungen im 19. Jahrhundert*, exhibition catalogue, Museum für angewandte Kunst, Munich, covers the great international exhibitions from 1851 to 1900. For architecture and industrial objects, see the exhibition catalogue of 1971, *Die Verborgene Vernunft. Funktionale Gestaltung im 19. Jahrhundert*, also at the Museum für angewandte Kunst, Munich.

10 On the Palladian model as taken up and used in one opera after another, see the amusing article by Daniel Rabreau, "Ce cher XIXe ou Palladio et l'éclectisme parisien" in *Monuments Historiques*, 1975, No. 2, pp. 56-65.

11 The area of Les Halles was the first to be tackled by Paris town-planners of the 19th century in their effort to open up the city centre. A considerable monograph (which, however, underestimates the 19th century contribution) was devoted to it by F. Boudon, A. Chastel, F. Couzy and F. Hamon, *Système de l'architecture urbaine. Le quartier des Halles à Paris*, C.N.R.S., Paris, 1977.

12 Much of what I have to say here stems from my study *Paris XIXe siècle*, A.P.U.R., Mairie de Paris, 1982.

13 For the renovation of Brussels, see the rich exhibition catalogue, *Bruxelles, construire et reconstruire. Architecture et aménagement urbain, 1780-1914*, Crédit Communal, Brussels, 1979.

14 Daniel Rabreau was the moving spirit behind the fine exhibition organized by Dominique Jarrassé, Claudine de Vaulchier and Thomas von Joest, *Gabriel Davioud. Architecte de Paris*, Délégation à l'action artistique de la Ville de Paris, Paris, 1981-1982. This exhibition led to the rediscovery of an extensive series of designs bequeathed by the Davioud family to the City of Paris, which had been mislaid in the attic storerooms of the Hôtel de Ville.

15 For the centenary of the Palais de Justice in Brussels, an authoritative monograph was published on the Belgian architect Joseph Poelaert (1817-1879), edited by Richard Vandendaele: *Poelaert et son temps*, Institut Supérieur d'Architecture Victor Horta, Brussels, 1980.

16 Opposite views of Viollet-le-Duc appear to be taken by Louis Grodecki and myself. But as pointed out by Bruno Foucart (in *Viollet-le-Duc*, exhibition catalogue, Réunion des Musées Nationaux, Paris, 1980, p. 14), his work is open to two possible readings, for it has "a Guimard side and a Le Corbusier side."

17 That six million francs were spent on La Païva's town house is stated by Victor Champier, "Une visite à l'hôtel Païva. La décoration sous le Second Empire," *Revue des Arts Décoratifs*, Paris, 1901, Vol. XXI, pp. 241-258.

18 Leonardo Benevolo, *Aux sources de l'urbanisme moderne*, Paris, 1972 (Italian edition, Bari, 1963), is a standard work on public housing. For France, see Roger-Henri Guerrand, *Les origines du logement social en France*, Paris, 1967, followed up by *Le logement populaire en France: sources documentaires et biliographie (1800-1960)*, Paris, 1979.

19 R.L. Delevoy and Annick Brauman, *Le familistère de Guise ou les équivalents de la richesse*, Archives d'Architecture Moderne, Brussels, 1976, and Annick Brauman, *Jean-Baptiste André Godin 1871-1888*, Brussels, 1980.

20 On suburban housing in France, see the three-volume study published by the Centre de Recherche d'Urbanisme: H. and M.G. Raymond and A. and N. Haumont, *L'habitat pavillonnaire*, N. Haumont, *Les pavillonnaires*, and above all M.G. Raymond, *La politique pavillonnaire*, Paris, 1966.

Bibliographical references

BENEVOLO Leonardo, *Histoire de l'architecture moderne*. Vol. 1 *La révolution industrielle*. Vol. 2 *Avant-garde et mouvement moderne (1890-1930)*. Vol. 3 *Les conflits et l'après-guerre*, Paris, 1978, 1979, 1980.
BIEHN Heinz, *Residenzen der Romantik*, Munich, 1970.
CAMERON Roderick, "Crystal Palace" in *L'Œil*, No. 62, February 1960.
CHRIST Yvan, *Les Métamorphoses de Paris*, Paris, 1967.
CHRIST Yvan, *Les Nouvelles Métamorphoses de Paris*, Paris, 1976.
CLÉMENT B., RIGNAULT B., SAUVAGEOT D., "L'architecture industrielle dans la communauté urbaine du Creusot-Montceau-les-Mines" in *Monuments Historiques*, No. 3, 1977.
CROOK J. Mordaunt, *Victorian Architecture. A Visual Anthology*, New York and London, 1971.
DYOS H.J. and WOLFF Michael, *The Victorian City: Images and Realities*, 2 vols., London, 1973.
FAVARDIN Patrick, "Nécessité et limites de la cité ouvrière en province" in *Monuments Historiques*, No. 3, 1977.
GIROUARD Mark, *The Victorian Country House*, Oxford, 1971.
GRODECKI Louis, *Pierrefonds*, Caisse Nationale des Monuments Historiques et des Sites, Paris, 1979.
GRUMBACH Antoine, "The Promenades of Paris" in *Oppositions*, No. 8, Spring 1977.
HAMMER Karl, *Jakob Ignaz Hittorff. Ein Pariser Baumeister, 1792-1867*, Stuttgart, 1968.
HARGROVE June Ellen, "L'hôtel de la Païva. L'architecture et le décor sous le Second Empire" in *Monuments Historiques*, No. 102, April 1979.
HUGUENEY Jeanne, "Napoléon III et Haussmann dessinateurs de jardins" in *Monuments Historiques*, No. 1, 1974.
JUIN Hubert, *Le Livre de Paris 1900*, Paris, 1977.
LAVEDAN Pierre, *Les villes françaises*, Paris, 1960.

MERCANTON Jacques, *Les châteaux magiques de Louis II de Bavière*, Lausanne, 1963.
METCALF Priscilla, *Victorian London*, London, 1972.
PLOUIN Renée, "La demeure française au XIXe siècle" in *Monuments Historiques*, No. 1, 1974.
PORT Michael H., *The Houses of Parliament*, New Haven, 1976.
SAALMAN Howard, *Haussmann: Paris Transformed*, New York, 1971.
SALMON M.-J., "Le château de Pierrefonds" in *Monuments Historiques*, No. 4, 1973.
SCHNEIDER Donald David, *The Works and Doctrine of Jacques Ignace Hittorff, 1792-1867*, 2 vols., New York, 1977.
TARN J.N., *Working-Class Housing in 19th-Century Britain*, London, 1971.
VAN ZANTEN David Theodore, *The Architectural Polychromy of the 1830's*, New York and London, 1977.
VINSON Robert-Jean, "Des monuments négligés" in *Connaissance des Arts*, No. 291, May 1976.
WIEBENSON Dora, "Le Parc Monceau et ses 'Fabriques'" in *Monuments Historiques*, No. 5, 1976.

Exhibition catalogues

L'Usine. Travail et Architecture, exhibition of the Centre de Création Industrielle, Pavillon de Marsan, Paris, 1973 (reviewed in *Architecture-Mouvement-Continuité*, No. 30, May 1973).
"Marble Halls", Drawings and Models for Victorian Secular Buildings, Victoria and Albert Museum, London, 1973.
Cerdá 1876-1976, centenary exhibition, Colegio Nacional de Ingenieros de Caminos, Canales y Puertos, Barcelona, 1976.

Chapter IV

The debate on architecture
(pages 111-139)

1 Its moral implications have rightly been singled out as a fundamental aspect of 19th century architecture by David Watkin, *Morality and Architecture: The Development of a Theme in Architectural History and Theory from the Gothic Revival to the Modern Movement*, Oxford, 1978.

2 Quoted from the speech of Emile Trélat at the opening of the Ecole Spéciale d'Architecture, Paris, 1875. This Ecole Spéciale, a competitor of the Ecole des Beaux-Arts, was born of the conflict of the rationalists with academicism. Trélat's speech was a hymn of praise to Labrouste and his ideas.

3 On the French architects awarded the Prix de Rome, see Pierre Pinon, "Les leçons de Rome" in the special issue of *Monuments Historiques* (No. 123, October-November 1982, pp. 18-24) devoted to the Prix de Rome award-winners. The Ecole des Beaux-Arts in Paris has become a much-discussed subject with the books of Arthur Drexler, *The Architecture of the Ecole des Beaux-Arts*, New York, 1977, and Robin Middleton, *The Beaux-Arts and Nineteenth Century French Architecture*, London, 1982. Pierre Pinon's article is of great interest as giving a concrete idea of the archaeological knowledge of these young Frenchmen in Rome, of their tastes and outlook–which the current Anglo-Saxon passion for these Beaux-Arts architects tends to mythify.

4 On the archaeological interests of these Prix de Rome architects, see the two exhibition catalogues, *Pompéi*, 1981, and *Paris-Rome-Athènes*, 1982, Ecole des Beaux-Arts, Paris. It was not till 1846 that they were authorized, during their study period at the Villa Medici in Rome, to range beyond Italy and visit Greece, where, however, they were attracted less by ancient Greek art than by Byzantine art, to which their eyes had already been opened in Sicily.

5 Georges Daux, secretary of the French School in Athens, published in 1956 an article on Normand's Athens photographs, "L'Athènes antique en 1851: photographies d'Alfred Normand," *Bulletin de Correspondance Hellénique*, Vol. LXXX, II, 1956, pp. 619-624, plates XI-XXIV. Some further work has been done by Philippe Néagu, *Alfred-Nicolas Normand architecte. Photographies de 1851-1852*, exhibition catalogue, Direction des Musées de France, Paris, n.d., and Pierre Saddy, *Alfred Normand architecte 1822-1909*, C.N.M.H.S., Paris, 1978. A comprehensive study of Normand is still needed.

6 In a brief polemical article for Maurice Culot ("Les traîtres sont dans les deux camps" in *Archives de l'Architecture Moderne*, No. 4, January 1976, pp. 12-13), I pointed out how very different theory and practice could be in 19th century architecture. I still hold this view, and indeed it is one of the underlying themes of the present book.

7 This forgotten architect, Florimond Boulanger, was rediscovered by the historian Roger Hanoune, who found some of his papers at the University of Lille and published an article on him: "De Douai à Rome et Athènes: un architecte oublié, Florimond Boulanger (1807-1875)," in *Revue du Nord*, No. 241, April-June 1979. See also Marie-Laure Blanchon, *Les architectes français en Grèce au XIXe siècle*, typescript thesis, D.E.A., Université de Haute-Bretagne, Rennes, 1980.

8 "Oh, you have some Etruscans, I said, laughing in spite of myself..." (letter from Viollet-le-Duc to his father, from Rome, 28 November 1836, quoted in *Le voyage d'Italie d'Eugène Viollet-le-Duc 1836-1837*, Ecole des Beaux-Arts, Paris, 1980. The so-called "Greek" style of elegant decoration, based on the surviving art of Magna Graecia and very fashionable under the Second Empire, was in fact a purely aestheticizing interpretation of academic teaching. Beside this "Greek" or "Etruscan" style, that of Ingres, who moved towards a form of Pre-Raphaelitism, could only appear as revolutionary!

9 The best study of Labrouste, all too brief, is that of Pierre Saddy, *Henri Labrouste architecte 1801-1875*, C.N.M.H.S., Paris, 1977, published for the Labrouste exhibition at the Hôtel de Sully.

10 In regarding Pugin as a rationalist, I realize that I differ from David Watkin. But it seems to me misleading to reduce Pugin's approach to ecclesiologism. (Likewise, in France, Bruno Foucart has emphasized the rationalist aspect of J.B. Lassus's ideas.) In the face of academicism, mysticism and rationalism could at times form a common front. The 19th century is full of these odd convergences between opposing views, in their common struggle against the establishment mentality.

11 The exceptional personality of Viollet-le-Duc has been well served by his descendants. Thanks to them it was possible to organize the exhibitions of P.M. Auzas, *Eugène Viollet-le-Duc. 1814-1879*, C.N.M.H.S., Paris, 1965, and Bruno Foucart, *Viollet-le-Duc*, Réunion des Musées Nationaux, Paris, 1980, the latter extended by two others, *Viollet-le-Duc, centenaire de la mort à Lausanne*, Musée de l'Ancien-Evêché, Lausanne, 1979, and *Le voyage d'Italie d'Eugène Viollet-le-Duc 1836-1837*, Ecole des Beaux-Arts, Paris, 1980.

12 Bruno Foucart, "La cathédrale synthétique de Louis-Auguste Boileau," *Revue de l'Art*, No. 3, 1969, pp. 49-66.

13 Prompted by some remarks made by the architect Mogens Prip-Buus, I pointed out this link between Gaudí and L.A. Boileau in the course of the Antoni Gaudí colloquium held in 1971 at the Musée des Arts Décoratifs, Paris.

14 J. Lobet, "L'architecture et Viollet-le-Duc à propos de l'église d'Aillant" in *L'Almanach historique de l'Yonne*, January 1868 (also quoted by B. Lemoine and C. Berger in *Viollet-le-Duc*, 1980, p. 189).

15 Jacques de Caso, "Le décor en 'motif détaché' dans l'ornement d'architecture et les arts décoratifs en France, 1840-1870" in *Actes du XXIIe Congrès international d'Histoire de l'Art*, Budapest, 1969 (Akademiai Kiado, Budapest, 1972), Vol. 2, pp. 293-301. To "motif détaché" I prefer the term "ornement-agrafe" (clip-on ornament).

16 In Chapter III I defined eclecticism more positively as a philosophical attitude based on freedom of choice. Hence my dissatisfaction with the current definition of the term. I would rather emphasize the notion of *analytical* architecture, meaning a collage of fragments whose significance springs from their unexpected arrangement. These analytics represent an essentially formal stance, a set of images removed from their frame of reference. Their unity then is not ideological but artistic; it lies in the intrinsic beauty of the arrangement. As for the implicit discourse, it is totally diverted by this collage principle which, without realizing it, makes the cultural reference an object of derision. All the ambiguity of the 19th century is present in this negative exaltation of the past.

17 In the proceedings of Robin Middleton's Beaux-Arts colloquium in 1982, Hélène Lipstadt aptly singled out the role of César Daly as the theorist of eclecticism. Ann van Zanten's Harvard thesis on Daly was completed before her untimely death.

18 Normand's work on the Pompeian House is well analysed by Marie-Noëlle de Gary, *La maison pompéienne du Prince Napoléon, 1856. Dessins de l'architecte Alfred Normand*, exhibition catalogue, Cabinet des Dessins, Musée des Arts Décoratifs, Paris, 1979.

19 Schooled as a sociologist, Paul Thompson has written a brilliant monograph on *William Butterfield*, London, 1971, well describing his role in Victorian England.

20 See Kristine Ottesen Garrigan, *Ruskin on Architecture. His Thought and Influence*, University of Wisconsin Press, 1973.

21 Paul Thompson, not without humour, analyses the opposition to Butterfield's "bad taste" and his relations with the nouveau riche mentality of the rising bourgeoisie. He makes clear how inadequate is the shallow sociological approach to Butterfield, whose style in its very directness and aggressiveness could only be understood by a highly cultivated public, able to appreciate its references and their reinterpretation.

[22] In Chapter III the Paris Opera was presented in its urban context, with the same arguments.

[23] So far, the only article of reference on Charles Garnier is that of Jean-François Revel, "Charles Garnier, dernier fils de la Renaissance" in *L'Œil*, No. 99, March 1963, pp. 2-11. An exhaustive monograph on him is being prepared by Editions Berger-Levrault, Paris: it will fill a surprising gap in the history of 19th century French art.

Bibliographical references

ANDRÉADIS Stratis G. and TRAVLOS Jean, *Architecture néoclassique en Grèce*, Athens, 1967.

AULANIER Christiane, *Histoire du Palais et du Musée du Louvre. Le nouveau Louvre de Napoléon III*, 2 vols., Paris, 1953.

BERCÉ Françoise, "Formation et Recrutement depuis 1830. Profession, Architecte en Chef des Monuments Historiques" in *Monuments Historiques*, No. 113, January-February 1981.

BÖRSCH-SUPAN Eva, *Berliner Baukunst nach Schinkel 1840-1870*, Munich 1977.

FOUCART Bruno, "Henri Labrouste et ses contemporains" in *Monuments Historiques*, No. 6, 1975.

GASCAR Pierre, "L'Opéra, une esthétique de l'accumulation" in *Zoom*, No. 31, 1975.

LENIAUD Jean-Michel, "Les architectes diocésains. Profession, Architecte en Chef des Monuments Historiques" in *Monuments Historiques*, No. 113, January-February 1981.

MANG Karl and Eva, *Wiener Architektur 1860-1930 in Zeichnungen*, Stuttgart, 1979.

MATTON Lya and Raymond, *Athènes et ses monuments du XVIIe siècle à nos jours*, Athens, 1963.

MIDDLETON Robin and WATKIN David, *Architettura dell'ottocento/I. L'Illuminismo in Francia e in Inghilterra. Architettura dell'ottocento/II. Diffusione e sviluppo del Classicismo e del revival gotico*, 2 volumes, Milan, 1980

ROCCA Roger, "L'observatoire de Nice. La boula blanca dei nissart" in *Lou Sourgentin*, revue culturelle bilingue français-nissart, No. 48, September-October 1981.

STANTON Phoebe, *Pugin*, New York, 1972.

STEINHAUSER Monika, *Die Architektur der Pariser Oper*, Munich, 1969.

Exhibition catalogues

Dessins d'Architecture du XVe au XIXe siècle dans les collections du Musée du Louvre, Musée du Louvre, Paris, 1972.

I calotipi della Società francese di fotografia. 1840-1860, Comune di Venezia, Venice, 1981.

Chapter V
Industrial architecture
(pages 141-173)

[1] Pierre Francastel's essay *Art et Technique*, Paris, 1956, remains a standard reference work, even though the artistic context to which he referred is no longer seen in the same light and the undiscriminating exploitation of his ideas has too often distorted them. The central problem of art's relation to industry was debated by architects for half a century, from the proclamations of Viollet-le-Duc to the book of Gabriel Davioud, *L'art et l'industrie*, Paris, 1874. The importance of this debate makes it a subject of continuing interest.

[2] In my study *Paris XIXe siècle*, A.P.U.R., Mairie de Paris, 1982, I tried to trace the technical transformation of the Paris apartment building, well before the appearance of modern comfort and sanitation. But a comprehensive study based on 19th century publications is needed.

[3] Historians unfamiliar with technology continue to confuse iron, cast iron and steel. There is a continual confusion between cast and wrought iron, and between iron and steel, throughout the books of Giulio Roisecco, *L'architettura del ferro* (*L'Inghilterra 1688-1914*, Rome, 1972, *La Francia 1715-1914*, Rome, 1973, and *Gli Stati Uniti 1776-1914*, Rome, 1980). This is not the case with Marie-Christine Gangneux, Bernard Paurd and Edith Girard, *Architectures, Paris 1848-1914*, n.d. (1976): these authors show a perfect understanding of this point. The best analysis of iron and cast iron is that of Henri Poupée, "Fer et fonte (Architecture)" in *Encyclopaedia Universalis*, Vol. 6, Paris, 1971, pp. 1027-1031.

[4] For an essay on the technology and originality of the Pont des Arts, Paris (before its destruction), see F. Loyer and M. Mosser, "Plaidoyer pour un pont" in *Architecture d'Aujourd'hui*, No. 176, November-December 1976, pp. 119-134.

[5] A fine series of drawings by Victor Baltard, showing the successive states of his designs for Les Halles (Central Markets), has recently been acquired by the Bibliothèque Historique de la Ville de Paris. From these one can now follow in detail the evolution of his ideas up to the elegant solution which he finally arrived at. On the stages of the project, see M.C. Gangneux, B. Paurd and E. Girard, *Architectures, Paris 1848-1914*, n.d. (1976), pp. 32-34, and also V. Baltard and F. Callet, *Monographie des Halles centrales de Paris*, Paris, 1863.

[6] Under the direction of R.H. Guerrand, an interesting study of the Wallace fountains was made in 1972 by the students of the Unité Pédagogique d'Architecture No. 8 of Paris (Patrick Delamotte, "1872-1972. Le centenaire des fontaines Wallace" in *Architecture-Mouvement-Continuité*, No. 29, June 1973, p. 50). See also Marie de Thézy, *Paris, la rue (le mobilier urbain du Second Empire à nos jours)*, Société des Amis de la Bibliothèque Historique de la Ville de Paris, Paris, 1976.

[7] French foundries have been studied by François Chaslin. His well-researched book, of great interest to historians, was reviewed in *Fontes ornées*, supplement to No. 45 of *Bulletin d'Information Inter-Etablissements*, C.E.R.A., Paris, 1979.

[8] E. Graeme Robertson and Joan Robertson, in *Cast Iron Decoration. A World Survey*, London, 1977, provide a prodigious documentation on the subject, showing in particular how very different was English cast iron from the use made of it in France and the United States.

[9] E. Graeme Robertson and Joan Robertson, in *Cast Iron Decoration. A World Survey*, London, 1977, ill. 322.

[10] Eugène Viollet-le-Duc, *Entretiens sur l'Architecture*, Vol. 2, Paris, 1872 (18e Entretien, p. 327).

[11] Carl W. Condit, *The Chicago School of Architecture*, Chicago, 1964.

[12] See Hugh Morrison, *Louis Sullivan, Prophet of Modern Architecture*, New York, 1935; John Szarkowski, *The Ideas of Louis Sullivan*, Minneapolis, 1956; Willard Connelly, *Louis Sullivan: The Shaping of American Architecture*, New York, 1960; and the interesting booklet of John Vinci, *The Art Institute of Chicago: the Stock Exchange Trading Room*, Chicago, 1977.

[13] Jean-Philippe Desportes, "Alavoine et la flèche de la cathédrale de Rouen" in *Revue de l'Art*, No. 13, C.N.R.S., Paris, 1971, pp. 48-62.

[14] The Noisiel factory was published by Jules Saulnier in *Encyclopédie d'Architecture*, 1874. See also M.C. Gangneux, B. Paurd and E. Girard, *Architectures, Paris 1848-1914*, Paris, n.d. (1976), pp. 40-41.

Bibliographical references

BLASER Werner, *Architecture en filigrane: construction en métal et en verre*, Basel, 1980.

CARMENT-LANFRY Anne-Marie, *La Cathédrale de Rouen*, Colmar-Ingerseheim, 1973.

CHADWICK George F., *The Works of Sir Joseph Paxton. 1803-1865*, London, 1961.

CONDIT Carl. W., *The Chicago School of Architecture. A History of Commercial and Public Building in the Chicago Area, 1875-1925*, Chicago, 1964.

GALLAND Noëlle and PISTRE Jean, "Noisiel, village et chocolaterie Meunier" in *Architecture-Mouvement-Continuité*, No. 30, May 1973.

GAYLE Margot, *Cast-Iron Architecture in New York*, New York, 1974.

GLOAG John and BRIDGWATER Derek, *A History of Cast Iron in Architecture*, London, 1948.

GRENIER Vincent, "Les débuts du métal dans l'architecture. Un matériau nouveau pour une technique traditionnelle" in *Monuments Historiques*, No. 1, 1974.

HENNIG-SCHEFOLD Monica and SCHMIDT-THOMSEN Helga, *Transparenz und Masse. Passagen und Hallen aus Eisen und Glas. 1800-1880*, Cologne, 1972.

HERBERT Gilbert, *Pioneers of Prefabrication: the British Contribution in the Nineteenth Century*, Baltimore, 1978.

MAYER Harold M. and WADE Richard C., *Chicago: Growth of a Metropolis*, Chicago, 1969.

PONENTE Nello, *Structures of the Modern World 1850-1900*, Geneva, 1965.

SPRAGUE Paul E., *The Drawings of Louis Henry Sullivan: a Catalogue of the Frank Lloyd Wright Collection at the Avery Architectural Library*, Princeton, 1979.

Exhibition catalogue

Victor Baltard. Projets inédits pour les Halles Centrales, Bibliothèque Historique de la Ville de Paris, Paris, 1978.

Chapter VI

Past and present 1870-1890
(pages 177-211)

[1] The competition for the Paris Opera opened in 1861 and the building was completed in 1874, the year of the competitions for the Hôtel de Ville and the Sacré-Cœur Basilica in Montmartre, the year too of the first group exhibition of the Impressionnists. Two years before, in 1872, appeared the second volume of Viollet-le-Duc's *Entretiens sur l'Architecture*, Saulnier finished the Menier factory at Noisiel, Richardson began Trinity Church in Boston and Furness began the Academy of Fine Arts in Philadelphia. These French and American dates, coming perhaps a little later than the key dates of English architecture, show the importance of the 1870s as a turning point.

[2] Quoted by Louis Hautecœur, *Histoire de l'architecture classique en France*, Vol. VII, Paris, 1957, p. 292.

[3] This was the generation of Guadet and Auguste Choisy. The great technical histories of architecture were the product of the analytical eye of the rationalists, wholly renewing the history of architectural styles. From this point of view, *L'Art de bâtir chez les Byzantins* by Auguste Choisy (1883) is surely the most important book of the century, after Viollet-le-Duc's *Entretiens sur l'Architecture*.

[4] H. Wieser-Benedetti, A. Brauman and P. Lenain, *Le paysage de l'industrie*, exhibition catalogue, Archives d'Architecture Moderne, Brussels, 1975, and above all Lise Grenier and H. Wieser-Benedetti, *Les châteaux de l'industrie. Recherches sur l'architecture de la région lilloise de 1830 à 1930*, Vol. 2, Archives d'Architecture Moderne, Brussels, 1979.

[5] On the Feldschlösschen brewery, see "Der Brauer als Schlossherr" in *Schweiz*, No. 3, 1977, pp. 54-65.

[6] This was the theme pointed up in the fine exhibition organized by Olivier Lépine, *Equivoques. Peintures françaises du XIXe siècle*, Musée des Arts Décoratifs, Paris, 1973, and reflected too in the exhibition of Geneviève Lacambre, *Le Musée du Luxembourg en 1874*, Réunion des Musées Nationaux, Paris, 1974.

[7] Françoise Boudon, "Recherche sur la pensée et l'œuvre d'Anatole de Baudot, 1834-1915," special issue of the review *Architecture-Mouvement-Continuité*, No. 28, March 1973.

[8] The competition for the reconstruction of the Hôtel de Ville, Paris, was of considerable importance; the 1982 exhibition at the Mairie de Paris failed to do justice to it. Equally important is its interior decoration, the most complete ornamental ensemble produced in France under the Third Republic. New light has been thrown on the Hôtel de Ville by the researches of Pierre Vaysse.

[9] On Anatole de Baudot, see above, Note 7.

[10] Mariana Griswold Van Rensselaer, *Henry Hobson Richardson and His Works*, Boston and New York, 1888, reprinted New York, 1969; Henry-Russell Hitchcock, *The Architecture of H.H. Richardson and His Times*, 3rd edition, Cambridge, Massachusetts, 1975.

[11] James F. O'Gorman, *The Architecture of Frank Furness*, Philadelphia Museum of Art, 1973.

[12] Peter Singelenberg, Manfred Bock and Kees Broos, *H.P. Berlage, bouwmeester, 1856-1934*, The Hague, 1975.

[13] Louis-Marie Cordonnier (1854-1941), winner of the competition for the Amsterdam Stock Exchange and a prominent architect in the Lille region (Mairie de la Madeleine, churches of Merville, Calonne and Coudry, Hôtel de Ville at Loos, etc.), was the son of the architect Jean-Baptiste Ferdinand Cordonnier (1820-?). He later collaborated with his own son, Louis S. Cordonnier (1884-1960), in building the basilica of Sainte-Thérèse de l'Enfant Jésus at Lisieux (from 1929). On the work of the Cordonnier family in the Lille area, see *Le siècle de l'éclectisme. Lille 1830-1930*, Archives d'Architecture Moderne, Brussels, 1979.

[14] George R. Collins, *Antonio Gaudí and the Catalan Movement, 1870-1930*, Charlottesville, N.C., 1973; Salvador Tarragó, *Gaudí*, Barcelona, 1974; María Lluisa Borrás, *Doménech i Montaner*, Barcelona, 1971 (text in English, French, German and Spanish).

[15] José Puig i Cadafalch, *L'Art wisigothique et ses survivances*, Paris, 1961.

[16] A. Cirici Pellicer, *Arquitectura gótica catalana*, Barcelona, 1973, is summarized in French in *Architecture-Mouvement-Continuité*, No. 36, May 1975, pp. 28-38.

[17] Françoise Choay, *L'urbanisme. Utopies et réalités. Une anthologie*, Paris, 1965. Coining the disputable but convenient term "culturalism," she lays emphasis on other theories than those of the modernists, and is the first to do so.

[18] First published in 1889 in the *Revue Indépendante*, Huysmans' biting criticism of the Eiffel Tower was republished that same year, under the title "Le Fer," in his book of essays *Certains*. Huysmans' judgment of it was shared and echoed by many professional architects both in France and abroad.

[19] M.C. Gangneux, B. Paurd and E. Girard, *Architectures, Paris 1848-1914*, Paris, n.d. (1976), pp. 62-130.

[20] J.K. Huysmans, *La Cathédrale*, Paris, 1898, starting from the example of Chartres, gives a fascinating synthesis of the mystical approach to medieval architecture typical of the late 19th century. His book had a strong influence both on architects (Gaudí in particular) and on art historians (notably Marcel Aubert and Denise Jalabert).

[21] A study of the Metz railway station has been made by Thomas von Joest, *La gare et la poste à Metz. A propos d'une architecture historiciste*, typescript *mémoire de maîtrise*, University of Strasbourg, 1979, briefly reviewed in *Monuments Historiques* ("Symbolique de la gare de Metz," No. 6, 1978, pp. 45-49). The work of Thomas von Joest, in particular on German historicism, extends well beyond the scope of this typescript study.

[22] I might never have realized the scope of Gaudí's work, were it not for the architect Mogens Prip-Buus, who, at the time of his collaboration with Joern Utzon on the Sydney Opera House, opened my eyes to its originality. Prip-Buus and Utzon went to Spain to study Gaudí's buildings, from which they drew inspiration in Sydney. On this experience, see my article "La chapelle Güell, laboratoire d'un nouveau langage plastique" in *L'Œil*, No. 198, June 1971, pp. 14-21.

Bibliographical references

BARTHES Roland and MARTIN André, *La Tour Eiffel*, Paris, 1964.

BECHER Bernhard and Hilla, *Die Architektur der Förder- und Wassertürme*, Munich, 1971.

BESSET Maurice, *Gustave Eiffel*, Milan, 1957.

DESWARTE Sylvie and LEMOINE Bertrand, *L'architecture et les ingénieurs: deux siècles de construction*, Paris, 1980, publication following up an exhibition at the Centre Georges Pompidou, Paris, December 1978.

EATON Leonard K., *American Architecture Comes of Age: European Reaction to H.H. Richardson and Louis Sullivan*, Cambridge, Mass., 1972.

FANELLI Giovanni, *Architettura moderna in Olanda. 1900-1940*, Florence, 1968.

HERBERT Eugenia W., *The Artist and Social Reform. France and Belgium, 1885-1898*, New Haven, 1961.

JOEDICKE Jürgen, *Architecture contemporaine. Origines et perspectives*, Stuttgart and Paris, 1958.

MAGNE Lucien, *L'architecture française du siècle*, Paris, 1889.

PRAT Véronique, "Les années-châteaux de New York" in *Connaissance des Arts*, No. 355, September 1981.

SABAT Antonio, *Palau de la Musica Catalana*, Barcelona, 1974.

SINGELENBERG Peter, *H.P. Berlage. Idea and Style. The Quest of Modern Architecture*, Utrecht, 1972.

Exhibition catalogue

Les concours des monuments historiques de 1893 à 1979, Caisse Nationale des Monuments Historiques et des Sites, Hôtel de Sully, Paris, 1981.

Chapter VII

The "Belle Epoque" 1890-1914
(pages 213-249)

[1] On workers' housing in general, see Lewis Mumford, *The City in History*, New York, 1961; for France, Marie-Geneviève Raymond, *La politique pavillonnaire*, Paris, 1966; for England, E. Gauldie, *Cruel Habitations: A History of Working Class Housing 1780-1918*, London, 1974.

[2] I have had to omit the problem of suburban housing in the late 19th and early 20th century, though examples are legion and the literature abundant in architectural journals and the writings of architects and builders themselves. This rich documentation calls for serial treatment, bringing out the basic features of the reference models; it calls above all for an economic and social study, beyond the competence of the art historian. What is flagrant, on the other hand, is the aesthetic mediocrity of the suburban house. It is not a satisfying subject for the specialist, unlike social housing, where the architectural work is of great interest. In sheer quantity, suburban housing is the most extensive of the 19th century, and a socio-economic study of it would help to clarify the relation of the middle classes to architecture.

[3] The view of style architecture conveyed by decorators, on the basis of simplified models, refers not to actual objects, whether furniture or buildings, but to a repertory of framing ornaments used initially for wainscoting and certain decorative objects, like goldsmith's work.

[4] *Le siècle de l'éclectisme. Lille 1830-1930*, Archives d'Architecture Moderne, Brussels, 1979, essay by Lise Grenier and Hans Wieser-Benedetti, "Ville et théâtre," pp. 28-31, illustrations 239-246 (pp. 286-290).

[5] The Hotel Lutétia, the work of two recent graduates of the Ecole des Beaux-Arts, was the first of the grand hotels with an accessible terrace roof (now disused). Treated as a hanging garden, it offered a model that was widely taken up in the 1930s (Hotel Miramar and Hotel Martinez at Cannes, for example). Boileau and Tauzin drew inspiration here from the Rue Trétaigne apartment building of Henri Sauvage (1903) and from François Hennebique's famous house at Bourg-la-Reine (1904). The terrace roof became a characteristic feature of modernism.

[6] The earlier Parisian apartment building of the 19th century answered to no original programme, for the constraints imposed upon it were crippling. From the 1880s on, however, it became the major concern of French architects, even more than the château or the church, and they made it a practice to call on sulptors and decorative painters to collaborate with them. On this point, see my essay "Art Nouveau Architecture in France" in the exhibition catalogue *Art Nouveau Belgium/France*, Institute for the Arts, Rice University, Houston, Texas, and The Art Institute of Chicago, 1976, pp. 378-403. Since then, several monographs have been undertaken, notably in the Unités Pédagogiques d'Architecture in Paris.

[7] M.C. Gangneux, B. Paurd and E. Girard, *Architectures, Paris 1848-1914*, Paris, n.d. (1976), pp. 112-115.

[8] Jacques Gubler, *Nationalisme et internationalisme dans l'architecture moderne de la Suisse*, Lausanne, 1975. This book deals chiefly with the 20th century, but the theme has deep roots in the 19th century.

[9] Franco Borsi and Ezio Godoli, *Paris 1900*, Brussels, 1976, is a convenient reference book, despite the poor quality of its illustrations.

[10] Apart from Serrurier-Bovy's *Pavillon Bleu* and Tronchet's *Belle Meunière*, the Paris World's Fair of 1900 turned its back on Art Nouveau. Samuel Bing was allowed no more than a small showing and the architects of the younger generation were reduced to erecting a few pavilions scattered in the gardens. The main buildings were in a vaguely exotic and superficial Louis XV style, beside which the Petit Palais of Charles Girault and the Grand Palais of Albert Louvet, Henri Deglane and Albert Thomas seemed austere, with their monumental classical colonnades and imposing interior volumes. René Binet's monumental gateway, a last echo of the large buildings of the 1878 and 1889 Paris Fairs, also disregarded the French Modern Style. This strange consensus in ignoring Art Nouveau recalls that of the 1893 World's Columbian Exposition in Chicago.

[11] Bernard Marrey, *Les grands magasins*, Paris, 1979.

[12] Meredith L. Clausen, "La Samaritaine" in *Revue de l'Art*, No. 32, C.N.R.S., Paris, 1976. The Samaritaine department store combines the example of Paul Sédille with that of Sullivan's Carson, Pirie & Scott Store in Chicago–but, to my mind, with a refinement surpassing Sullivan himself.

[13] *Encyclopédie d'Architecture*, 1876, p. 120.

[14] It is not by chance that Louis Hautecœur's *Histoire de l'architecture classique* stops at 1900. Since then, though the neo-classical movement has had its good moments, the fact remains that the classical spirit is foreign to the 20th century.

[15] For a brief listing of French seaside resorts and some of their most famous buildings, see the special issue "Retour aux Sources" of *Monuments Historiques*, No. 1, 1978.

[16] The only recent study of Hébrard is that of Gwendolyn Wright and Paul Rabinow, "Savoir et pouvoir dans l'urbanisme moderne colonial d'Ernest Hébrard" in *Cahiers de la Recherche Architecturale*, No. 9, Paris, 1982, pp. 26-43. Vittel, luckier in this than Evian or Vichy, is well documented in the exhibition catalogue of Marie-Héléne Contal, *Vittel 1854-1936. Création d'une ville thermale*, Institut Français d'Architecture, Paris, 1982.

[17] Some of these architect's villas are included in the exhibition catalogue *Henri Sauvage 1873-1932*, Archives d'Architecture Moderne, Brussels, 1976; some too in the special issue "Retour aux Sources" of *Monuments Historiques*, No. 1, 1978, chiefly in the article of Nathalie Glon, "Villas balnéaires de la Manche," pp. 34-40. The subject is well worth further study.

[18] This description is based in part on oral accounts, stored in my memory, of a way of life which has now receded into the past. For some literary records of it, see François Loyer, "Châtelains et châteaux au XIXe siècle dans l'Ouest de la France" in *Arts de l'Ouest*, 1, 1978, pp. 45-77.

[19] This has been well described for the Château de Bel-Air at Le Pertre (Mayenne) by Odile de Charry, *Histoire d'un château. Le château de Bel-Air, exemple de reconstruction castrale dans l'Ouest de 1870 à 1914*, typescript memoir, D.E.A., Université de Haute-Bretagne, Rennes, 1982.

[20] For the period 1910-1920, see for example the books of Maurice Leblanc featuring the personality of the gentleman burglar Arsène Lupin.

[21] In France the so-called diocesan architects *(architectes diocésains)* were charged by the Administration Française des Cultes, then part of the Ministère de l'Instruction et des Cultes, with the upkeep and construction of religious buildings, until the separation of Church and State in 1905. Their work was often the same as that of the architects of the Monuments Historiques, administered by the Direction des Beaux-Arts, which was also part of the Ministère de l'Instruction et des Cultes. This structure had been set up under the guidance of Viollet-le-Duc at the beginning of the Second Empire (1852 on). The diocesans thus competed with the Prix de Rome architects of the Bâtiments Civils and the Palais Nationaux, who had the privilege of public commissions in other fields. With the rise of the Municipal and Departmental architects in provincial France, and the almost exclusive control exerted here by the "D.P.L.G." architects (holding government diplomas), the rivalry between diocesans and Prix de Rome architects slowly waned towards the end of the 19th century.

[22] Viollet-le-Duc, *Dictionnaire raisonné de l'architecture française du XIe au XVIe siècle*, 10 volumes, 1854-1868, articles Construction (Vol. IV, p. 233, fig. 130-131) and Château (Vol. III, p. 169, fig. 30-31).

[23] One of the first models of the grand hotel was the Hôtel de l'Impératrice Eugénie at Biarritz, built under the Second Empire; the building was even given the form of the letter E, reproducing the Empress's monogram. The first of the grand hotels were connected with a railway station, as in London; then they sprang up in the seaside resorts, as at Brighton, and later in France.

[24] Elisabeth Walter, "1850-1930. Le décor dans les établissements thermaux et les casinos" in *Monuments Historiques*, 1, 1978, special issue "Retour aux Sources," pp. 65-74. This essay admirably completes the preliminary account by Bruno Foucart, "Au plaisir des architectes. Les villes d'eau et leur architecture aux XIXe et XXe siècles" in the same issue of *Monuments Historiques*, pp. 2-11.

[25] Michel Mohrt and Guy Feinstein, *Paquebots. Le temps des traversées*, Paris, 1980.

[26] The works of art decorating Baron Vitta's Villa La Sapinière were published by Roger Marx, "Une Salle de Billard et une Galerie Moderne (Salon de la Société Nationale)" in *Art et Décoration*, July-December 1902, Vol. XII, Librairie Centrale des Beaux-Arts, Paris, pp. 1-13, and Léonce Bénédite, *Hauts Reliefs pour une Décoration d'Architecture et pointes sèches par A. Rodin*, exhibition catalogue, Musée National du Luxembourg, Paris, February-March 1905. Roger Marx refers in his article to "a deluxe book on the subject published by the *Gazette des Beaux-Arts*": he himself was the author of it. So the decorations of the villa were publicized at once. Not so the medallions of Falguière and the architecture of Formigé. These were noticed in architectural journals, whose circulation however was much more restricted than that of the art magazines.

[27] A. Tournaire, *Notice sur la vie et les travaux de M. Camille Formigé (1845-1926)*, Paris, 1930, a paper read before the Academy on 20 December 1930.

[28] The 1905 exhibition at the Musée du Luxembourg (see above, Note 26), showing Rodin's drypoints, an unexpected aspect of his work, appears to have met with little success. What would his admirers have said if they had seen Rodin's actual bas-reliefs for the Villa La Sapinière, "wedged into the masonry of the vestibule where their stone is due to merge insensibly into that of the walls they are designed to decorate, which thus accounts for the masses left in reserve in the upper part of the reliefs" (Léonce Bénédite)?

Bibliographical references

CHAMPIGNEULLE B., *L'Art Nouveau*, Paris, 1972.

GUERRA DE LA VEGA Ramón, *Madrid. Guía de Arquitectura (1800-1919)*, Madrid, 1980.

HARRIS Bill, *The Plaza*, Secaucus, New Jersey, 1981.

HENNIG-SCHEFOLD Monica and SCHAEFER Inge, *Struktur und Dekoration. Architekturtendenzen in Paris und Brüssel im späten 19. Jahrhundert*, Werk-Buch 4, Winterthur, 1969.

JOHNSON Marc, *Jules Chéret. Divertissements*, Lausanne, 1983.

La Laurentine et l'invention de la villa romaine, Institut Français d'Architecture in collaboration with Pierre Pinon, Paris, 1982.

L'Œil, No. 75, Paris, March 1961, special issue "L'architecture du XXe siècle" with an essay on "L'évolution du gratte-ciel."

LOYER François, "Paris assassiné" in *L'Œil*, No. 191, November 1970.

NIERMANS Marianne, "Niermans, l'architecte des palaces 1900" in *Connaissance des Arts*, No. 280, June 1975.

RHEIMS Maurice, *L'art 1900 ou le style Jules Verne*, Paris, 1965.

SALCH Charles-Laurent and MARTINEZ Dominique, *Les plus beaux châteaux d'Alsace*, Strasbourg, 1978.

TAFURI Manfredo, "Vie et mort des gratte-ciel, la dialectique de l'absurde" in *L'Architecture d'Aujourd'hui*, No. 178, March-April 1975.

Exhibition catalogue

Art Nouveau Belgique, Palais des Beaux-Arts, Brussels, 1980-1981.

Chapter VIII
Modern times
(pages 251-293)

[1] Charles Bourgeois, active at Tourcoing in northern France from about 1900 to 1930, is particularly interesting as an architect who moved on from Art Nouveau to the pastiche of period architecture. See *Le siècle de l'éclectisme. Lille 1830-1930*, Archives d'Architecture Moderne, Brussels, 1979, pp. 99-101.

[2] Durand, Letarouilly and Gromort continued to figure on the entrance programme of the Ecole des Beaux-Arts, Paris, until 1968, though admittedly their work was not studied with much conviction. A few years later this programme might have seemed up to date in the context of Post-Modernism.

[3] Between the wars, in Berlin in the 1920s, at the Bauhaus and in Paris with Le Corbusier and André Lurçat, architects put a distinct emphasis, in contradictory ways, on their political convictions and continually sought to wed style with political commitment, all too often with confusing results.

[4] The term "School of Paris" fails to cover the work of these men, who represent fundamentally divergent tendencies.

[5] A point well brought out by Philippe Boudon in his study of Le Corbusier's work at Bordeaux-Pessac and its rejection by the local population (*Pessac de Le Corbusier*, "Aspects de l'Urbanisme," Paris, 1969).

[6] This is clear from the difficult adjustment to history of the Post-Modernists, despite the interesting approach of Charles Jencks in *The Language of Post-Modern Architecture*, New York, 1977.

[7] The exhibition of Henri Sauvage and his friends, organized by Frantz Jourdain, was entitled *Un grenier d'architectes*, Galerie Le Barc de Boutteville, Paris, 1896. See the exhibition catalogue *Henri Sauvage 1873-1932*, Archives d'Architecture Moderne, Brussels, 1976, p. 16.

[8] M.C. Gangneux, B. Paurd and E. Girard, *Architectures, Paris 1848-1914*, give a good account of Samuel Bing's Paris gallery.

[9] Frantz Jourdain, "L'architecture à l'Exposition universelle. Propos à bâtons rompus" in *Revue des Arts Décoratifs*, Vol. XX, Paris, 1900, p. 245.

[10] On Serrurier-Bovy, see Jacques-Grégoire Watelet, *Gustave Serrurier-Bovy, architecte et décorateur, 1858-1910*, Brussels, Académie Royale de Belgique, Mémoires de la classe des Beaux-Arts, Vol. XIV, fasc. 3, 1975.

[11] J.C. Groussard and F. Roussel, *Nancy architecture 1900*, exhibition catalogue, Secrétariat d'Etat à la Culture, Office du Tourisme de la Ville de Nancy, Nancy, 1976.

[12] F. Loyer, "Paul Hankar: l'Art Nouveau critique" in *Revue de l'Université de Bruxelles*, special issue "Art Nouveau. Littérature et Beaux-Arts à la fin du XIXe," 3, 1981, pp. 93-100.

[13] Though written in French, the autobiography of Henry van de Velde has only been published in German (*Geschichte meines Lebens*, Munich, 1962) and later in Italian.

[14] Filippo Alison, *Charles Rennie Mackintosh as a Designer of Chairs*, Milan, New York, London, 1973.

[15] Le Corbusier, *L'Urbanisme*, Paris, 1959, quoted by F. Choay, *L'urbanisme. Utopies et réalités. Une anthologie*, Paris, 1965, p. 259.

[16] Antoine Grumbach, "Le pur et l'impur" in *Architecture-Mouvement-Continuité*, No. 37, November 1975, pp. 46-48. Sauvage's "tiered" apartment house at 26, rue Vavin, Paris, was finished in 1914, while his post-Haussmannian building next door, at 137, boulevard Raspail, was not built till 1925, so that the more modern of the two is the earlier one.

[17] On these apartment blocks set round a large courtyard, see the excellent study by J. Castex, J.C. Depaule and P. Panerai, *Formes urbaines: de l'îlot à la barre*, "Aspects de l'Urbanisme," Paris, 1977.

[18] A study of the Fondation Rothschild competitions by Marie-Jeanne Dumont is soon to be published by the Institut Français d'Architecture, Paris.

[19] On the garden city, see the special issue of the review *Architecture-Mouvement-Continuité*, No. 34, July 1974, by Olivier Girard, Olivier Nicoulaud and Georges Teyssot; and Marcel Smets *L'avènement de la cité-jardin en Belgique. Histoire de l'habitat social en Belgique de 1830 à 1930*, Brussels, 1977.

[20] The "politics of fashion" ("le système de la mode") is an expression coined by Michel Foucault.

[21] This quotation from Walter Gropius comes from his famous Bauhaus manifesto of 1919.

[22] On the Mathildenhöhe art colony in Darmstadt, see the exhaustive, lavishly illustrated exhibition catalogue, *Ein Dokument deutscher Kunst 1901-1976*, 5 volumes, Hessisches Landesmuseum, Darmstadt, 1976.

[23] Dennis Sharp and Maurice Culot, *Van de Velde, Theatre Designs 1904-1914*, exhibition catalogue, The Architectural Association, London, 1974.

[24] For Berlage's large unbroken wall surfaces, see Holland House, London (1914), for example.

[25] Henri Sauvage, *La boutique à treize*, Paris, 1923.

[26] Brian Brace Taylor, "Sauvage et l'habitat hygiénique ou la Révolution de la Propreté à Paris" in the exhibition catalogue *Henri Sauvage 1873-1932*, Archives d'Architecture Moderne, Brussels, 1976, pp. 71-78.

[27] Apart from Wright's own writings, the best reference work on him at present is probably the exhibition catalogue by Alberto Izzo and Camillo Gubitosi, *Frank Lloyd Wright*, documenting his designs from 1887 to 1959, Palazzo Reale, Naples, 1976 (in English, *Frank Lloyd Wright: Drawings 1887-1959*, Centro Di, Florence, 1980).

Bibliographical references

ADLMANN Jan Ernst, "Pomp and Common Sense: Wagner's Architecture as Transition" in *Art in America*, May-June 1979.

BILLCLIFFE Roger, *Architectural Sketches & Flower Drawings by Charles Rennie Mackintosh*, London, 1977.

BILLCLIFFE Roger, *Mackintosh Watercolours*, London, 1978.

BILLCLIFFE Roger, *Charles Rennie Mackintosh. The Complete Furniture, Furniture Drawings & Interior Designs*, Guildford and London, 1979.

BLONDEL Alain and PLANTIN Yves, "Pionniers du XXe siècle. L'expressionnisme naturaliste de Guimard au Castel Béranger" in *L'Œil*, No. 194, February 1971.

BUDDENSIEG Tilmann and ROGGE Henning, "Peter Behrens e l'architettura della AEG" in *Lotus International*, No. 12, September 1976.

BUDDENSIEG Tilmann and ROGGE Henning, *Peter Behrens und die AEG 1907-1914*, Berlin, 1981.

DELEVOY Robert L., *Dimensions of the 20th Century 1900-1945*, Geneva, 1965.

FANELLI Giovanni, *Il disegno Liberty*, Rome-Bari, 1981.

FISHMAN Robert, *Urban Utopias in the Twentieth Century. Ebenezer Howard, Frank Lloyd Wright and Le Corbusier*, New York, 1977.

GIROUARD Mark, *Sweetness and Light: the "Queen Anne" Movement, 1860-1900*, Oxford, 1977.

HOWARTH Thomas, *Charles Rennie Mackintosh and the Modern Movement*, London, 1952.

LARNER Gerald and Celia, *The Glasgow Style*, London, 1979.

MAEYER Charles de, *Paul Hankar*, Brussels, 1963.

MASSOBRIO Giovanna and PORTOGHESI Paolo, *Album del Liberty*, Rome-Bari, 1975.

PEHNT Wolfgang, *Die Architektur des Expressionismus*, Stuttgart, 1973; 2nd edition, 1981; *Expressionist Architecture*, London, 1973.

PEVSNER Nikolaus, *Pioneers of Modern Design*, New York, 1949; Penguin Books, 1960; first published as *Pioneers of the Modern Movement*, London, 1936.

SHARP Dennis, *A Visual History of Twentieth-Century Architecture*, London and Greenwich, Connecticut, 1972.

SCHLUMBERGER Eveline, "La colonie d'artistes du grand-duc de Hesse-Darmstadt" in *Connaissance des Arts*, No. 344, October 1980.

SCHMUTZLER Robert, *Art Nouveau–Jugendstil*, Stuttgart, 1977.

SCHREYL Karl Heinz and NEUMEISTER Dorothea, *Joseph Maria Olbrich. Die Zeichnungen in der Kunstbibliothek Berlin*, Berlin, 1972.

TAFURI Manfredo and DAL CO Francesco, *Architettura Contemporanea/I. Architettura Contemporanea/II*, Milan, 1979.

WRIGHT Frank Lloyd, *The Imperial Hotel, Tokyo, Japan. 1915-1922*, edited by Yukio Futagawa in *GA 53 (Global Architecture)*, Tokyo, 1980.

Exhibition catalogues

Otto Wagner. Das Werk des Wiener Architekten 1841-1918, Hessisches Landesmuseum, Darmstadt, November 1963-February 1964.

Antoine Pompe et l'effort moderne en Belgique. 1890-1940, Archives de l'Architecture Moderne. Musée d'Ixelles et Ecole Nationale Supérieure d'Architecture et des Arts Visuels, Brussels, 1969.

Pionniers du XXe siècle. Guimard, Horta, Van de Velde, Musée des Arts Décoratifs, Paris, March-May 1971.

A. et G. Perret. Architectes français. Conservatoire National des Arts et Métiers, Paris, 1976.

List of Illustrations

ILLUSTRATIONS FOR THE INTRODUCTION

FRONTISPIECE ILLUSTRATIONS FOR CHAPTERS I TO VIII

ILLUSTRATIONS BY ORDER OF PLACE

FRONTISPIECES AND COVERS

FURNITURE AND DECORATIONS

ILLUSTRATIONS AND POSTERS

PAINTINGS AND SCULPTURES

PLANS AND MAPS

TRANSATLANTIC LINERS

UNEXECUTED DESIGNS AND STAGE SET

Index of Names

Book design and layout by
Sylvia Saudan-Skira

Printed by
IRL Imprimeries Réunies Lausanne S.A.

Binding by
Ateliers Roger Veihl, Geneva.

Printed in Switzerland